Early Ontario Potters:
Their craft and trade

Early Ontario Potters:
Their craft and trade

David L. Newlands

McGRAW-HILL RYERSON LIMITED
Toronto Montreal New York St. Louis San
Francisco Auckland Bogotá Guatemala Hamburg
Johannesburg Lisbon London Madrid Mexico
New Delhi Panama Paris San Juan São Paulo
Singapore Sydney Tokyo

EARLY ONTARIO POTTERS: Their Craft and
Trade

Copyright © McGraw-Hill Ryerson Limited,
1979.

ISBN 0-07-082972-1

1 2 3 4 5 6 7 8 9   BP   8 7 6 5 4 3 2 1 0 9

Printed and bound in Canada

Canadian Cataloguing in Publication Data

Newlands, David L., date
    Early Ontario potters

Bibliography: p.
Includes index.

ISBN 0-07-082972-1

1. Potters — Ontario. 2. Pottery — 19th century
— Ontario. 3. Pottery, Canadian — Ontario.
I. Title.

NK4030.05N39   738.3'09713   C79-094333-6

Contents

Acknowledgments

I would like to express my appreciation to those publications that have permitted me to re-tell the story of potteries which I originally wrote up for their pages. These include the *Canadian Collector, Rotunda, Archaeological Newsletter, Material History Bulletin, Ontario Potter,* and *York Pioneer.*

Several chapters of this book were "tested" on local historical societies who had graciously welcomed me as a speaker. These include the North York Historical Society, the Paris (Ontario) Historical Society, the Brant County Historical Society, and the Peterborough Historical Society.

I would like to record my appreciation to Mr. Claus Breede, Director of the Bruce County Museum, Southampton, who prepared some of the maps for this book. Mr. Bill Robertson and Mr. Brian Boyle, of the Photography Department, Royal Ontario Museum, were helpful in photography work. Mr. Donald B. Webster, Curator, Canadiana Department, Royal Ontario Museum, kindly permitted me to photograph pottery in the collection of the Royal Ontario Museum. Dorothea Hecken of the ROM carefully reviewed the information in Appendix One, "The Care and Handling of Pottery Collections," and made extensive revisions and suggestions for improvement of the information on recordkeeping, insurance, packing and shipping, and the export and import of pottery. I am indebted to Ms. Hecken for her interest and valuable assistance.

During the past five years many individuals and institutions have shared information on pottery and in some cases have permitted me to photograph wares in their collections. I would like to acknowledge my personal appreciation to these individuals and institutions, including D. Arlene Alyea, of Picton; James Anderson, of Stratford; Mrs. Keith Angel, of Kilsyth; The Archives of Ontario, Toronto; Mr. Jon Aristone, London; Mr. Andrew Armitage, Owen Sound; Jean Bacso, Toronto; Mr. and Mrs. Joseph Batchelor, Owen Sound; Clay Benson, Port Hope; Wayne Berry, Cannington; Dr. Michael Bird, Waterloo; Fred Bishop, Burlington; Black Creek Pioneer Village, Toronto; Bill Boden, Strathroy; Bob Bowen, Mississauga; David Bowman, Brantford; Bowmanville Museum, Bowmanville; Brant County Museum, Brantford; Brantford Public Library, Brantford; Reg Broomfield, Drumbo; Ken Brown, Peterborough; Bruce County Museum, Southampton; Mrs. Robert Bull, Etobicoke; Brian Butler, Strathroy; Doug Caley, Bloomfield; Mr. & Mrs. Robert Cline, Paris; Elizabeth Collard, Ottawa; Mrs. J. E. Connell, Toronto; Harry Crowfoot, St. Catharines; Lillie Davis, Willowdale; Gerald Fagan, Listowel; R. B. Fleming, Woodville; John Forbes, Guelph; Edwin Foster, Burlington; Dr. & Mrs. John H. Fowler, Toronto; Hyla Fox, Toronto; Laberta Fralic, Toronto; Gibson House Museum, Willowdale; Reg Good, Kitchener; Gil Graham, Kincardine.

Other persons and institutions who have helped are Betty Haight, London; Mr. and Mrs. Carl Handley, Picton; Mrs. George Harrison, Hamilton; Muriel Harrison, Toronto; Bill Hart, Seaforth; J. H. Harvey, Toronto;

Dorothea Hecken, Toronto; A. G. Hitchon, Brantford; Henry Hodges, Kingston; Janet Holmes, Toronto; Gerry Houston, Port Hope; Lewis Humberstone, Toronto; Ted Hunt, Port Hope; Dr. Irmgard Jamnik, Brantford; Jordan Historical Museum of the Twenty, Jordan; Joan Kadoke, Belfountain; Kitchener Public Library, Kitchener; Mr. and Mrs. Richard Knowles, Toronto; Peter Koenig, Toronto; Bruce Krug, Chesley; Howard Krug, Chesley; Wayne Landen, Owen Sound; the late Werner Leavens, Bolton; Brenda Lee-Whiting, Deep River; Joyce Lister, Toronto; Mr. and Mrs. Mervyn Lobb, Clinton; John Lunau, Markham; Markham District Historical Museum, Markham; A. V. Mason, Brantford; Harvey Mercier, Harriston; Margaret Morrison, Brantford; Marianne MacKenzie, Peterborough; James McCartney, Toronto; John McCutcheon, Owen Sound; Mary McGill, Beaverton; Dr. and Mrs. William McGill, Brantford; National Museums of Canada, Ottawa; Jack Newstead, Brantford; Ontario Agricultural Museum, Milton; Ontario Department of Mines, Toronto; Steve Otto, Toronto; Paris (Ontario) Public Library, Paris; Bruce Parker, Port Hope; George Pawlick, Toronto; James D. Percival, Brantford; Peterborough Centennial Museum, Peterborough; Mr. and Mrs. Ebor Pollard, Guelph; Prince Edward County Museum, Picton; Public Archives of Canada, Ottawa; Kenneth Richardson, Kerwood; M. N. W. Robertson, Burford; Mrs. John Rock, Bridgeport; Alex Ross, Toronto; Ted Rowcliffe, St. Mary's; Royal Ontario Museum, Toronto; Gladys Rush, Rochester, N.Y.; Dr. David Rupp, St. Catharines; Frank Ryan, Newmarket; Jean Saunter, Gilford; Don Savage, Markham; the late G. Blake Schuler, Brantford; Barbara Seargeant, Prescott; Wilfrid Shaver, Brantford; Harold Stankaitis, Weston; Strathroy & District Historical Museum, Strathroy; Mrs. Roy Summers, Fonthill; Sonja Tanner, Toronto; Jean Tebbutt, Hamilton; Harry Thompson, Clinton; William Tolton, Mississauga; Mr. and Mrs. Nick Trainor, St. Catharines; Marion B. Veinot, Bowmanville; Leighton Warren, Toronto; Wellington County Museum, Fergus; Mrs. E. Arnold Wilkinson, Toronto; Don Witherspoon, Kilsyth; Pearl Woodyatt, Brantford; William Yeager, Simcoe.

A nearly complete set of issues of the *Mercantile Agency Reference Book* is in the library of Dun and Bradstreet, Toronto. I would like to express my appreciation to that company for permission to use the credit-rating information contained in those books.

If I have failed to acknowledge the help of any individual or institution, I extend my apologies.

This book is dedicated to my sons, Joshua David Newlands and Nathaniel Kenneth Newlands.

1.
Introduction

The name and location of the first pottery in Ontario probably will never be known, for local records were few in the early period of the European and American settlement of Ontario, and the records that have survived are even fewer. It is likely that when Samuel Humberstone opened his workshop in 1796 in Augusta Township, Grenville County, he was one of the earliest immigrant potters to produce redwares using local clay.

The waves of immigration into Ontario during the nineteenth century saw the opening of many small potteries throughout the southern area of the province. Wherever settlers were establishing homes and farms, there was a need for pottery for handling, storing and transporting food. The earthenware and stoneware containers produced by the province's pot shops were an easily available and inexpensive source of containers for the needs of these settlers. The pottery industry reached its zenith by the 1880s and then began a rapid decline, so that within two decades most of the shops had disappeared, except for a handful of smaller enterprises operated by determined craftsmen. The last operating pottery in Ontario was the Foster Pottery Co., of Hamilton, which produced flowerpots until it was destroyed by fire in 1974, but by this time the means of production and marketing had changed considerably from that of the potteries begun in the nineteenth century.

A field survey of Ontario pottery sites, conducted by Mr. David Porter of Kitchener, and funded by the Ontario Ministry of Culture and Recreation, has shown that no pottery buildings remain, and that only a few sites have any potential archaeological significance. The rapid change in the urban landscape long ago destroyed the remains of potteries in the cities, but it was not until the growth of suburban communities after the Second World War that the final sentence of death was pronounced on rural sites, which until the mid-1950s had remained undeveloped. The loss of architectural remains of nineteenth-century potteries is not unique to this industry, and historians can, no doubt, point to the fact that glass factories, bell foundries, and most small furniture factories (to name but a few of the many early enterprises) have suffered no less harshly from population expansion and an indifferent public.

The *Ontario Heritage Act* of 1974, with its provisions to encourage the study, preservation, restoration and controlled archaeological exploration of significant aspects of our heritage, should help to change our attitude toward the remains of the industrial past. Unfortunately, those interested in potteries will realize that the Act came too late to prevent the destruction of most of the remains of the pottery industry.

During the past two decades there has been a growing interest in the products from the early potteries. Many people with capital to invest in antiques and an interest in Ontario history have started to collect Ontario earthenware and stoneware. In some cases these new collectors have been a stimulus in the development of new local museums. Collectors have contributed generously to these museums, and by so doing have enriched the heritage resources in the public domain. I believe that the interrelationship between the growth of private collections and the development of new community museums is the result of the realization that important objects of the past are a shared heritage, and that ownership (whether by an individual or an institution) is a trust and a responsibility taken on behalf of the people — those alive today and those who will come later.

I have written this book with the conviction that there are many individuals and institutions who agree with me that we have a responsibility to preserve and interpret the significant objects of the past. What I believe is necessary is that information on the history and products of the potteries, and knowledge about the care and handling of artifacts, should be widely available to the public.

1

There have been a number of publications on Ontario pottery since 1964. Donald B. Webster's *Early Canadian Pottery*, published in 1971, was the first widely available book on pottery, but since it's scope went beyond Ontario, it was possible to include only a limited amount of information on the Ontario shops. Webster has also contributed to our knowledge of Ontario pottery through archaeological explorations at the Brantford and William Eby potteries. Reports on these two sites, while of interest primarily to the historical archaeologist and museum curator, are helpful for those with special interest in these two factories. Philip Shackleton's "Potteries of 19th Century Ontario," completed in 1964, is an unpublished manuscript report of Parks Canada, Ottawa. Shackleton listed the names of potters and potteries that he located in directories, gazetteers, newspapers, and correspondence with persons who recalled a particular pottery in operation. The most complete checklist of potters and potteries in Canada was published in 1967 as an appendix in Elizabeth Collard's *Nineteenth Century Pottery and Porcelain in Canada*. Collard had expanded and documented Shackleton's list. Since 1974 I have been researching the history of each of the more than one hundred and fifty potteries in the province, following the life history of individual potters, and conducting excavations at two pottery sites in Huron County. In addition to this, I have systematically examined all the basic documentary sources from land-title records to credit ratings and fire insurance maps. Each summer has been devoted to field trips to different parts of the province to record the recollections of those who as children remembered the potteries in operation. As a result of my study I have obtained many more details on the known potteries and located many new sites in the province.

There are still important gaps in the history of the local workshops, created in part by the absence or loss of local records, and the vagaries of early craftsmen who preferred to call themselves farmers, labourers or manufacturers, rather than record for posterity that they were potting. I have been unable to locate two potteries reported in Essex County, or a small pottery in Renfrew County; all three of these workshops were in operation in the 1880s. I would welcome information on these or any other pottery in the province. Therefore, this book is written with the acknowledgment that the last words have not yet been written about the province's pottery industry, or the steadfast workmen who shaped clay into useful and beautiful objects. If this book stimulates further interest in the history of the pottery industry I will feel that one of its objectives will have been achieved.

This book has concerned itself with the history of the potteries that produced utilitarian containers for the home or industry, rather than those potteries that flourished at the end of the nineteenth century by producing artistic wares for decorative purposes. Many of the crocks made in Ontario were both useful and beautiful, but the distinction in functions has been clearly established in the study of potteries in Europe and the United States. It is hoped that a volume on the art potteries of Canada will be produced so that those interested in Ecanada Art Pottery, Sovereign Pottery, or the McMaster pottery will find information of help to them.

Over the past three years I have shared information on Ontario potteries through articles in a number of journals. The public response to these has encouraged me to bring the information together into a large and more complete work, one that would recapture the feeling of the potter's trade, and be of practical use to the collector, dealer, museum curator, and local historian.

2.
The Potter's Craft

The pottery workshop in Ontario during the nineteenth century varied from a shed to a large factory of two or more storeys. The majority of earthenware shops were one to three rooms, built of wood (sometimes of brick or stone) and with a work force of three or four men. There were a small number of stoneware and industrial pottery factories which employed ten or more men, but these were always a minority.

The size of the pottery shop, and the number of men employed, determined the organization of production and the amount of specialization.

THE POTTERY WORKMEN

The size of the work force at any particular pottery is difficult to determine. Sources such as the census returns and assessment rolls for a district usually include under the occupation of potter only those actually trained as a potter. The person who owned the pottery business was also listed as a potter, as distinct from the "labourer" who, while working at the pot shop, did not actually make the pottery. In the larger factories the name potter was usually used for those who made the wares, while other workmen were called "helpers," "apprentices," "teamsters," or "travelling salesmen."

The helper performed routine chores around the workshop, including sweeping the floor, charging and drawing the kiln, and loading pottery onto the wagon for delivery to merchants. The helper would be thirteen to sixteen years of age and might in time become an apprentice. George Taylor, of Port Hope, the last of the earthenware potters, told, in a taped interview in 1965, how his father, James Taylor, first became acquainted with the pottery business as a helper. James Taylor worked for $4 a month and board at the William Brownscombe pottery in Peterborough.

An apprentice was a young man (no woman has ever been reported as an apprentice in an Ontario pottery) between the ages of sixteen and eighteen, who by agreement with a potter would spend a number of years, generally three to five, working at a shop and learning the trade. The apprentice worked for a very small amount of money and board, but had the advantage of first-hand experience in the craft. James Taylor worked as an apprentice in the 1870s for $10 a year and board. Apprenticeships were common in potteries in the early nineteenth century, but later declined in number. This decline was a result of the general decrease in the number of small potteries, the specialization (demanding less dependence on skilled workmen) in the larger factory potteries, and the lack of interest in the apprenticeship system by the children of potters.

A pottery would employ one or more labourers, men who would do all the routine heavy work in the shop, except for the actual making of the wares. Factory potteries employed more labourers than potters, as shown by the census returns which consistently report far fewer potters than the total number of workmen who were reported by the owners.

Most potters hired one or more salesmen, called "travellers" or "travelling salesmen," who took orders for pottery from village stores. The salesmen were usually paid a commission, and this had to be deducted from the advertised price of the wares, along with the discount allowed the merchant, to determine the money the potter actually received. The use of the salesman appears to have been a very effective way to sell pottery. The records of a general store in Harriston, Wellington County, indicate that the firm purchased pottery from shops as distant as Paris, Picton, and Mount Forest. The distance between Harriston and Picton is about 350 kilometres. The network of travelling salesmen crossing the province influenced the spread of the products of local workshops, while maintaining competition between factories.

The teamster delivered by horse and wagon, or as it was called, "teamed-out," the finished wares to the local shops. The teamster's job could be very dangerous, especially during the spring thaw, when roads were almost impassable. The case of Philip Burgard, son of Ferdinand Burgard, of Egmondville, illustrates the danger involved in using local roads. He was injured in a road mishap and lost a load of pottery as a result of the road conditions. The family sued the township for the loss. The case was eventually appealed to a higher court in Toronto, and as a result Ferdinand Burgard and his son received payment for damages caused by the poor roads.

The potter was either a person trained to make pottery or the owner of a pottery business, whether trained as a potter or not. Sometimes the records describe as a potter a person who is making brick and drainage tile, but further research usually clarifies this situation. In larger factory potteries, the term "potter" was often replaced by more specific titles, such as "thrower," "turner," "moulder," or "presser," which describe the specialized work of these potters.

POTTERY CLAY

Clay was the basic ingredient for pottery and a good supply was important in determining the location and success of any enterprise. In Ontario there were two basic kinds of clay used to make pottery: *earthenware* and *stoneware.*

Throughout southern and southwestern Ontario, *earthenware* clay is found as surface deposits dating to the Pleistocene and Recent Ages, the result of glacial activity. The major problem with these local clays is the large amount of impurities they contain, such as gravel, lime, and organic matter. In the nineteenth century, the government of Ontario had not yet published a study of clay deposits, and so the potter would have to rely on his own exploration and local reports to locate a good clay bed.

The locations of commercially useful clay for pottery manufacture in eastern Ontario were few, as clay deposits were generally restricted to the Ottawa River Valley, the north shore of the St. Lawrence River, and the banks and lowlands of inland rivers and lakes.

Although local clays were a grey or blue-grey colour when dug, they invariably became a terra cotta or buff colour when fired at a relatively low temperature. High iron content clay would fire to a terra cotta colour and the low iron but high lime clay would fire to a buff colour; hence the origin of the terms "redwares" and "yellow (cane) wares," terms used in popular literature of the period in Ontario.

From the time of the opening of the first stoneware pottery in Ontario in 1849 until the closing of the last such pottery in 1906 there were a total of nine businesses that depended on the import of stoneware clay from the states of New Jersey, Ohio, and Pennsylvania, or Devon, England. *Stoneware* clay was more refractory (heat resistant) than local clays and therefore produced a more durable product: because of its composition it had to be fired at a higher temperature, approximately 1100°C to 1200°C. Stoneware factories were established in port towns near the Great Lakes and in cities in southern Ontario, so that bulk shipments of clay could be delivered by boat or railroad to the factory.

While earthenware clays were usually available at a low cost, or free, stoneware clay might cost anywhere from five dollars to ten dollars a ton at the source, and to this was added the cost of shipping and import. The dependence of stoneware factories on imported raw materials was a major influence in their demise during the last two decades of the nineteenth century.

The R. Campbell's Sons pottery in Hamilton was one of the few industrial potteries that blended clays, the exact mixture depending on the type of ware being produced, the composition of the glazing, and the firing temperature. These factors were especially important for factories that produced industrial wares because of the specialized needs of their customers — restaurants, hospitals and chemical industries.

DIGGING CLAY

Local clay was usually dug in the spring for processing in the summer; clay dug in the fall was "weathered" during the winter and used in the pottery during the next spring. Since most of the clay was found as surface deposits, no expensive equipment was required to dig the material. The potter or one of the labourers had only to remove the layer of topsoil and then shovel clay directly into a wagon for

2.1 *A pugmill in operation at an early Canadian brickyard. Pugmills of similar construction were used to mix clays at potteries.*

transport to the workshop. An interesting account of clay digging is reported in the Wilmot Township Council minutes, where concern was expressed for the activity of Xavier Boehler, of New Hamburg, who dug clay from the road in front of his pottery, creating a hazard for horses and wagons. A final deposition of the matter has not been recorded.

An earthenware pottery producing $1600 a year worth of articles would require between forty and fifty tons of clay a year. This need could be met if the potter found a small deposit within a few kilometres of his workshop. It would probably take many years for a potter to have exhausted all the local sources of clay, and in most cases economic conditions had determined the fate of the workshop before the shortage of clay became an issue.

PREPARING THE CLAY

When clay arrived at the workshop or factory it had to be cleaned and mixed before it could be used to make pottery. The potter would begin by picking out stones, leaves or other impurities. The clay was then put into a *pugmill,* which mixed the clay to make it homoge-

neous. The pugmill consisted of a wooden bin in the centre of which was a vertical shaft with fitted knives. The knives were placed at an angle so as to press the gravel and other coarse material downward toward an opening at the base. The shaft was rotated by a long wooden beam, three or four yards long, which was turned by a horse. Clay was shovelled in the top of the pugmill, water added to make a "soupy" mixture, and the shaft rotated. When it had reached a smooth consistency, the clay would be drained off, sieved into a settling tank and allowed to stiffen. The clay might also be allowed to stiffen in the pugmill, after which it would have to be cut in blocks and removed. Although no photograph of a pugmill in Ontario is known, a similar device from a Canadian brickyard (plate 2.1) illustrates a general view of the device.

The steps in processing clay varied from one pottery to another depending on the clay being worked and the types of pottery being made. For example, if the clay was too plastic, burnt and crushed clay or fireclay (commonly called *grog*) would be added. The addition of grog would also help the clay dry evenly during firing, prevent denting during the early stages of firing and avoid excessive shrinkage of the pottery. At the R. Campbell's Sons pottery in Hamilton, the clay was processed in a

2.2 *Mixing clay and water in a blunger to make
a slip of "heavy cream" consistency.* Courtesy
Ontario Archives.

blunger (see plate 2.2), a device similar to a
pugmill. The blunger blended the clay and
produced a liquid mixture, called a *slip*. The
slip could then be pumped into a filter press.
After the filter press the clay was pugged again
before being used to make hand-pressed or
moulded wares. In comparison the Foster Pottery Co., of the same city, pugged clay and
then stored it for three to six weeks before
pugging it a second time. It was then ready to
be made into flowerpots. Storing helped to
break down the clay aggregates and made the
clay more plastic and workable.

The *filter press* was used in the larger potteries. Clay slip was pumped into the press, a
device consisting of a series of parallel com-
partments. Each compartment was lined with

porous filter cloths and connected to a common intake pipe. As the liquid clay was
pumped into a compartment, excess water
passed through the filter cloths and dropped to
the floor. When the compartment was full, the
entrance tap was turned off, and the next
compartment filled. When all the compart-
ments had been filled the plates were com-
pressed by means of a fly-wheel moved by a
central screw, forcing the remaining excess
water out of the clay. The clay was then left in
each compartment until it was firm, after which
time it was pugged again to remove air and
was then ready for use. A filter press at the R.
Campbell's Sons pottery of Hamilton is shown
in plate 2.3.

MAKING POTTERY
The simplest way to make pottery was by
hand-forming (*throwing*) on a wheel. A ball of
prepared clay of a specific size was first

2.3 *A filter press in operation at R. Campbell's Sons pottery, Hamilton. The filter press was used to* *remove excess moisture from slip.* Courtesy Ontario Archives.

kneaded and worked to remove air pockets and lumps (a process that is called *wedging*), before being thrown on the potter's wheel. The wheel was a horizontal, revolving disc, powered by the potter who kicked a large flywheel at the bottom of a central shaft. As the wheel revolved, the potter formed a vessel by pulling the mass of clay with his hands. As the potter pulled the clay to form the pot, the height could be controlled by using a wooden measuring gauge. It was important to make the ware to established sizes in order to have the pottery hold an identifiable amount of liquid, such as one Imperial quart. Since many people would be using the pottery to buy or sell specific amounts of liquids or solids, the potter had to be as accurate in his work as possible. The rim of the pot could be shaped with a small wooden hand-held template, called a *rib,*

which gave the piece a particular profile. A group of ribs from a nineteenth-century pottery in West Virginia is shown in plate 2.4. By standardizing the height and width of pottery it was possible to load the kiln more easily.

The pot was cut off from the wheel disc with a turning tool or a piece of wire (like a cheese wire) pulled taut along the surface of the disc. The base of pots cut off in such a way had a series of concentric circles on the base. When the ware had become a leathery texture, then handles, spouts, knobs and incised decoration or the potter's name or the name of a merchant could be added. The pots could then be remounted on a lathe and shaped to remove any rough or uneven features on the surface of the ware.

Throwing was generally replaced in factory potteries by "jiggering and jolleying." The *jig-*

2.4 *Pottery "ribs" used to shape the rim and body of earthenware pottery. These ribs were from a West Virginia pottery that was discontinued in the late 1890s. Photo from Walter Hough, "An Early West Virginia Pottery," in Annual Report of the Smithsonian Institute for 1899.*

ger was a revolving head on which a plaster mould was mounted. The potter would take a pancake of clay, somewhat thicker than was required for the finished pot, and place it inside a plaster form that was attached to the jigger. The *jolley* was a lever with an attached rib in the shape of the inside of the bowl or the back of a plate. As the jigger revolved, the jolley was lowered to press the clay firmly to the surface of the mould, giving the correct thickness to the vessel. Surplus clay was removed from the edge of the mould. The piece could be set aside for the clay to stiffen, after which time it could be removed from the plaster mould, marked and incised with decoration, according to the wishes of the potter. A jigger and jolley in use at the R. Campbell's Sons pottery

is shown in plate 2.5. Jiggering and jolleying enabled workmen to produce large quantities of plates, bowls, cups and other containers where uniform size and shape were desired.

While throwing and jiggering and jolleying were used to produce plain ware, fancy wares such as teapots or lawn ornaments were usually made by casting or pressing. In the casting of wares, slip was poured into a plaster mould. Water in the clay slip along the face of the mould was absorbed into the plaster, causing a layer of clay to adhere to the surface of the mould. As a layer of stiff clay began to form, the excess slip was emptied out. When the clay had become firmer, the mould could be taken apart and the pottery removed (plate 2.6). It was then possible to add handles, spouts and other appendages, as is being done in the photograph (plate 2.7) from the R. Campbell's Sons pottery. Moulds could be dried and re-used many times, depending on their quality. A part of a plaster mould used to make a finial is shown in plate 2.8. This was recovered during excavations at the Huron Pottery, Egmondville.

Plaster moulds enabled the potter to copy popular designs from wares made elsewhere, and in this way helped his wares to compete with other domestic and imported wares. Stoneware potteries such as Brantford, and Hart Bros. & Lazier, Picton, were casting wares by the early 1850s. Casting was a popular method of producing fancy wares during the last half of the nineteenth century.

Pottery was also made in Ontario workshops by hand or mechanical pressing. In *hand pressing* a ball of clay was spread to make a pancake using a knocker, a plaster block about six inches in diameter, attached to a clay handle. A batter (without the plaster block) which was recovered during excavations at the Huron Pottery, Egmondville, is shown in plate 2.9. In *mechanical pressing*, a pancake of clay was placed on a mould, the shape of a plate or lid. An arm with a "negative" of the desired shape was pressed down on the pancake, forming it into the desired object. Excess clay was scraped away from the edge of the form.

In hand pressing, each part of the plaster mould would have to be pressed separately. The different parts would then be assembled

2.5   *Making bowls by "jigger and jolley" method at R. Campbell's Sons pottery.* Courtesy Ontario Archives.

and bound together, so that the seams could be joined by using a small ball of clay and the fingers. A clay form for making a pressed turkshead mould is shown in plate 2.10. This was also recovered from the Huron Pottery site. The turkshead mould was used to bake fancy ring-shaped cakes, or to make jelly. The name "turkshead" was derived from the twists reminiscent of those in a Turkish turban. To make a turkshead mould, the potter pressed a pancake of clay on the form. When the clay had stiffened, it could be removed from the

form. The central cone was thrown separately and attached. Jugs. pitchers and teapots were some of the fancy wares that could be made by hand-pressing.

The only machine for making pottery that was developed and used in Ontario was used for the manufacture of flowerpots. Stanley and Fred Foster, of the Foster Pottery Co., of Hamilton, patented an automatic flowerpot machine in 1909. Two of their patent drawings are shown in plate 2.11. A "blank" of clay (a predetermined part of a column of clay extruded from an auger machine) was placed in the cup (marked U on the drawings), which rose to meet a rotating plunger (R). The plunger spread the clay along the inside of the

2.6 *Removing a slip-cast jug from a plaster of Paris mould. Picture is from R. Campbell's Sons pottery ca. 1895.* Courtesy Ontario Archives.

cup, and according to the distance between cup and plunger, controlled the thickness of the flowerpot. Excess clay was removed from the top of the cup by a movable arm. As the cup returned to its original position, the

2.7 *Turner removing excess clay and attaching a spout to a "Champion" teapot at R. Campbell's Sons pottery.* Courtesy Ontario Archives.

flowerpot was partially lifted out of the cup so the operator could remove it. The pot was placed on a plank and carried to the drying room (plate 2.12). One of these automatic flowerpot machines is still in use at Halton Ceramics, Burlington. The machine is in its original condition except for the replacement of the drive shaft sheave (C) by V-belt drive.

The use of an automatic machine enabled the company to produce large quantities of low-priced pottery for the horticultural trade. Without such machinery the business could not have survived. Flowerpots were the only pottery made by machine in Ontario throughout the nineteenth century.

DRYING

When pottery was taken from the wheel or plaster mould, it had to be dried before it could be fired in the kiln. Potters would dry their wares on wooden planks outdoors in dry and warm weather, or in a drying room during wet and cold weather. The drying room was usually located near the kilns and would be equipped with a cast iron stove. The characteristics of a good drying room were a constant dry heat and a clean environment. The drying room at the R. Campbell's Sons pottery is shown in plate 2.13.

2.8 *Part of a plaster mould with finial made from the mould. Both were recovered during excavations at the Huron Pottery, Egmondville.*

Unfired pottery, called "green ware," would be kept in the drying room, after being dipped in slip or glaze and awaiting firing in the kiln.

MARKING POTTERY

There were three different types of marks that might be placed on a pot: a number indicating the capacity of the container (usually in Imperial measure), a crown, used by a few potteries to distinguish Imperial from American measure, and the name or mark of the potter or pottery, or of the merchant for whom the pottery had been made.

Six of the most common ways of marking pottery are described below, in the order of their frequency of use on Ontario pottery. These marks are illustrated in the checklist in Appendix Three.

1. *Impressed marks*
By far the most common type of mark on Ontario earthenware and stoneware is the impressed mark. The mark is made by applying a metal die, or metal letters forming a name, to the ware before decoration (occasionally after) and firing.

2. *Incised marks*
Incised marks are scratched into the clay, often on the base, before decoration or glazing. Most incised marks on Ontario pottery are the names of potters (signature marks), or the person for whom the piece was made. Incising was never used as a standard method of marking the products of a particular factory. An incised mark can be identified by the uneven edges, caused by the movement of the incising point.

2.9 *The handle of a "batter" for making a pancake of clay for use in hand-pressing wares. A plaster of Paris base would be attached to the handle by means of the grooves, shown in the picture. Handle was excavated at the Huron Pottery, Egmondville.*

3. *Printed marks*
Printed marks were usually made by painting over a stencil or by applying a rubber stamp. The printed mark is applied before glazing.

4. *Mould marks*
A mark can be part of a mould so that when the pot is formed by casting or pressing, the maker's name is an integral part of the ware, usually on the base of the piece.

2.10 *A pottery mould from which turkshead moulds would be made by hand-pressing. The clay mould was recovered during excavations at the Huron Pottery, Egmondville.*

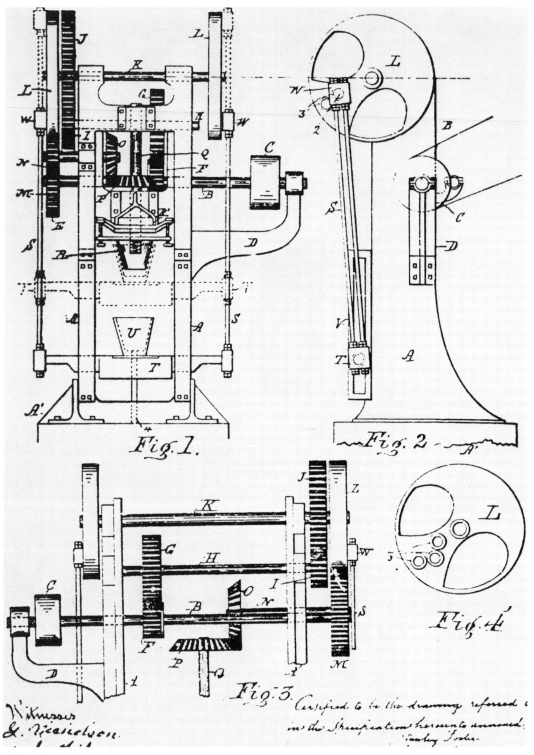

2.11 *Portions of patent drawings for the auto-matic flowerpot-making machine patented in 1909* by Fred & Stanley Foster, of the Foster Pottery Co., Hamilton.

2.12 *Unfired flowerpots are carried to a drying room where they are allowed to dry before being fired in the kiln.* Courtesy Mrs. Edward Hamilton.

2.13 *Green ware stored on wooden planks prior to being loaded into the kiln for the first, or bisque, firing.* Courtesy Ontario Archives.

5. *Hand-painted marks*
Hand-painted marks were applied by a brush on the bisque ware before glazing.
6. *Applied moulded marks*
Applied marks are not common on Ontario pottery. The impressed name is first applied to a separate raised pad of clay, and then the pad is attached to the base of the ware.

DECORATING POTTERY
Most of the earthenware and stoneware pottery produced in Ontario during the nineteenth century was never marked or decorated. This was a reflection not of the lack of aesthetic sensibility of the potter, but of the fact that he produced so many pieces that it was only the exceptional one that received the attention necessary to decorate it. Most of the pottery in private collections and museums today represents these exceptions, rather than the usual production of the factories.

The green ware could be decorated by incising one or more lines or a floral motif into the

fabric. David Burns, of Holmesville, Huron County, placed a characteristic single line around the outside of bowls (see plate 11.11), while fragments of pottery from the B. Lent site in Jordan, Lincoln County, had incised floral decorations reminiscent of a technique dating back to the early nineteenth century in New England and Upper New York State. Incised decoration was not widely used in Ontario.

The Ontario potter also impressed decorations into the green ware. A plaster coggle-wheel recovered during the excavations at the Huron Pottery, Egmondville (plate 2.14), was used to give an impressed pattern on the rim of flowerpots and on the base of special pieces such as water container stands. The wheel would have been mounted on a wooden handle and used similarly to the pie crimper of the pastry cook. At the Huron Pottery and B. Lent pottery, simple impressed designs were used on pottery. These were diamond, square and star-shaped. No doubt further examples could be found at other Ontario pottery sites.

Applied raised decorations were used to adorn the products of many Ontario potteries. The best example of this practice comes from the Huron Pottery, where during excavations in the years 1975 and 1976 I recovered twenty-two clay moulds, called *sprig moulds,* for producing clay appliqués — sprigs. The moulds were easy to use, durable, and cost little to produce. They were therefore made in a wide variety of designs. Examples of the sprig moulds from the Huron Pottery are shown in plates 2.15a and b and 2.16. These illustrate the range of sizes and complexity of design of the spriggings used to decorate pottery. Another sprig mould is shown in plate 11.5 with a lid of a water container which has attached identical spriggings.

To make a sprigging, a ball of clay was forced into the mould and the excess clay scraped away. When the clay had stiffened, the sprigging could then be removed. It could be attached to the green ware with a slip, which would hold it in place until the pottery had been slip dipped and then glazed. When the pottery was fired, the sprigging would be firmly attached.

The use of raised appliqués was not re-

2.15a, b *Two views of one of a number of sprig moulds recovered during excavations at the Huron Pottery, Egmondville. Sprig moulds were used to make relief decorations.*

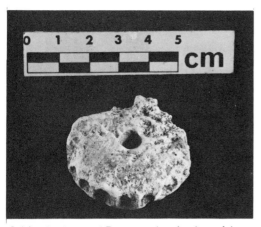

2.14 *A plaster of Paris coggle wheel used (on a handle) to decorate the rims of flowerpots at the Huron Pottery, Egmondville.*

2.16 *Sprig moulds could also be large and ornate, such as is shown in this example, also from the Huron Pottery, Egmondville.*

stricted to earthenware potteries, as shown by the stoneware water container in plate 12.24. That there are fewer examples of spriggings on stoneware may be explained by the fact that the stoneware potters could decorate their product with cobalt oxide, which was not generally possible with earthenware clays.

Occasionally potters produced special pieces with raised decorations, such as are shown in the clay jug in plate 9.8. This example is covered with scorpions, swastikas, snakes, death faces, etc. George Taylor, of Port Hope, in a taped conversation, stated that his father, James Taylor, made applied leaves, stems and flowers on earthenware pottery. Lawn vases, cemetery urns and special presentation pieces are also known to have been decorated with the Canadian coat of arms, floral motifs, and beaver motifs.

Another method of decoration used in Ontario pottery was a *slip* (usually of contrasting colour to the body of the vessel). The ware was dipped in a tub of slip, and occasionally the slip would be poured into the inside or over the piece. Slip-covered pottery was dried and then given a low temperature firing in the kiln.

There are no authenticated cases of *sgraffito* ware produced in Ontario. This tradition of covering a piece of pottery with a contrasting slip and then decorating it by scraping away the slip to expose the contrasting colour of the body beneath was a German and English pottery-making tradition that is not known to have been practised in Ontario during the nineteenth century. Some pottery was decorated by trailing slip over the green ware to produce a pleasing design, but this method also, although common in England and the United States during the nineteenth century, was only rarely practised in Ontario (see plate 7.24). Larger pottery factories at Brantford, London, and Hamilton produced mocha ware, which was banded with white, brown, yellow or blue slip. This practice of slip-banding produced a bowl that was very popular for kitchen use.

Stoneware was decorated with designs painted in cobalt oxide, applied in a liquid with a brush or the fingers. The cobalt oxide produced a blue colour. Since all but one of the stoneware potteries were established by persons trained in the United States, particularly New York State, it is not surprising that the decorations were similar (and in some instances identical) to those on New York State stoneware. Stoneware was also decorated by dipping it in a dark chocolate brown slip, an "Albany slip," which upon firing became a glaze. Earthenware pottery could also be decorated by painting with a metallic oxide as shown in plates 9.3, 9.4 and 10.3.

A few potters painted unglazed pottery with ordinary oil paint after firing. Outdoor ornamental vases and flowerpots would be covered with bright blue, red or green paint. Examples of such work were recovered in the excavations at the Huron Pottery, Egmondville.

Glazing

Most earthenware produced in Ontario was covered with a glass-like coating called a *glaze,* which made the pottery less porous, easier to clean and more attractive. Glazes used on earthenware had as their basic ingredients silicates and borates, and a flux. The exact glaze mixture depended on the source of the components, the clay body of the pottery, and the firing temperature. The development of glazes suited to the clay body was an important part of the potter's training. The glaze and clay had to "fit," i.e., the coefficient of contraction of the melted glaze had to be roughly equal to that of the clay, or the glaze would craze into a fine network of cracks. Likewise, if the composition of the slip and glaze was unsuitable for the clay fabric, the glaze would flake off. Impurities in the clay body might also cause blistering during the firing process. Earthenware potters were resourceful in obtaining the various ingredients for the glazes. Lead sheets from locally found tea chests could be heated and ground into lead oxide, and silicates could be obtained from white sand or flint.

A lead glaze was transparent, and the final colour of the pottery would be determined by the colour of the clay body and the firing temperature. By the addition of oxides of tin, iron, copper or manganese, it was possible to colour the glaze a milky white, shades of red, of blue-green, or purple-black, respectively. The range of colours of glazes in the nineteenth century was generally restricted to colours produced by the above four oxides.

In the latter part of the nineteenth century the potter could obtain prepared ingredients for glazes, extending the range of possibilities. Ingredients were imported from Great Britain, Germany and the United States to produce bristol ware which had an opaque glaze with zinc oxide as the main flux. Glazes such as "Rockingham" were popular throughout England and North America and were reproduced in Ontario as purple-brown glazes. Some potters describe a solid brown glaze as "rock," and advertised the pottery as "Rockingham ware," whether or not it had relief such as the traditional Rockingham ware had.

Most of the glazes used in the nineteenth century in Ontario were in the fritted form. *Fritting* was done by the potter in his workshop. The soluble constituents of the glaze were mixed with the insoluble ingredients and melted together over a hot fire. The premelting of the soluble part with the insoluble part produced a frit that was insoluble. After the ingredients had been mixed, the hot liquid was poured into cold water, shattering the mixture. The fritted glaze was then ground to a fine powder and added to water to make a glaze ready for use. The pottery would be dipped into the glaze, or the glaze could be swirled inside the vessel and the excess poured out. Sometimes the glaze was brushed on the pot. After glazing, the wares were transferred to the drying room. At this stage the glaze was a fine powdery layer on the pottery.

Earthenware pottery as "green ware" could be glazed, but the firing would have to be slow until the moisture from the clay body was evaporated. The pottery would then be given a rapid and higher temperature firing to fuse the glaze. It was usual for green ware to be given a first firing, called the *bisque* or biscuit firing, before the pottery was dipped into glaze. It was also possible for the biscuit ware to be covered with a slip before it was glazed. The exact steps in the manufacture of the pottery would depend on the decoration intended for the pottery and the use of the wares.

Stoneware pottery was given a *salt-glaze,* formed by throwing common salt on the fire. The salt volatilises and ionizes to sodium and chloride ions. Sodium ions combine with silica in the body to form a glaze; chloride ions are carried away in vents largely as hydrochloric acid. The surface of the stoneware had a rough texture, like an orange peel. Stoneware that was underfired could be finished with a bristol glaze, using zinc oxide as the flux. The London Crockery Manufacturing Co., London, produced large quantities of bristol ware at the end of the nineteenth century.

FIRING

Pottery, no matter how well made or how attractive, had to be fired if it were to be of any use. The kiln, or oven, for firing pottery was a vital part of the workshop. A trained potter would have to know how to build a kiln, how to use it under different weather conditions, and how to repair any damage that might occur. Unfortunately, no intact kiln remains, and all that is known about construction techniques is what can be deduced from evidence obtained from archaeological excavations and documentary references. From the information we have, it is clear that potters' kilns were not built to any standard specification, but according to the training and experience of the potter. It is not unusual to find that kilns in the same district of the province are quite different in construction.

Ontario pottery kilns were of three types: up-draft, cross-draft and down-draft. The up-draft kiln had the heat from the fire passing through the wares and out one or more vents in the crown. The earliest known up-draft kiln, which is also the best preserved example of a pottery kiln in Ontario, was recovered at the Lent Pottery, Jordan. The kiln was a rectangular multi-flued up-draft kiln with a single chamber. It had an over-all dimension of ca. two and one-half yards by three and one-quarter yards. The kiln is believed to have had a vaulted roof of flat stones laid in clay mortar, forming a number of openings.

At the David Burns Pottery, Holmesville, archaeological excavations revealed a rectangular cross-draft kiln, of the Cassel or Newcastle type.[1] The footing was of stone, upon which a brick superstructure was built. The kiln was two and one-half yards by four yards in dimension and had two parallel flues running the length of the structure. These were connected by two cross-flues, one at the eastern end and a second two feet from the eastern end (fig. 11.4). At the western end of each flue was a square firebox. Two cast iron doors were found, one in front of each firebox. Although the superstructure was not found intact, the arrangement of flues suggests that the kiln had a single chamber with the heat of the fires passing through the wares and out a chimney, presumably located at the eastern end.

The large up-draft kilns were bottle-shaped with a singular or multiple chamber, a circular or square base, and a circular superstructure. The kilns were from five to eleven yards high. A central chimney enabled the heat to pass through the wares and directly out of the structure. The bottle kilns were of brick construction, although the kiln at the William Eby pottery had a stone base.

The up-draft had certain disadvantages, including the fact that the wares could be damaged from exposure to the flames and smoke; the kiln was also very inefficient in the use of fuel. It was difficult to control the distribution of heat in the kiln with the wares closest to the fire being baked sooner than those near the crown of the kiln. Workshops with up-draft kilns had a great amount of wastage. Damaged pieces were broken and cast aside, forming large waster dumps at pottery sites. Examples of up-draft kilns are the Ahrens Pottery (plate 12.10), and the Humberstone pottery (plate 7.3). In spite of the disadvantages of the up-draft kilns, as long as wood was available and at a low cost, the kiln could be operated economically. A trained potter learned to control the firing of the kiln and keep wastage down to a reasonable amount.

The down-draft kiln appears to have been the most common type in Ontario. It was circular or rectangular in floor plan, and anywhere from three to six yards high. The down-draft kiln usually had an arched crown and therefore was often referred to as a "beehive" kiln. In the downdraft kiln, the heat from the fires passed up to the crown where it was deflected downward through the wares, through openings in the floor, and then through flues to the chimney. The advantages of the down-draft kiln were its efficiency in the use of fuel, and an even distribution of heat throughout the kiln.

At the Huron Pottery, Egmondville, all that remained of the down-draft kiln was the stone footing and one or two courses of brick that had been laid in mortar on top of the footing (plate 2.17). The kiln was circular in shape, with an outside diameter of about four yards.[2] There were four fireholes and the fragmentary remains of the chimney at the north end of the structure (plate 2.18). In general plan this kiln was similar to the brick and tile kilns of the period.

The kiln shown in plate 2.19 at the

2.17 *The remains of the base of a down-draft kiln at the Huron Pottery, Egmondville, after excavations had been completed.*

Richardson Pottery and Tileyard, Kerwood, was reported to have been used to fire pottery. This is the only known picture of a pottery kiln indicating the shape of the doorway, and the shape of the down-draft kiln.

The kiln at the R. Campbell's Sons pottery, Hamilton, was about eleven yards and composed of two chambers. The upper one was used to give the green wares a first firing and was of the up-draft type; the lower chamber (which was the hotter), was used to glaze the wares and was of the down-draft type.[3]

Unglazed green ware, such as flowerpots, stove tubes , and lawn ornaments, were given only one firing, as this was adequate to harden the clay. The green ware could be fired without any problems, provided the wares were not exposed to the flames, in which case the pot-

tery would have to be placed in protective containers ("saggars"). All the potter had to do in firing unglazed ware was to stack the pottery so that the weight of the columns was not so great as to damage the lowermost wares, and to place the pottery in positions that ensured an even firing.

Glazed ware required special attention when placed in the kiln, for if the pottery touched, it would stick together. The easiest way to separate large containers, when a little flaw of the glaze would not be unsightly or reduce the value of the piece, was to use two or three small sherds placed between the rim of one crock and the base of the one above. After the firing the pieces could be physically separated.

When a blemish was not acceptable, the potter would use small pieces of specially shaped fireclay, called separators, to keep the wares apart. There was a wide range of kinds of separators (or kiln furniture) in use in On-

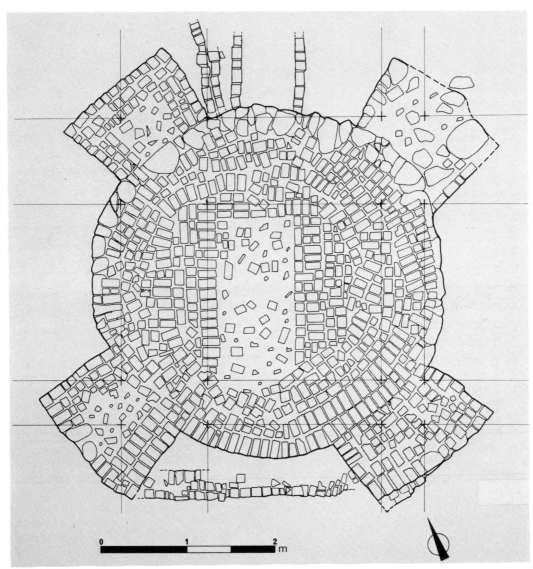

2.18 *Scale drawing of Egmondville Pottery kiln showing the location of four fireboxes and the remains of the chimney (top, centre).*

tario potteries, including wedges, tripods, pan rings, slabs and cockspurs (spurs). The shape and size of the separators was based on the potter's own preferences, the types of wares being fired, and the method of placing the wares in the kiln.

The loading of the kiln (called *charging*) at the Foster Pottery Company of Hamilton is shown in plate 13.4. This illustrates how unglazed flowerpots were stacked or placed for

the firing. When the kiln had been charged, the door was sealed with clay (called clamming). The kiln was fired and the temperature raised slowly so that the water in the clay could be driven off. At a temperature of 600°C to 700°C, the water of chemical combination would be driven off in the form of steam. The temperature of the wares could then be raised to ca. 1000°C to 1100°C. Although wood was adequate for low-firing temperatures, coal would be required to produce temperatures high enough for stoneware firing. The firing process could take thirty-six hours. The pottery was then left to cool slowly before being

2.19 *The kiln at the Richardson Pottery & Tile Yard, Kerwood, Ontario.* Courtesy Strathroy-Middlesex Museum.

2.20 *Packing teapots in a wooden crate at R. Campbell's Sons pottery, ca. 1895.* Courtesy Ontario Archives.

2.21 *Packing pottery in a willow crate at R. Campbell's Sons pottery. Straw was used as packing material.* Courtesy Ontario Archives.

removed from the kiln. The cooling process might take several days.

The firing temperature for glazed pottery had to be raised slowly so that the water in the clay body could escape without damaging the glaze on the surface. After all the water had been driven off, the temperature could be raised rapidly to melt and fuse the glaze. The whole process took several days, after which the wares would cool and then be ready to ship to the customers.

STORAGE, PACKING AND SHIPPING
Saleable pottery would be stored until enough wares were available to complete outstanding orders. The wares produced during the cold months would accumulate until the early spring when the roads were passable and the pottery wagon could make its visits to the local stores.

Pottery was packed for shipment in either wooded crates (plate 2.20), willow crates (plate 2.21), barrels, cartons, or directly into the potter's wagon. Straw was generally used as the packing material. The cost of packing and shipping was usually paid by the purchaser. A wooden crate as shown in plate 2.20 could hold twenty to twenty-five dozen assorted pieces of pottery.

3.
The Ontario
Pottery Industry

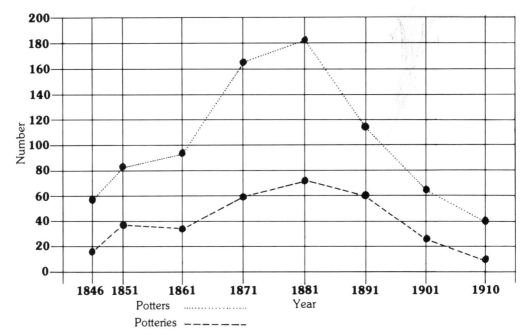

Fig. 3.1   *Graph showing development of potteries and number of potters in Ontario from 1846 to 1910.*

The pottery industry of Ontario spanned the period from ca. 1796 to 1974. During this time more than 150 potteries were operating in the province, producing a wide variety of earthenware and stoneware products.

The general development in the numbers of potteries and potters in the industry from 1846 until 1910 is shown in the graph of figure 3.1. The growth of the industry was sustained until the 1880s when a decline began that continued at a rapid pace until about 1910. The evidence for the development of the industry and the factors affecting this are discussed in three general categories: the formative period (1796-1845), the period of development (1846-1880), and the period of decline (1881-1910).

THE FORMATIVE PERIOD
(ca. 1796-1845)

The exact number and location of the earliest potteries is not known, as government records were not kept or have been lost over the years. In the late 1820s and early 1830s the movement of potters from the United States into Southern Ontario was part of a general migration of people from the eastern seaboard of the United States westward into Michigan and Indiana. The arrival in Upper Canada of potters such as B. Lent, of Jordan, and Cyrus Little, of Beamsville, are examples of such migration. A second source of potters was the immigration of German-speaking craftsmen to Waterloo County and the Niagara Peninsula. These immigrants were either Pennsylvania Germans or those who came from Germany to Canada by way of the United States. The great migration of potters from Great Britain had only begun, and the arrivals in this early period were the vanguard of the movement that was a response to the decline of the urban potteries in Great Britain in the 1850s and 1860s.

It is not an easy task to document the migration of the potters in the formative years. The first census for Ontario was not until 1842, and the returns were incomplete. I have been able to locate only seven potters in this earliest census. The names of these seven were John Marlatt, Cyrus Little, Patrick McGaw, Samuel Horning, Andrew Biehn (all of Beamsville, Lincoln County), Joseph P. Elson (of London Township, Middlesex County) and John Harvey (of Yarmouth Township, Elgin County). Street directories, gazetteers and historical atlases for Ontario were not published until after 1846, except for the city of Toronto, which, although not listing inhabitants by occupation, did have its first directory in 1833. Petitions for grants of land from the Crown, although useful for genealogical or local history work, are indexed by name of petitioner and not by profession. Likewise, there were few immigration records until late in the nineteenth century.

In some townships there were assessment rolls in the late 1840s and early 1850s, but many of these have subsequently been lost by fire, flood, and indifference. Despite the severe limitations imposed by the absence of documentary sources, we can locate many pioneer pottery sites.

I have located twenty-seven potteries in operation during part or all of the formative years. The name of the owner of each pottery and the location of the workshop is shown in figure 3.2. This list may not be complete, but it represents those workshops for which there is some documentary and archaeological evidence. These potteries were located near military and colonization roads. The potters in Grenville, Northumberland, Durham, York, Wentworth, Lincoln and Welland Counties were located in important military roads bordering the shores of Lake Ontario. The potteries in Waterloo, Brant, Elgin and Middlesex Counties were near settlement roads and local rivers.

It is difficult to obtain personal information on the potters of this early period. It would be helpful if, for example, we knew where they learned the trade, and where they worked before coming to Canada. We have, unfortunately, only the most general information on these workmen. Of the potters that we do have information about, Samuel Eby and John Yeigh were from Pennsylvania. B. Lent may have been the same person active in New Jersey and later in New York State in the 1830s. S.V. Carroll was working in New York State in the 1830s. Lyman Gleason had established a pottery with his brother Fortunatus at Morganville, New York State, in the 1830s.

The earliest known potter of German origin was Jacob Bock, who inscribed his name on two moulded earthenware jars, both decorated with a relief portrait of "S. AMBROSIUS." Other potters of German origin were William Schwab and Michael Steumpfle, both of whom had established a pottery in Preston, Waterloo County. I have given details of the potters of German origin because they established a pattern of settlement in Waterloo County that continued until the 1860s. After this time they spread over a larger area, including Brant, Grey, Lincoln, and Middlesex Counties, but never became concentrated enough to establish a regional "Germanic tradition" of pottery making.

THE PERIOD OF DEVELOPMENT
(1846-1880)

During this period, there was a rapid increase in the number of potteries and potters in the province, and a wealth of original sources of information on them became available. The first comprehensive gazetteer was published in 1846 and the first dominion-wide census was in 1851-52. This census reported the names of all members of a household, their profession, age, marital status, and country of origin. The reporting of the profession "potter" continued from 1851 until the census of 1900-01, when the practice was discontinued and potters were presumably included under brickmakers.

Unfortunately, the census of 1851-52 is incomplete as the records for the cities of Toronto and London and the townships of Halowell, Hope, Woolwich and Beverley have been lost. In these municipalities there were important potteries. The data from the 1851-52 census is not only incomplete, but is also often inaccurate.Frequently the census-taker noted a person's occupation as "potter" but did not report, as was required, on the pottery business itself. For example, the aggregate returns for 1851-52 indicate there were seven potteries in operation at the time, employing sixty-six potters. A district by district check of the returns indicates that there were at least thirty-eight potteries employing eighty-seven potters.

In the 1860s, potteries became established in more northerly areas such as Bruce, Grey, Simcoe and Ontario counties. The northernmost extent of the potteries can be marked by a line connecting (from east to west) the communities of Peterborough, Beaverton, Orillia and Owen Sound, with Owen Sound being the northernmost point at 44°40' north latitude. Potteries in these communities not only supplied wares to local shops but also packed earthenware for shipment by railroad or steamer across Georgian Bay to more remote areas. The location of potteries active in the 1846-1880 period is shown in figures 3.3a and 3.3b.

An important influence on the development of the pottery industry was the establishment in 1849 of two stoneware potteries, at Brantford and Picton. During the next twenty-two years there were stoneware potteries established in Paris, Toronto, Hamilton, York Township, Cornwall and Belleville, so that by 1870-71 there were eight workshops operating in the province. These urban factories had become a major force in the decline of the smaller earthenware factories.

Fig. 3.2   *The distribution of potteries active in Ontario in the period 1796-1845.*

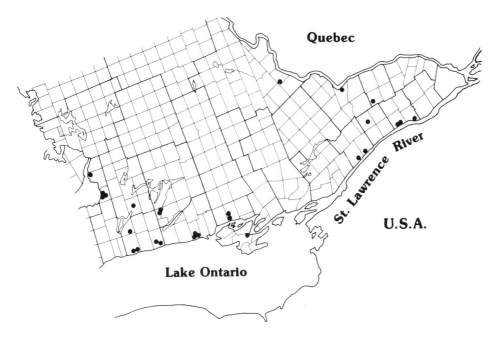

Fig. 3.3a *The distribution of potteries in Eastern Ontario in 1846-1880.*

The census returns of 1860-61, 1870-71, and 1880-81 illustrate the stranglehold that stoneware potteries had on the industry. In the 1860-61 returns, three of the fourteen potteries that reported figures were stoneware factories. These three plants accounted for $8,900 worth of pottery, or 52% of the total dollar value of the wares produced during the year 1860. By the 1870-71 census there were eight stoneware factories of the fifty-eight potteries reporting. These eight factories produced $110,000 of the total of $186,405 worth of pottery produced in the census year. This means that by this date a small number of potteries accounted for 59% of the dollar value of all wares produced in the province. The trend continued and in the 1880-81 census the ten stoneware potteries, of a total of ninety-six reported operating, produced $207,000 of the total of $314,645 worth of pottery produced, or 66% of the total dollar value. Although the census returns of 1890-91 show a marked decline in the pottery industry, the stoneware factories continued to show a better performance than their earthenware counterparts.

A statistical analysis of the returns for indus-

trial establishments in the 1870-71 census shows other factors indicative of the favourable position of the stoneware potteries. The average wage per month per employee in a stoneware pottery was $27.24, while the wage for an employee of an earthenware pottery was $21.94. This means that the stoneware potters earned $63.64 more per year than the earthenware potters, a difference of 24%. Stoneware factories also employed a larger work force than the local earthenware concern. The average number of employees for each stoneware factory was ten, while the earthenware pottery employed an average of two and one-half.

The dominance of stoneware factories illustrates a pattern of industrial activity that developed in the nineteenth century in many Ontario businesses. The founders of the stoneware factories in Brantford, Picton, Cornwall, and Toronto were from the United States. They came to Canada with capital, know-how, and in some cases, potters trained in the United States. These factories were also dependent on the importing of clay from New Jersey, Ohio, and in later years, England. As

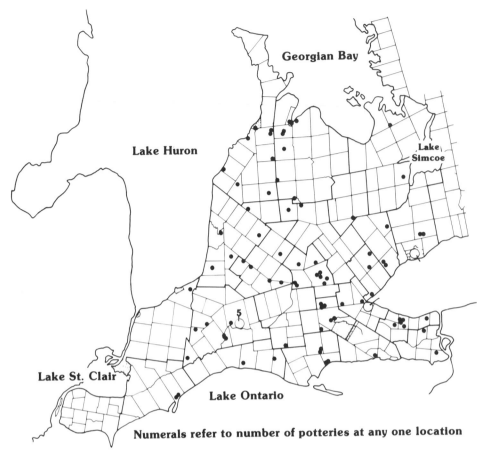

Fig. 3.3b *The distribution of potteries in Western Ontario, 1846-1880.*

stoneware was fired at a higher temperature than earthenware, the fuel for the kilns was coal, and this too had to be imported into Canada. The stoneware factories were, in summary, dependent on imported skills, capital and raw materials.

Economic common sense dictated that stoneware should be produced closer to the source of the raw materials and fuel; this is what ultimately doomed the Ontario stoneware industry. The last major stoneware business was the Toronto Pottery Co., Ltd., a wholly-owned subsidiary of the Robinson Clay Products Co., of Akron, Ohio. The Toronto outlet never produced a single pot in Ontario, but acted as a distribution centre for wares produced in Ohio. In the year 1924 the Toronto Pottery Co. was selling close to $100,000 worth of stoneware in Canada. A

Canadian catalogue, dated 1912-14, is a replica of the United States catalogue, except for the prices, which were generally twenty-five percent higher in Canada.

In order to break the control of foreign-made stoneware, a group of thirteen Ontario potters assembled in Hamilton, Ontario, in January, 1873, to form the Ontario Earthenware Manufacturers Association, with the aims of the organization being to forge a network of potteries that would not undersell other members of the association. Stiff penalties were set out for any infractions of the agreement by the signators, and the association appears to have had some influence in establishing uniform prices. Jacob Henry Ahrens indicates on a price list of his firm that his charges were in conformity with the rates agreed upon by this association. Signators to the agreement, made with Robert Campbell of Hamilton, and his brother William Campbell as witnesses, were: John Davis, S. T. Humberstone, McGlade & Schuler, William A. Brown, J. H. Ahrens, J. Bradwin, Robert Irwin, Samuel Burns, Joseph Brown, James Harrison Burns, Arthur Doidge and William Taylor. The Association does not appear to have had any long-term impact on the Ontario industry, and it is not heard of again after the initial agreement.

PERIOD OF DECLINE
(1881-1910)

By the late 1880s the pottery industry began its irreversible decline. First, the change in the United States shipping tariffs on clay and coal doubled and sometimes tripled the cost of raw materials from the price quoted at the pit, thus escalating the cost of manufacturing stoneware in Ontario. As the pottery owners themselves wrote to the Canadian Minister of Finance in the 1880s, the Americans were at a distinct advantage by having their factories much closer to the source of raw materials. The fact that Canada did not adequately protect the domestic market from the large flow of

cheaper imports from the United States and Great Britain meant that Canadian stoneware factories could not survive the stiff competition for the domestic market. The locations of potteries during this period are shown in figures 3.4a and 3.4b.

There were other influences that caused the decline of the potteries, including the growing affluence (disposable income) of Ontarians, which meant that when they had the money they preferred to purchase imported porcelain and stoneware, even if at a higher cost that the plain domestic earthenware. There was also the improvement in transportation and therefore in the distribution of goods. By the 1880s there was a network of railroads connecting the major centres of population, enabling the potter to ship his goods throughout the province, and at times to Western Canada. It also meant that imported goods from the United States could be shipped to Ontario without any difficulty.

The most direct cause of the decline of Ontario potteries was the development of alternative ways to store and process farm and household foods. The ice box replaced pickling crocks, mechanical cream separators re-

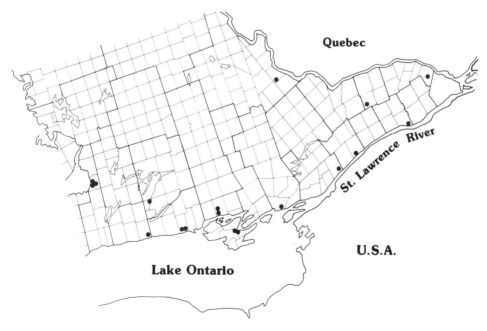

Fig. 3.4a *The distribution of potteries in Eastern Ontario in 1881-1910.*

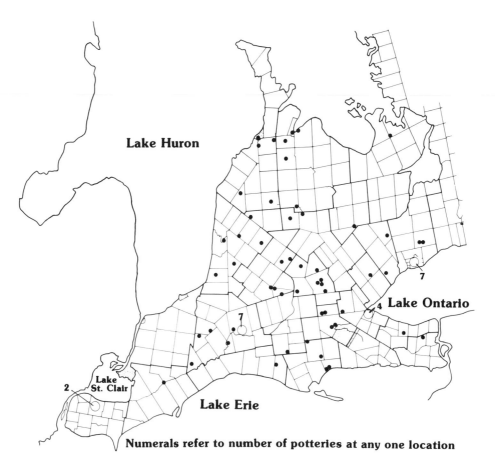

Fig. 3.4b *The distribution of potteries in Western Ontario, 1881-1910.*

placed the milk-skimming pan, glass jars replaced the pottery fruit and preserve jars. One by one the traditional products of the pottery were superseded by lighter, more attractive alternatives.

In the early twentieth century the major product of potteries for which sustained demand persisted was flowerpots. Foster Pottery Co., John Davis & Son, and John Cranston & Son were the three major producers of flowerpots until the early 1920s.

The Brantford Stoneware Manufacturing Co., Ltd. produced brightly coloured jardiniéres, hanging flowerpots, umbrella stands and other decorative wares in the hopes of being able to recapture the Ontario market, but their experiment, which lasted some eleven years, ended with the company being dissolved.

EPILOGUE

There were eleven potteries that continued to produce wares beyond 1910. These are shown in figure 3.5. The last major pottery which produced a wide variety of institutional products was the R. Campbell's Sons, of Hamilton. This business was brought to an end by a disastrous fire in 1947. The Foster Pottery Co., also of Hamilton, produced flowerpots using automatic machines, until 1974, when the plant caught fire and the business closed.

As the once busy potters became too old to

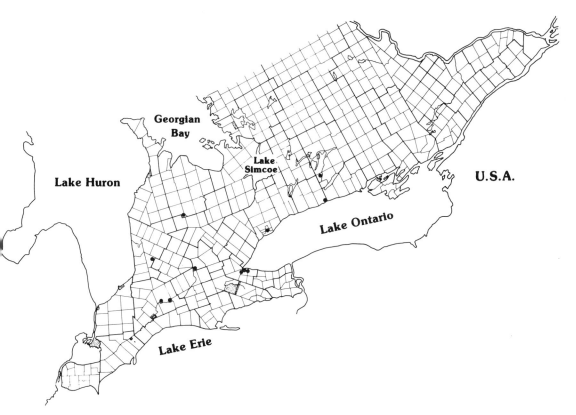

Fig. 3.5   *The distribution of potteries active in On-*
tario after 1910.

continue their trade, or turned to other pursuits
that promised a better living, the shops closed.
Little public notice was made of the disappear-
ance from the community of these once proud
craftsmen. The history of each of the more

than 150 potteries from 1796 to 1974, including the location, dates of operation, the products and major achievements of their owners
and workmen, is the purpose of the next chapters of this book.

4.
Potteries of
Eastern Ontario

Renfrew County • Ottawa   St. Eugene

• Russell

Inkerman   • Cornwall
•   • Aultsville

•Johnstown
•/Prescott
•/Augusta Township
•Brockville

Cataraqui •

Fig. 4.1 *Location of potteries in eastern Ontario during the nineteenth century.*

Few potteries existed in the eastern counties of Ontario, due to the sparse population and the limited sources of clay. The businesses that were founded were located, with few exceptions, along the north shore of the St. Lawrence River.

The location of the potteries in the eastern counties during the nineteenth century is shown in figure 4.1.

GRENVILLE COUNTY

Augusta Township

The earliest known pottery in the province was established by Samuel Humberstone, who by 1796 was living on a two and one-half acre part of the southeastern corner of lot 27, concession 1, Augusta Township. In the deed for the land, dated January 31, 1823, a pottery building is listed.[1] Apparently, the pottery had been operating for some time before Samuel Humberstone acquired title to the land only months before his death, in March of the same year. Samuel Humberstone bequeathed his glaze-grinding wheels and his tools to his son, Thomas Humberstone, who had begun his own pottery in York County.[2]

Prescott

The earliest pottery in Prescott was operated by Asabel Gerards, Jr. In an 1837 issue of the *Prescott Herald & Grenville General Advertiser*, a notice reads:

A. Geralds Junior, begs leave to inform the public that he keeps constantly on hand at his earthenware establishment, at the lower extremity of Main Street in the Village, a general assortment of WARE. Comprising jugs from one quart to five gallons, large and small butter crocks, milk pans, preserve jars, flower pots, stove crocks of various lengths from three to twenty inches, pitchers, candlesticks & c. together with other activities too numerous to mention; He ventures to assert that his WARE is inferior to none manufactured in America, and that he can with confidence recommend it to the Public.[3]

The location of Gerald's pottery in 1837 is not certain for he did not purchase land in Prescott until 1840, when he bought lot 7 on the north side of King Street.[4] Geralds sold the property in 1845, and this brought his business to an end.

The Mooney family was active in pottery-making in Prescott and the nearby town of Johnstown, during the last half of the nineteenth century. Prominent potters in the family were James and John Mooney, two of the sons of Patrick Mooney, a grocer in the community. By 1847 James Mooney advertised:

MOONEY'S EARTHEN WARE POTTERY

The subscriber begs to inform the public that he has constantly on hand a large assortment of ware in the pottery business, manufactured by the best mechanics, and of excellent materials.[5]

Mooney's property was lot 9 on the north side of King Street, at the east end of town near Fort Wellington's parade grounds.[6] A jug made by James Mooney and stamped with his name is shown in plate 4.1.

The operator of the business in 1856 was John Mooney, who in that year won a first prize in the Provincial Exhibition for the best specimen of pottery and the best assortment of pottery.[7] An 1869 directory lists Hugh Mooney, formerly of Johnstown, as operating the pottery.[8] Presumably, Hugh Mooney took over the business from John Mooney.

The Prescott pottery closed before 1870, as it is not reported in the census of that year. Instead, the pottery in Johnstown is described.

Johnstown

James Mooney, Sr., moved from Prescott to Johnstown sometime between 1847 and

4.1 *An earthenware jug made by James Mooney of Prescott. The jug is of red earthenware with a clear lead glaze.*

1852 and established a pot shop on the south side of King Street.[9] The 1851-52 census indicates that James Mooney employed his sons Hugh, James Jr., and John. James Mooney, Sr., died in 1855 and willed his business to his son James Jr.,[10] who had left in 1853 for Ottawa, where he opened a shop on the south side of Rideau Street in the Sandy Hill area. Hugh Mooney had moved to Prescott by 1869, leaving John Mooney to operate the

Johnstown business. In the 1870-71 census the business was reported as operating all year and employing two men and one boy to produce twenty kiln loads of earthenware valued at $1200.[11] The Johnstown pottery had closed by 1902, when the property was sold.[12]

CARLETON COUNTY

Ottawa

James Mooney, Jr., moved from Grenville County in 1853 and founded a pottery on lot 54 on the south side of Rideau Street, at the intersection of Wurtemberg Street.[13] The shop, which was known as the Ottawa Pottery Co., produced flower pots, stove tubes, preserve jars, liquor jugs, cream and butter pots and milk pans.[14] Mooney died in 1869 and pottery-making was discontinued.[15]

RENFREW COUNTY

A pottery was operating in the southern townships of Renfrew County during the 1880s, but I have not been able to determine the name of the potter nor the location of the works. The 1880-81 census indicates that the business employed one male hand to make articles valued at $600 a year.[16] This was a very small enterprise, perhaps explaining its absence from contemporary records of the county.

RUSSELL COUNTY

Russell

A small earthenware pottery was begun by Adam Elliott in 1873 on a two-acre parcel of lot 11, concession 3, Russell Township, near the town of Duncanville, now called Russell.[17] The pottery was a marginal enterprise, producing only $300 worth of goods in 1870, and $200 worth in 1890.[18] The pottery continued until late in 1890, when Elliott sold the land.[19] He is still listed as a potter in a directory of 1899, but since there is no credit rating for his business after 1890, the business probably did not continue beyond the earlier date.[20]

PRESCOTT COUNTY

St. Eugene

Antoine Lambert is listed as a potter in St.

Eugene in an 1865-66 directory.[21] He had purchased a fifteen-acre parcel of land known as part of the east half of lot 5, concession 8E., Hawkesbury Township.[22] There is no further evidence of a pottery in Prescott County until the 1890-91 census, which indicates one pottery operating in the county. It is not known if this latter reference is to Lambert, or another workshop. In any case, it was hardly a full-time job, as the census returns indicate that the business employed one male hand at a yearly wage of $40 to produce $100 worth of pottery.[23]

DUNDAS COUNTY

Inkerman

Frederick Merkley is listed as a potter in Inkerman, Mountain Township, in an 1865-66 directory,[24] but if he owned a pottery it is unlikely that he actually worked there, as credit ratings for 1872 through 1876 list Frederick Merkley & Son as owners of a very prosperous general store and mills in the region.[25]

John Irving, an eighteen-year-old potter in 1870, is reported in the census of that year as working as a potter in Williamsburgh Township, but no further mention is made of a pottery in the list of industrial establishments in the same census.[26]

STORMONT COUNTY

Aultsville

Two potteries operating in Aultsville were owned by members of the Elliott family. John Elliott immigrated to Canada from Ireland ca. 1848, and by 1853 we have evidence of the location of his pottery. In that year he purchased three-quarters of an acre of the east half of lot 32, concession 1, Osnabruck Township.[27] The land was located on the south side of the Queen's Highway, now Highway 2, and bordered the St. Lawrence River. Elliott produced pottery and bricks, the latter being in great demand in the area for building construction.[28] Also living in Aultsville at the time of the 1860-61 census were John Elliott's brothers, William James and Alexander. The pottery was reported in a directory as Elliott & Brothers,[29] so presumably they were partners in the enterprise.

By the late 1870s Alexander Elliott is operating a pottery in Cannifton, Hastings County. In 1864 John Elliott purchased a half-acre piece of land owned by Gordon Empey, who had been listed in an 1851 directory as proprietor of a pottery.[30] The extent of the Elliott pottery in 1870 is reported in the census, where the business is listed as employing three men to produce earthenware valued at $1,000.[31] John Elliott, Sr., worked at the business until ca. 1879, when his son John Jr., who also owned a hotel, took over the workshop. The pottery was sold by John Elliott, Jr., in 1901.[32]

William Elliott, brother of John Elliott, Sr., is first listed in 1865, apparently working with his brother. In 1870 he purchased a quarter-acre part of the east half of lot 32, concession 1, Osnabruck Township from Richard Dafoe.[33] He was now operating independently. The census of 1870-71 indicates that he produced assorted types of earthenware valued at $2,000 yearly.[34] William Elliott produced pottery until 1893, as indicated in credit-rating manuals,[35] and then made only bricks until ca. 1907.

The 1851-52 census indicates that Richard Dafoe, Sr., and his son, Erastus Dafoe, were operating a pottery in Aultsville.[36] The "wood pottery shop" may have been located on land later purchased by William Elliott in 1870.

The town of Aultsville was flooded by the development of the St. Lawrence Seaway project, making it impossible to do a field study to determine the location of the potteries in the region.

Cornwall

The first pottery in Cornwall was begun by Oren L. Ballard, who by 1864 had leased part of hydraulic lot 4 in the town, at the foot of Canal Street, from William Mattice.[37] Ballard had operated a pottery in St. John's, Quebec, and wares with his name and the Quebec location are found in private collections and museums. Examples of stoneware made by Ballard while working in Cornwall are shown in plates 4.2 and 4.3. Ballard's business was purchased in 1869 by David Andrew Flack and Isaac Hatfield Van Arsdale.[38] Both of these men were Americans who had worked in New York State before moving to Canada.[39]

4.2 *Three-gallon stoneware preserve jar with the impressed mark O.L.BALLARD/CORNWALL, C.W.*

Cornwall was well situated for the shipment of stoneware clay to the factory and the transport of finished pottery to communities along the north shore of the St. Lawrence. The demand for stoneware must have been very great, for less than two years after Flack & Van Arsdale had purchased Ballard's business, the census taker reports that the partners had $11,000 invested and employed ten men all year to make $30,000 worth of stoneware. This required 550 tons of clay valued at $3,000.[40] The pottery workshop was powered by water, and is the only pottery in the province to use this type of motive power.[41] The business continued to grow in the 1880s and 1890s, with credit ratings indicating that it had a pecuniary worth of $10,000-$20,000 in 1881 and $20-$40,000 in 1891.[42] Beginning in the year 1900 the credit ratings of the company began a rapid decline, and early in the year 1907 the business was sold.[43] The closing of the business was hastened by the death of Isaac Van Arsdale in 1907, the partner most active in the daily operation of the pottery. David A. Flack, although originally trained as a

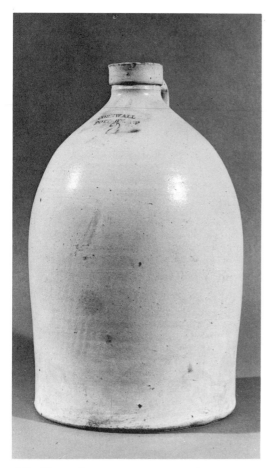

4.3 *Two-gallon stoneware jug with impressed mark, CORNWALL/POTTERY, C.W. This piece was made during the time O. L. Ballard owned the business.*

4.4 *Five-gallon stoneware jug with impressed mark FLACK & VAN ARSDALE/CORNWALL, ONT.*

CORNWALL, O. are shown in plates 4.4, 4.5, and 4.6.

LEEDS COUNTY

Brockville

potter, became an entrepreneur in Cornwall and controlled a batting factory, a coal business, and railway ticket agency. Potters known to have been employed at the factory include William Heck, Gordon Runions, Samuel McKnight and Philip Carpenter.

A characteristic decoration of Flack & Van Arsdale pottery is the stylized bird made in cobalt-blue colour on the grey stoneware body. Although this design is not exclusively used by Flack & Van Arsdale, the majority of extant pieces made by the firm have this decoration. Examples of stoneware made by the firm, and frequently marked with the impressed name FLACK & VAN ARSDALE/

For less than a decade a small stoneware pottery was operating on Hartley Street in Brockville. The pottery was known as White & Handley (John A. White and Edward Handley) or White, Handley & Co. when it began in 1884.[44] A two-gallon stoneware butter crock with the impressed mark WHITE & HANDLEY/BROCKVILLE, ONT. is shown in plate 4.7. After 1884 the pottery appears to have been taken over by new owners, although H.A. White, presumably related to John A. White, is listed as a potter as late as 1886. In this year the business is known as Comstock's Pottery.[45] In 1890 the pottery produced $500

4.5 *Three-gallon FLACK & VAN ARSDALE crock with cobalt-blue bird motif.*

4.7 *A two-gallon stoneware butter crock with impressed mark WHITE & HANDLEY/BROCKVILLE ONT. This business was in operation ca. 1884-1886.*

4.6 *An unusual decoration on a Flack & Van Arsdale jug. Most jugs made at the pottery had a stylized robin in cobalt blue.*

worth of wares.[46] There is no information on wares produced by the plant during the Comstock period. The business closed in the 1890s.

FRONTENAC COUNTY

Cataraqui

James Elliott established a pottery on a twenty-acre part of the northwestern part of lot 17, concession 2, Kingston Township. Elliott purchased the property in 1881,[47] and worked at the site for a year before selling it to William D. Martin.[48] The nearest post office was Cataraqui, a village about five kilometres northwest of the town of Kingston. The 1880-81 census reports that a pottery in the county, presumably that of Elliott, produced crockery valued at $2,000 annually.[49]

William D. Martin is listed frequently in directories until 1899, when he is reported as owning a "pottery and toll gate."[50] The pottery was discontinued around 1900,[51] and Martin sold the business in 1904, thus bringing to an end pottery-making in Frontenac County.[52]

5.
Kilns of Prince Edward and Hastings Counties

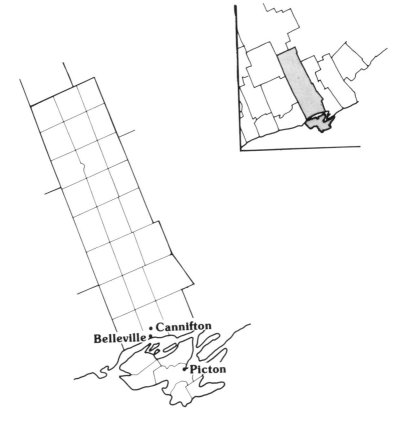

Fig. 5.1 *Locations of potteries in Prince Edward County and Hastings County.*

Prince Edward County and Hastings County are closely linked in the history of the pottery industry through the business activities of the firm of Hart Bros. & Lazier. Established first in Prince Edward County, this pottery moved in 1879 to Belleville.

In the 1890s a second, much smaller pottery was operating in Picton; likewise, there was a village pottery in Cannifton as early as 1857. The locations of the potteries in Prince Edward and Hastings Counties are shown in figure 5.1.

PRINCE EDWARD COUNTY

Picton
The William Hart pottery in Picton shares with Morton & Co., of Brantford, Brant County, the

distinction of being the first stoneware factories in the province. Both firms were established in 1849, with the Picton pottery probably being earlier than the Brantford firm.

The history of the Picton stoneware pottery follows the names of the potters who either operated or owned the business.

5.1 *A five-gallon stoneware crock with stylized bee design in cobalt-blue colour. Piece is marked with impressed name W. HART. &. CO.*

W. Hart & Co. (1849-1855)

William Hart came to Picton in 1849 from Ogdensburg, New York State, where his father, James Hart, had established a pottery in 1841.[1] In 1849 William Hart, with the financial assistance of his uncle Samuel Hart, of Fulton, New York, purchased part of lot 6, North West Carrying Place, Hallowell Township, from Samuel Skinner who was Samuel Hart's nephew.[2] Samuel Hart was also a potter, but throughout the history of the Picton stoneware business he remained a financial backer, and never worked at the pottery himself.

A note in the 1851-52 census gives us the only detailed financial information we have about the pottery under William Hart:

William Hart Stoneware factory cost £300; wrought by horsepower; amount of ware manufactured about £1,000; amount invested to carry on the pottery yearly £350; 5 persons usually employed.[3]

The census reports the names of three of the potters working at the plant in 1851-52: Samuel Skinner, Henry Whitman and Sapress (*sic*) Storz (*sic*).

Pottery produced during William Hart's time was marked with the impressed name W. HART &. CO/PICTON, C.W., or just W. HART &. Co. Examples of pottery produced in this period are shown in plates 5.1 and 5.2.

5.2 *A two-gallon stoneware water container with painted, stylized bee in cobalt-blue colour. The piece is marked W. HART. &. CO.*

On October 17, 1855, William Hart sold his interest in the pottery to his uncle, Samuel Hart, for £475.[4] William Hart returned to Ogdensburg, New York, and worked in the pottery there until his death on November 12, 1869.[5] Samuel Hart leased the Ontario pottery to Samuel Skinner, who was then the foreman in the plant.

S. Skinner & Co. (1855-1864)

Samuel Skinner operated the business until 1864, when he sold his one-third part of the lot to Samuel Hart for $4,600.[6] Skinner marked the wares he produced with S. SKINNER & CO. or the fuller name S. SKINNER & CO./PICTON, C.W. or PICTON, P.O. Examples of pottery produced during this period are shown in plates 5.3 through 5.7. The pieces

5.3 A stoneware preserve jar with cobalt-blue bird and with impressed maker's mark of S. SKINNER & CO./PICTON, P.O. The piece was produced at Picton between 1855 and 1864.

5.5 A very attractive six-gallon stoneware butter churn with bird and flower motif, similar to design elements found on New York State pottery at this time. Piece is marked S. SKINNER & CO./PICTON, C.W.

5.4 A five-gallon stoneware butter crock with elaborate flower design in cobalt blue.

5.6 A two-gallon stoneware crock with design elements similar to piece shown in plate 5.4.

5.7 *The pine-tree motif was popular on stoneware produced during Skinner's time at the Picton pottery.*

are all decorated with cobalt blue designs, including flowers (plate 5.4 and 5.6), bird and flower (plate 5.5), and a pine tree (plate 5.6). These contemporary motifs are characteristic of stoneware produced in New York State.

Very little information is known about the pottery during the Skinner years, and local government records, which might have helped to describe the business and list the potters who worked in Picton, have been destroyed by fire.

G.I. Lazier (1864-1879)

After the departure of Samuel Skinner, the potter George I. Lazier, the husband of Samuel Hart's daughter Alcena, took over the operation of the pottery. From 1864 until 1879, when Alcena Lazier and her two brothers formed the partnership of Hart Bros. & Lazier, George I. Lazier produced crockery with his own name on it.

The census of 1870-71 indicates the extent of the pottery at the beginning of that decade. The works employed six men to produce stoneware and Rockingham ware valued at $5,000. This required 150 tons of stoneware clay, worth $1,350,[7] all brought in from New Jersey.

A price list from Lazier's time is shown in plate 5.8, indicating the variety of wares that were in supply at the pottery, and the contemporary prices. Examples of pottery produced

in Picton are also shown, including a crock with two dog handles (plate 5.9), a six-gallon butter churn with a hen and the date "1875" (plate 5.10), and a three-gallon stoneware crock with a personal inscription (plate 5.11). The pieces are impressed with the mark G.I. LAZIER/PICTON, C.W.

In 1874 Samuel Hart sold his interest in the Picton pottery to his daughter Alcena M. Lazier for $4,600, thus ending his financial interest in the Canadian enterprise.[8]

Hart Bros & Lazier (1879-1887)

The partnership of Hart Bros. & Lazier was formed late in 1879 to accommodate the expansion of the business to a newly leased pottery in Belleville.[9] The three members of the new organization were Alcena Lazier, who owned the Picton pottery operated by her husband, George I.; Charles A. Hart, who managed the Belleville part of the business;[10] and Edwin E. Hart, who remained in Fulton, New York State, and remained a financial backer, but was not otherwise active in the business.

During the 1880s both factories were busy turning out stoneware products, although the more convenient location of the Belleville plant saw a gradual shift away from the Picton works. This is also reflected in the census of 1880-81, which reports that the Picton plant had two male employees compared with the six employees of a decade earlier. Although the value of the wares produced in 1880-81 was $1,000 more than 1870-71, the dollar value of imported stoneware clay was less than half of that of a decade earlier, suggesting that they produced far less stoneware in 1880-81 than in the 1870-71 period.[11]

On the death of George I. Lazier in 1887, the Picton plant was closed and the business continued at Belleville. The Picton property was sold by Alcena Lazier in 1892.[12]

The types of ware produced under the partnership did not differ noticeably from that produced under the firm of G.I. Lazier. An example of the impressed mark H.B. & L./PICTON, C.W. of this period, a relatively rare mark, is shown in plate 5.12. The abbreviation of the firm name as H.B. & L. was also used at this time for products from the Belleville plant, but the different name for the location distinguishes the origin of the product.

PICTON, Ont., *April 2 d* 1872

Mr C. McJohn

Bought of **George I. Lazier,**

Manufacturer of Every Description of

STONE AND ROCKINGHAM WARE.

Wholesale Price List adopted by Convention of Potters of the Dominion of Canada.

5.8 *Price list of G. I. LAZIER showing the types of pottery produced, and the cost of stoneware.* Courtesy Royal Ontario Museum.

5.9 *Stoneware crock with dog handles and cobalt-blue leaf design. Piece is marked G.I. LAZIER/PICTON, C.W. Courtesy National Museums of Canada, Ottawa.*

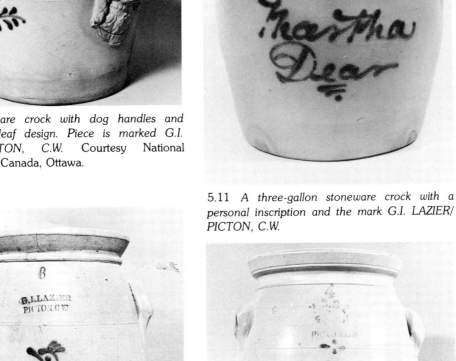

5.11 *A three-gallon stoneware crock with a personal inscription and the mark G.I. LAZIER/PICTON, C.W.*

5.10 *An elaborate six-gallon stoneware butter churn with hen and the year 1875 in cobalt-blue colour and with impressed mark G.I. LAZIER/PICTON, C.W.*

5.12 *A four-gallon stoneware churn with mark H.B. & L./PICTON, C.W. The same abbreviations for the firm with the location BELLEVILLE/ONT. are used for the other pottery operated by the firm.*

5.13 *Photo of the Handley pottery in Picton. This small earthenware workshop was in operation from 1891 to ca. 1899.* Courtesy Mrs. Percy E. Rush.

5.14 *Earthenware spaniel with dark brown glaze and marked HANDLEY BROS./PICTON.* Courtesy Mrs. Ruth Pollard.

On July 19, 1978, a plaque was erected on the site of the Picton pottery to commemorate the enterprise of the potters — the only pottery in the province to be so recognized.

Handley Brothers
William J. and Henry Handley were working for Hart Bros. & Lazier in Belleville when, in 1891, they purchased lots 131, 132 and 133 on the north side of Spencer Street in Picton for the site of an earthenware pottery.[13] The site bordered on the Bay of Quinte, and was an ideal spot for obtaining water necessary for the cleaning of the clay. A picture of the pottery building (plate 5.13) shows the windmill for pumping water. The kiln was located left of the area shown in the picture. Henry Handley and his family lived above the workshop. Pottery produced during this period was marked HANDLEY BROS/PICTON. An earthenware poodle made by the Handleys is shown in plate 5.14.

On December 31, 1894, William J. Handley

5.15 *Close-up of the Handley workshop shown in plate 5.13, with the pottery produced, including churns, jugs, spittoons, cuspidors, flowerpots, and* lawn or cemetery vases. Courtesy Mrs. Percy E. Rush.

sold his share in the pottery to his brother Henry. Henry continued the business until about 1899, although he did not sell the property until 1905.[14] It is not certain that the Handley brothers actually worked at the pottery beyond the first year, as Belleville tax assessment rolls list William Handley as residing in that place in 1892 and 1893, and Henry Handley as living there in 1893.[15]

The Handley pottery produced both glazed wares and unglazed flowerpots and lawn and cemetery ornaments. Plate 5.15 is a close-up of the pottery shown in plate 5.13. The five-gallon butter crock shown in plate 5.16 is a rare piece of earthenware from this workshop. It is marked with the impressed name H. HANDLEY/MANUFACTURER/PICTON, ONT.

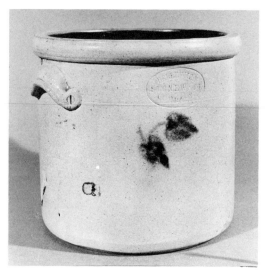

5.17 *A decorated stoneware crock made by the Belleville Stoneware Company (1870-ca. 1873).*

5.16 *A five-gallon earthenware butter crock with clear lead glaze and impressed mark of H. HANDLEY/MANUFACTURER/PICTON, ONT.*

After the pottery closed Henry Handley returned to work for Hart Bros. & Lazier in Belleville.

HASTINGS COUNTY
Belleville

The pottery in Belleville was founded by

James Simeon McCuaig in 1868, the year he purchased lot 15 on Mill Street.[16] McCuaig was operating a forwarding business in Picton at the time, so L.J. White managed the pottery business. In an 1869 directory the business is listed as McCuaig's Pottery and J.C. Lake is listed as manager.[17] Early in 1870 McCuaig sold the business to the Belleville Stoneware Company, whose principal stockholder was John Montgomery Scott.[18]

An advertisement in a local newspaper at the time reports:

The undersigned having purchased the Belleville Stoneware Company, all their rights, title and interest in the above Factory, begs to intimate to former patrons of the Company that, having had an extensive experience in the business, he has perfected the facilities of the establishment, and is now turning out work second to none in Canada or the United States. In his store rooms will now be found Rockingham and Stoneware in all varieties made from the best imported clay, and by first-class workmen. Orders solicited. J.M. Scott.[19]

The new company did not seem to have prospered for by the fall of the same year Scott had become the sole owner of the property.[20] Scott defaulted on the mortgage and McCuaig

5.18 *Hart Bros. & Lazier frequently advertised in provincial directories. This advertisement mentions* *the two potteries and wares produced during the time.* Courtesy Ontario Archives.

became the official assignee of the property.[21] Pottery with the impressed mark BELLE-VILLE/STONEWARE/COMPANY probably dates to this early period (plate 5.17).

During the early years of the pottery, a large quantity of stoneware was produced in Belleville. The 1870-71 census report on industrial establishments shows that their business employed seven men, who used 400 tons of clay a year to produce stoneware valued at $16,000.[22]

After another series of changes in ownership, the land was purchased by James McDonald in 1873.[23] He does not appear to have been a potter himself, although he was listed as the operator of the workshop during the years 1873-75.[24] He leased the business to J.M. Read (Reid) in 1876 and 1877 but the building remained vacant in the two succeeding years.[25] It was then that Hart Bros. & Lazier of Picton obtained a lease from McDonald for the business. The pottery offered the Picton firm an outlet on the mainland that was closer to communities bordering the north shore of the lake, and was within easy shipping distance of inland villages. Belleville itself was a rapidly developing commercial centre, which meant that stoneware would be in demand. By 1882 the property had passed to Curtis Bogart, from whom Hart Bros. & Lazier leased the business. An advertisement from the 1880s indicates

that Hart Bros. & Lazier maintained two operating potteries (plate 5.18), not just one pottery at Picton and a warehouse in Belleville, as proposed by some writers. The published summary of the 1880-81 census indicates that the pottery had nine men working to produce $6,000 worth of pottery.[26] At that time the potters who had worked at the business had been associated with the Picton works and included the Handleys and Wheelers. Thomas Wheeler had been with John Marx, owner of the London Pottery, London, Ontario, in the 1870s, but returned to Belleville in 1882 and continued at the plant until his death in 1895. Newlove Handley worked at the pottery from 1883 until 1910. The manager of the Belleville business was Charles A. Hart, who also continued to work at the pottery into the second decade of the twentieth century. The picture of the Belleville pottery (plate 5.19) shows Newlove Handley on the right, William Handley standing fourth from the right. Displayed on the stands in front of the potters are jugs, butter crocks, and lawn vases. A unique picture of the interior of the pottery (plate 5.20) shows the racks for drying bisque ware and the area at the right rear where the pottery was thrown. These two pictures were probably taken at the same time, as some of the potters are in both.

The Belleville pottery continued to prosper in the last decades of the nineteenth century.

5.19 *Picture of the Belleville pottery shop of Hart Bros. & Lazier (1897-1901), showing potters and* *examples of wares produced.* Courtesy Mrs. Ruth Pollard.

5.20 *Interior of Belleville pottery with drying shelves (left) and area for turning wares (right rear).* Courtesy Mrs. Percy E. Rush.

5.21 *A four-gallon decorated crock with impressed mark HART BROS. & LAZIER/BAY OF QUINTE WORKS. Piece was made at Belleville between 1879 and 1901.*

5.22 *A spittoon of the same period as the piece in plate 5.5 with the impressed mark HART BROS. & LAZIER/BELLEVILLE/ONT. This mark was also used at the same time as the mark on the piece in plate 5.5.*

For example, the 1890-91 census indicates that the annual value of articles produced had risen to $18,100. It took ten men working all year to produce this ware.[27] The Belleville pottery produced stoneware, Rockingham ware, and yellow ware. The range of products included household crockery, drain tiles, fire bricks and water filters. They imported stone-

ware and fire clay from New Jersey, which made the product more expensive than ware made of local clays. The pottery was marked HART BROS. & LAZIER/BAY OF QUINTE WORKS (plate 5.21), or the same name, with BELLEVILLE/ONT. but without the name of the works (plate 5.22). A directory advertisement from this period describes the

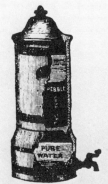

Filter and Cooler.
Six Sizes and Designs.

HART ᴮᴿᴼˢ· ⳤ LAZIER
BAY OF QUINTE WORKS.
Stoneware, Rockingham & Yellow-ware.
BELLEVILLE, ONT.

All Filters are packed with best bone charcoal, and are suitable for offices or family use.

5.23 *An advertisement from* Ontario Directory of 1884-85 *describes the products of the Belleville*

pottery, including water filters produced for public places. Courtesy Ontario Archives.

5.24 *A three-gallon plain butter crock with sten-cilled mark B.P. Co./BELLEVILLE/ONT. enclosed in a heart-shaped shield. The Belleville Pottery Company was founded in 1901 to continue the business begun by Hart Bros. & Lazier.* Courtesy Black Creek Pioneer Village, Toronto.

products made at the pottery and illustrates their specialty water filter (plate 5.23).

In 1901 the Hart Bros. & Lazier firm was succeeded by the Belleville Pottery Company, with James Blake Ives as owner of the new firm. Charles A. Hart continued to work at the pottery until the late 1910s. The new company marked its wares BELLEVILLE POTTERY COMPANY/SUCCESSOR TO HART BROS. & LAZIER, or BELLEVILLE POTTERY COMPANY, or just B.P. Co./BELLEVILLE/ONT. in a heart-shaped shield (plate 5.24). An interesting picture of the company's display wagon at the local Belleville agricultural fair shows spittoons, jugs and crocks manufactured during the early part of the twentieth century (plate 5.25).

James Blake Ives purchased the pottery property in 1925 from Ellen Bogart, widow of Curtis Bogart, for $2,050.[28] The firm continued to sell pottery, drain tiles, and other clay

5.25 *The Belleville Pottery Co., display wagon at the local Belleville agricultural fair.* Courtesy Prince Edward County Museum.

products until the late 1930s, but it is believed they did not make ware after 1914, but imported pottery and china for resale. Finally, in 1947, the widow of Ives sold the property to the Station Street Marketeria. The land has recently been redeveloped by a local recreational centre, and the pottery lot is now the site of a building.

Cannifton

A pottery was established in the village of Cannifton, Thurlow Township, by James Bryce around 1857. The location of the pottery has not been determined, and therefore a more precise date for the founding of the business cannot be established. A directory of 1857-58 lists Bryce as "manufacturer of pottery,"[29] but does not provide any details of the business. Bryce had worked earlier in York Township, York County, on lot 31, concession 3, probably the site of Joseph Walmsley's pottery. Bryce died ca. 1864, as a directory the following year lists his widow only. The pottery continued to operate under management not now known until 1879, when Alexander Elliott is reported as operating the business. An 1869 directory records that Cannifton has "some other factories of less importance ..(including) a pottery."[30] Elliott is reported as working in Cannifton until 1899.[31] The 1880-81 census describes one pottery in Hastings County East, which must have been the Elliott works. The census indicates that three men worked at the business to produce pottery valued at $1,000 a year.[32] Nothing more is known of the pottery wares produced in Cannifton.

6.
Potteries of East Central Ontario

Fig. 6.1 *Locations of potteries in East Central Ontario during the nineteenth century.*

Potters moved from one workshop to another, sometimes with the hopes of learning about the trade, and at other times to establish their own business. The pattern of migration is illustrated in the history of the potters and potteries of East Central Ontario. Potters moved from Peterborough to Durham to York to Ontario counties, from Durham to Peterborough, and from Victoria to Durham, to name only a few of the movements. The locations of the potteries in the east central Ontario region are shown in figure 6.1.

NORTHUMBERLAND COUNTY

Colborne
The village of Colborne, in the eastern part of Northumberland County, was the location of three potteries in the nineteenth century. The first pottery was established by S.V. Carroll in

1842.[1] Carroll was born in the United States and worked in Rochester, New York , before migrating to Canada.[2] An 1851 directory indicates that there was one pottery in Colborne, probably Carroll's.[3] Carroll appears to have gone out of business, for in an 1853 directory, Orchard J. Fowler, originally from New Haven, Connecticut, is listed as a potter in the village, and was also a successful merchant. Although he continued to be listed in credit records as the owner of the pottery as late as 1868, it was his three sons, George O., Timothy, and Harvey who actually worked at the pottery, located on lot 7, Old Percy Road.[4]

From the year 1854, George O. Fowler is listed as a potter in Colborne, presumably on land he later purchased.[5] In 1858 he took his brothers Timothy and Harvey into the business, and it became known as George Fowler & Co.[6] By 1866 Harvey Fowler was described as a tanner and furrier, and had presumably left the pottery business.[7] The pottery continued as a partnership of George and Timothy until 1870, when the brothers decided to operate separately. George O. continued to run the pottery on lot 7, Old Percy Road, while Timothy is listed as being on lots 21 and 22 on the north side of Park Street, land located a short distance south of the Percy Road site.[8]

The census of 1870-71 indicates that the Percy Road pottery was the larger of the two, with $1,000 capital invested. The business employed two men to make earthenware valued at $1,000 annually.[9] By comparison, Timothy Fowler's pottery had $100 invested, hired one male employee, and produced earthenware valued at $800 a year.[10] The Percy Road pottery continued under George O. Fowler until 1877, when Harvey Fowler returned to the business. He purchased the land in 1880[11] and continued the enterprise until 1888, when he sold the business to his son William H. Fowler.[12] The business continued until ca. 1893. In that year W. H. Fowler is also listed as a potter on part of lot 21, concession 1, Cramahe Township, near the hamlet of Salem.[13] The Colborne pottery was no longer in operation in 1896, when W. H. Fowler is reported as a baker and grocer.[14]

During the years 1866 to 1870, Caleb Gilbert worked at the Old Percy Road pottery. He left Colborne in 1870 and is reported working in Belleville in 1871.

There is no record of potters or potteries in Colborne ever marking their wares, and no pieces can be attributed to the community.

DURHAM COUNTY

Bowmanville

The first pottery in the Bowmanville area was established by John Wilson by the year 1845.[15] Wilson is listed in census returns of the area for 1845, 1848, and 1849.[16] He purchased a one-acre piece of land in Bowmanville in 1848 for £25.[17] Wilson's pot shop was discontinued by 1853 as a directory of that year lists him under "removed, discontinued or altered" since 1851.[18]

Listed with Wilson in the 1848 census was James T. Bailey, who in 1846 was part of a pottery partnership known as Bailey & Williams, located on land leased from Charles Bowman and described as on the northwest side of Dundas (now King) Street, adjacent to the mill dam.[19] The partnership had been dissolved by 1848, the year Bailey is listed as working with John Wilson.

In 1849 the partnership of Bailey & Brown was formed. Their workshop was north of Scugog Street and west of King Street in Bowmanville, described at the time as a one-acre parcel known to be on the west part of lot 12, concession 2, Darlington Township.

An 1849 advertisement of the firm announces:

Messrs. Bailey & Brown of Bowmanville, Township of Darlington, have commenced the manufacture of fine earthenware and moulded ware, after the manner of the Staffordshire Potteries, at their establishment in the village. The clay, which we understand is sufficiently good, is put through the same process as in Staffordshire, and from the samples produced there appears to be no doubt but that the Canadian plates, dishes & c will equal those of England . . .[20]

This partnership did not last beyond the spring of 1851, as an advertisement in the Bowmanville *Messenger* of April 25, 1851 (plate 6.1) reports the dissolution of the firm. Bailey continued to produce pottery until ca. 1855.

John Brown operated his own pottery on a one-and-one-half-acre parcel of land he purchased on May 2, 1853.[21] This was adjacent to Bailey's holdings. A price list for John Brown's pottery, dating around 1855, indicates the pottery produced milk pans, cream pots, preserve jars, molasses jugs, butter pots, as well as moulded bedroom sets, bedpans, butter jars, water pitchers, spittoons, dishes, mugs, teapots and bowls. Of special importance was his production of drain tiles and stove tubes, the latter article advertised as "the safest in use."[22] In the 1855 Provincial Exhibition John Brown received a first prize for the best specimen of pottery and a first prize for the best assortment of pottery.[23] Brown closed the pottery and left for York County in 1856.

In 1851, Bailey & Brown had introduced into Upper Canada the first commercial tile-making machine. It may be that drainage tiles which won awards were the products of these new machines.[24]

Bowmanville Pottery.

THE Subscriber takes this method of returning thanks to his friends, and the public at large, for the liberal patronage bestowed upon the late firm of BAILEY & BROWN and begs to inform them that he intends to carry on the business as heretofore, and hopes, by strict attention to business, to merit a continuation of their support. Merchants, by sending a written order, can have any description of Pottery Ware, on the following terms :—

COMMON WARE.

			£	s	d
Large Cream Pots, per dozen,	-	-	1	10	0
2d size do.	do.	-	0	15	0
3d size do.	do.	-	0	7	6
Large Butter Pots, with Covers, per dozen.	-	1	4	0
2d size. do.	do.	-	0	18	0
2 Gallon Preserve Jars, per dozen,	-	1	4	0
1 Gallon do.	do.	-	0	18	0
½ Gallon do.	do.	-	0	15	0
¼ Gallon do.	do.	-	0	7	0
3 Gallon Jugs, per dozen,	-	-	1	16	0
2 do.	do.	-	1	7	0
1 do.	do.	-	0	18	0
½ do.	do.	-	0	12	0
¼ do.	do.	-	0	7	0
Large Milk Pans, per dozen,	-	-	0	15	0
2d size do.	do.	-	0	12	0
3d size do.	do.	-	0	7	6
Large Milk Crocks, per dozen,	-	0	12	0
2d size, do.	do.	-	0	7	6
Chamber Pots, per dozen,	-	-	0	12	0
Wash Bowls, do.	-	-	0	12	0
Churns, large size, do.	-	-	3	0	0
do. small size, do.	-	-	2	0	0
Stove Tubes, large,	-	-	0	15	0
do. small,	-	-	0	12	0

MOULDED WARE.

			£	s	d
Spittoons, per dozen,	-	-	0	18	0
Oval Bakers, do.	-	-	0	7	6
Large Beaded Nappeys, per dozen,	-	0	12	0
2d size, do.	do.	-	0	7	6
3d size, do.	do.	-	0	4	0
Moulded Fancy Flower Pots, per dozen.	-	0	18	0

Large Platters. Covered Dishes, Moulded Pitchers, Mugs. Toys, and other descriptions of Ware, too numerous to mention. All orders will be punctually attended to, and a liberal discount allowed to wholesale purchasers.

JAMES BAILEY.

Bowmanville. April 25. 1851. 7-12m.

6.1 *Pottery advertisement from Bowmanville Messenger, June 18, 1851.* Courtesy Metropolitan Toronto Library Board.

Cartwright Township

A pottery was established by Robert Wilson on a half-acre part of lot 20, concession 4, Cartwright Twp. in 1855.[25] The 1860-61 census indicates that the pottery produced "all kinds of p(ottery) ware, only just commenced." There was $1200 invested in the business. One man was hired to work in the shop.[26] It may have been at this site that Francis Bailey and his son, William J., worked, for they are listed as potters in the township in the 1960-61 census.[27] The relationship between the Baileys of Bowmanville and Cartwright Township is not known. Wilson's pottery ceased

6.2 *Red earthenware jug with clear lead glaze and impressed maker's mark F. BAILEY.* Courtesy Royal Ontario Museum.

operation in 1862 when he sold his holdings.[28] A red earthenware jug with a clear lead glaze and the mark F. BAILEY may have been produced at this short-lived pottery operation (see plate 6.2).

Welcome

John Brownscombe, Sr., came to Canada from England ca. 1843 and settled in Hope Township. In the year 1851 John Sr., his son William, and his son-in-law, Henry Pethick, moved to Peterborough where they established a pottery early in the year 1852. John Jr., stayed in Welcome at the family homestead, located on a part of lot 13, concession 3, until 1871.[29] In that year he moved to Kinloss Township, Bruce County.[30] John Brownscombe, Sr., did not place his name on the pottery he produced while at Welcome, making it impossible to identify his pottery.

Port Hope

James Taylor potted on a half-acre piece of lot 3, concession 2, Hope Township from 1876 until his death ca. 1915.[31] Born in Peterborough County, as a boy he worked at William Brownscombe's pottery as a helper. He left there to become an apprentice at John Brownscombe's in Welcome, a village a short distance west of Port Hope. From Welcome, James Taylor went to work at S.T. Humberstone's pottery in Newton Brook, York County, then in 1873 left York County to join his brother William, who was operating a pottery and brickyard in partnership with Arthur Doidge, in the town of Beaverton, Ontario County. James Taylor eventually established his own business in Hope Township. At his death his son, George N. Taylor, took over, and he continued until 1918, when the business disbanded.

An interview with George Taylor, done shortly before his death in 1967, gives intimate and first-hand details of the life of the Taylor family and its association with the pottery trade in Ontario. The interview has been summarized in an article in the *Canadian Collector.*[32]

VICTORIA COUNTY
Lindsay
Thomas Rawlings and William Taylor set up a pottery in Ops Township, south of Lindsay, in 1869. The pottery, which was situated on a two-acre part of the northeast corner of lot 15, concession 5, near the intersection of modern-day highways 7 and 35,[33] continued until 1872.

The 1870-71 census indicates that the pottery employed three men and one boy to produce 30,000 pieces of earthenware a year. The wares were valued at $3,000.[34]

Rawlings had been born in England and had immigrated to the United States. By 1861 he had moved to Canada. His son George was active in the pottery trade in Peterborough. William Taylor learned about the pottery and brick industry in Peterborough before coming to Ops Township. He left after 1872 for Beaverton, Ontario County, where he was a lumber and coal merchant and owner of a pottery and brickyard.

William Davey, an Englishman, came to Canada in 1855 and worked in Peterborough for a number of years before accompanying Taylor to Ops Township. After the closing of the Lindsay pottery, Davey returned to Peterborough.

Although the Ops Township building disappeared long ago, the intersection is still known by local residents as "pottery corners."[35]

PETERBOROUGH COUNTY
Peterborough
There were two potteries in this town during the nineteenth century. The histories of the two sites, though intertwined, are here presented separately.

William Brownscombe
About 1851 John Brownscombe, Sr., his son William, and son-in-law Henry Pethick arrived in Peterborough from Durham County. On January 1, 1852, William Brownscombe and Henry Pethick purchased a half-acre piece of land known as lot 2 on the south side of Murray Street, west of George Street, for £100 and established a pottery business.[36] Henry Pethick sold his interest in the business to William Brownscombe in 1856.[37] A directory advertisement of 1858 indicates that he (Brownscombe) produced earthenware including "cream and milk crocks, pans . . . bottles, jars, flower pots & c."[38] By the time of the 1861 census the pottery had grown. Five men were employed to produce 15,000 pieces of pottery a year, with a value of $2,000.[39] Sixty tons of clay were required to produce the wares.[40] The employees were Richard Kingdon, John Goodenough, H. Bacon, William Oakley and Francis Pethick.[41]

On March 22, 1867, fire destroyed Brownscombe's pottery, leaving only a $600 fire insurance policy as the remaining assets.[42] The pottery was rebuilt and Brownscombe worked at the site the next year, but after 1868 he rented the pottery to other potters.

An example of a jug produced by Brownscombe during the period 1851-68 is shown in plate 6.3. The piece is marked with the impressed name W. BROWNSCOMBE, above which a crown motif appears. An unsigned picture frame made by Brownscombe (with his picture inside) is shown in plate 6.4.

In 1868 Brownscombe moved to a farm south of Peterborough in North Monaghan Township. During 1868-1880 he was listed at different times as a farmer, Justice of the Peace, and lockmaster on the Trent Canal.

6.3 *An earthenware jug with clear glaze and impressed mark W. BROWNSCOMBE with a crown above.*

Robert Westcott (also spelled Wescott) had first come to the pottery as a workman in 1865, and took over the business upon Brownscombe's retirement in 1868. Westcott continued at the site until 1871 when he estab-

6.4 *Small earthenware picture frame with marbled blue-green glaze. The piece is unmarked and has been in the Brownscombe family to this day. The photograph is of William Brownscombe.*

lished his own workshop in North Monaghan Township.

The 1870-71 census indicates that Westcott employed five men who produced pottery valued at $3,000 annually.[43]

The Brownscombe pottery was rented to William Saunders and his son, William J., for 1874 and 1875, then to the partnership of Baker & Davey (Henry Baker and William J. Davey) from 1876 to 1879.[44] Baker had come to work at the pottery in 1870 and Davey had joined the business in 1869. A second disastrous fire struck the pottery, this time on May 6, 1877. The fire destroyed the pottery, adjacent outhouses and an adjoining business.[45] The pottery was rebuilt and the partnership of Baker & Davey continued at the site until 1879.

In November, 1878, William Brownscombe and his son-in-law Frank Goodfellow, previously working as a printer, formed a partnership known as "Brownscombe & Goodfellow" to manufacture pottery. This was duly registered in the land registry office.[46] In 1880 and 1881 the new partners made stoneware and earthenware at the Murray Street site; during the same period they also leased the Westcott pottery, which had by this time been discontinued by Westcott. Frank Goodfellow died in October, 1881, ending the family involvement in pottery-making. An example of a stoneware crock made during the time of the partnership is shown in plate 6.5.

In 1881 Samuel F. Allin, who prior to this date had been a teamster with Brownscombe, took over the Brownscombe and Westcott potteries. The next year he leased only the Westcott site.

Robert Westcott
Robert Westcott's was, after Brownscombe's, the second pottery in the town of Peterborough. It was located on park lot 7, part of lot 14, concession 12, North Monaghan Township, east of Westcott and George Streets and west of Crescent Road.[47] An advertisement in the Peterborough *Examiner* describes the business in 1877:

WESTCOTT'S PRIZE POTTERY
The proprietor of the Peterborough Pottery Works is still manufacturing the leading wares

of the Dominion including his well-known make of Rockingham and stone enamelled ware. Special attention is at present being devoted to fancy wares such as flower vases, flowerpots, water fountains, & c. and a first class article is now offered at lower prices than by any other pottery in the Province . . . Peterborough Pottery Works, opposite Little Lake. Robert Westcott, Proprietor. [48]

Westcott made pottery until 1880, when he leased the pottery to Brownscombe & Goodfellow.[49] After the death of Frank Goodfellow in 1881, Samuel F. Allin assumed the lease and continued the business until his death in 1884.[50] His widow, Mrs. Grace Allin, continued to operate the business until 1890. During this time her son, John F., Henry Baker, James W. Davey (son of William J.), and George Rawlings (son of Thomas Rawlings) worked at the pottery. John F. Allin ran the business from 1891 to 1904, when George Rawlings purchased it.[51] His death in 1912 finally ended the pottery.[52]

ONTARIO COUNTY

Atherley
Early in the year 1871, Gerhart Dryer purchased a part of the southern half of lot 27, concession 13, Mara Township, (now in Simcoe County) to begin a pottery business.[53] A description of the project appeared in Orillia's *Northern Light* on August 25, 1871:

Large quantities of excellent pottery clay have been discovered on Mr. G. Dryer's farm . . . The clay has been tested and manufactured into a number of culinary and dairy utensils by Mr. Dryer, who professes a thorough knowledge of the business and proposes to build a pottery immediately in order to utilize this important discovery . . .

The pottery ware was fired at the nearby brickyard of Beard & Sutherland. In spite of the above glowing prospects of a pottery business, Dryer advertised the sale of the business on July 12, 1873, in the Montreal *Gazette:*

Pottery for Sale
To Rent, or on shares, the
only one in District

6.5 *Stoneware crock with impressed maker's mark BROWNSCOMBE & GOODFELLOW/ PETERBOROUGH ONT.*

For Particulars apply G. Dryer,
Orillia, Ont.

By 1873 Dryer was listed as a resident of Orillia in assessment rolls of the town. The pottery property was sold in 1875.[54]

Beaverton
The town of Beaverton, located on the shores of Lake Simcoe, was a port of call for steamers plying their trade along the lakes. The town also had a link with the Port Hope, Lindsay, and Beaverton Railroad. The region was fortunate to have extensive deposits of high quality clay, providing the stimulus for the establishment of brickyards and potteries.

During the nineteenth century there were three potteries in the Beaverton/Thorah Township area. The first was established by William Taylor and Arthur Doidge in 1872. The second pottery, located to the east of the town, was owned in succession by George Drake, William Taylor, and Robert McCallum. The third pottery was founded by James Bemister. The story of these potteries follows.

Arthur Doidge & Co.
William Taylor arrived in Beaverton in 1872

from Lindsay and in partnership with Arthur Doidge established a pottery firm, known as Arthur Doidge & Co., on part of the north half of lot 14, concession 5, Thorah Township. This was later incorporated into the town of Beaverton and became lot 12 on Elizabeth Street.[55] In 1873 William Taylor's brother, James W., came to help in the newly established business,[56] and worked at the site until his move to Port Hope in 1875.

The pottery was discontinued in 1885, when William Taylor purchased the Drake pottery and brickyard in Thorah Township.

George Drake/William Taylor/
Robert McCallum
George Drake began making brick in Thorah Township as early as 1856.[57] In 1869 he purchased the south half of lot 10, concession 5, Thorah Township, later called Drakesville, where a deep deposit of high quality clay had been found.[58] In 1873 he and Thomas Rawlings became partners in the firm known as Drake & Rawlings. This did not last for more than a year and Drake continued to make pottery and bricks at the site. During the next twelve years he operated both a pottery and brickyard, the pottery being known as the Thorah Pottery. In 1885 Drake sold his eighty-nine acres to William Taylor.[59] At this time the land had kilns, a pottery shed, barn, and a branch line of the Port Hope, Lindsay and Beaverton Railway. Drake moved south of Beaverton to lot 11, concession 4, Thorah Township, where he is listed as a brickmaker into the early years of the twentieth century.

When Taylor purchased the Drake business in 1885, he concentrated on the development of the brickyard, the most profitable part of the business. During the next years he leased the pottery part to different individuals. In the years 1886 to 1890 his brother, James W. Taylor, appears as the tenant on the pottery lot, on the southwest corner of the eighty-nine-acre tract of land. A piece of pottery made by J. W. Taylor during these years is shown in plate 6.6. By 1892 Robert McCallum was renting the pottery and on May 3, 1898, Taylor sold it to him.[60] Two years later, Taylor sold the remainder of his holdings at the lot to the Beaverton Brick & Tile Co.[61] The clay pit had been dug so deep that water flooded the pit

6.6 *Earthenware two-gallon crock with impressed mark J.W. TAYLOR/BEAVERTON.*

and made it too difficult to continue the brick business. In 1913 brickmaking ceased and the land was sold to a local farmer.[62]

McCallum continued the pottery business until ca. 1903.[63] During his years at the site, he produced a range of wares typical of many of the potteries of nineteenth-century Ontario. A price list of McCallum's pottery is shown in plate 6.7. McCullum sold the pottery business in 1918, at which time he was working as a carpenter in Wainfleet, Albeta.[64]

James Bemister/Walter Bryan Bemister
James Bemister was a veterinary surgeon until he was fifty-three years old, and then he decided to make a career in the pottery trade. With the assistance of his son, Walter Bryan, he founded a pottery on lot 16 on the north side of Simcoe Street, Beaverton, in 1876.[65] In 1878 he purchased lot 25 on the same side of the street.[66] The pottery was run by James Bemister until ca. 1888, when the business became known as James Bemister & Son. After James Bemister's death in 1897 his son took over the shop. Walter Bemister continued the business until ca. 1904. In 1905 the pottery was rented as a hand laundry.[67] In later years Walter Bemister served in the Northwest Mounted Police (for five years) and in the war

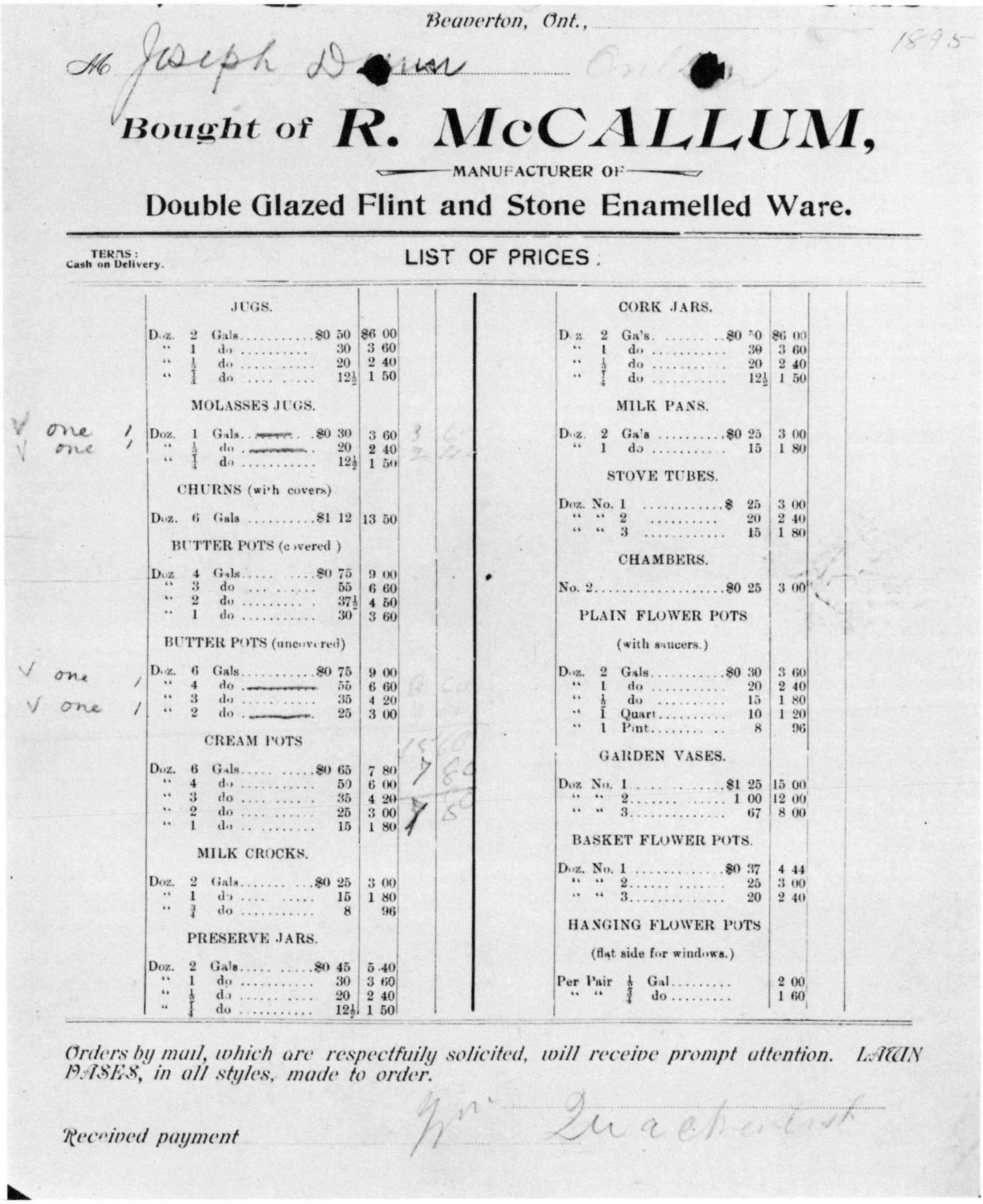

Beaverton, Ont.,

Mr. Joseph D____   ____ 1895

Bought of R. McCALLUM,

MANUFACTURER OF

Double Glazed Flint and Stone Enamelled Ware.

TERMS:
Cash on Delivery.

LIST OF PRICES.

JUGS.

Doz.	2	Gals..........	$0 50	$6 00
"	1	do	30	3 60
"	½	do	20	2 40
"	¼	do	12½	1 50

MOLASSES JUGS.

√ one /
√ one /

Doz.	1	Gals..........	$0 30	3 60
"	½	do	20	2 40
"	¼	do	12½	1 50

CHURNS (with covers)

Doz.	6	Gals..........	$1 12	13 50

BUTTER POTS (covered)

Doz.	4	Gals....	$0 75	9 00
"	3	do	55	6 60
"	2	do	37½	4 50
"	1	do	30	3 60

BUTTER POTS (uncovered)

√ one /
√ one /

Doz.	6	Gals....	$0 75	9 00
"	4	do	55	6 60
"	3	do	35	4 20
"	2	do	25	3 00

CREAM POTS

Doz.	6	Gals....	$0 65	7 80
"	4	do	50	6 00
"	3	do	35	4 20
"	2	do	25	3 00
"	1	do	15	1 80

MILK CROCKS.

Doz.	2	Gals..........	$0 25	3 00
"	1	do	15	1 80
"	¾	do	8	96

PRESERVE JARS.

Doz.	2	Gals..........	$0 45	5 40
"	1	do	30	3 60
"	½	do	20	2 40
"	¼	do	12½	1 50

CORK JARS.

Doz.	2	Ga's.	$0 50	$6 00
"	1	do	39	3 60
"	½	do	20	2 40
"	¼	do	12½	1 50

MILK PANS.

Doz.	2	Ga's	$0 25	3 00
"	1	do	15	1 80

STOVE TUBES.

Doz.	No. 1	....	$ 25	3 00
"	" 2	....	20	2 40
"	" 3	....	15	1 80

CHAMBERS.

No. 2.	....	$0 25	3 00

PLAIN FLOWER POTS

(with saucers.)

Doz.	2	Gals..........	$0 30	3 60
"	1	do	20	2 40
"	½	do	15	1 80
"	1	Quart	10	1 20
"	1	Pint..........	8	96

GARDEN VASES.

Doz	No. 1	....	$1 25	15 00
"	" 2	....	1 00	12 00
"	" 3	....	67	8 00

BASKET FLOWER POTS.

Doz.	No. 1	....	$0 37	4 44
"	" 2	....	25	3 00
"	" 3	....	20	2 40

HANGING FLOWER POTS

(flat side for windows.)

Per Pair	½	Gal.		2 00
" "	¼	do		1 60

Orders by mail, which are respectfully solicited, will receive prompt attention. LAWN VASES, in all styles, made to order.

Received payment   Wm Quackenbush

6.7 *Price list of R. McCallum, Beaverton. The pottery was run by McCallum from ca. 1892 until about 1903.* Courtesy Royal Ontario Museum.

6.8 *Walter Bemister (centre) standing in front of the pottery shop on Simcoe Street, Beaverton.*

" BEMISTER'S POTTERY."

W. B. BEMISTER,

MANUFACTURER OF

DOUBLE - BURNED STONE AND FLINT - GLAZED ROCKINGHAM AND FANCY GARDEN WARE OF EVERY DESCRIPTION.

MODELLING FOR HAND PAINTING A SPECIALTY.

Goods packed by experienced hands and delivered F. O. B. Cars or Boat here. Crates when returned free and in good order, credited the same as charged.

BEAVERTON,   -   -   ONTARIO.

6.9 *Advertisement of Bemister pottery from a county directory.*

of 1914-18. He died in 1949 at the age of eighty-seven. A picture of the pottery during the last years of the nineteenth century is shown in plate 6.8. Walter Bemister is standing in the doorway of the frame building.

The Bemister family home on lot 36 on the north side of North Street is set on the banks of the Beaver River. Fragments of pottery from the Bemister business can be found here, on the steep slopes of the river edge. It is probable that the pot sherds were used as fill for the family homestead. Pieces of pottery retrieved from the banks of the River are shown in plate 6.10. The lawn vase had part of Walter Bemister's name inscribed on the base.

The closing of the Bemister pottery marked the end of pottery-making in the Beaverton area. Few pieces of local pottery have been found in the area, and those attributed to the Beaverton workshops usually have no identifying maker's marks to make their identification certain.

6.10 *Fragments of pottery recovered from Bemister homestead on North Street, Beaverton. Fancy lawn stand (right rear) is inscribed with part of* the name of Bemister. Teapot and unglazed lids (left, and right front) were also produced by the Bemisters.

7.
The Workshops of York County

Fig. 7.1 *Locations of potteries during the late eighteenth and nineteenth centuries, York County.*

The County of York, with the bustling centre of York (now the City of Toronto), is located in central Ontario, north of Lake Ontario. The county was one of the areas settled in the late eighteenth century. Beginning in 1793, when John Graves Simcoe moved the capital of the province from Niagara to the Town of York, the population of the county increased rapidly. Settlers took up land along newly surveyed roads leading north to Lake Simcoe and west and east to the interior of the province. Along these roads developed early communities (now often indistinct from Toronto because of twentieth-century urban development), where the potter established his workshop to produce crockery.

Potteries were established during the late eighteenth and nineteenth centuries in three areas of the county: York Township, Markham Township and the City of Toronto. The location of these potteries is shown in figure 7.1.

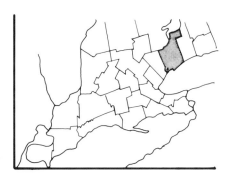

YORK TOWNSHIP

Humberstone Pottery
The earliest recorded pottery in the township was several kilometres north of the town of York, in the area called Newton Brook. Here in 1798, Thomas Humberstone, Sr., who had moved from Augusta Township, Grenville County, established a pottery on a 200-acre farm on lot 14, concession 1 of York Township, on the west side of Yonge Street. C. B. Robinson, in the *History of Toronto and County of York, Ontario*, gives a detailed biographical sketch of the Humberstone family.[1] Thomas Humberstone, Sr.'s father, Samuel, had emigrated from Staffordshire, England, to Pennsylvania, where Thomas was born in 1766. The outbreak of the American Revolution forced the family, with other Loyalists, to move to Grenville County, where Thomas learned pottery-making. He settled in York Township and continued pottery-making, in conjunction with farming, until the outbreak of

60

7.1 *Five-gallon crock with cobalt-blue bird design. Crock is marked S.T. HUMBERSTONE/NEWTON-BROOK.*

the War of 1812. After the war he resumed his trade until his death in 1849. Thomas Humberstone, Jr., his second son, took over the pottery business. Thomas Humberstone, Jr., was born in York Township and learned pottery-making in the family workshop. He moved the business to York Mills; later the pottery was moved north again, only to be plagued by fire, which destroyed the workshop twice. After the retirement of Thomas Humberstone, Jr., his son, Simon Thomas, continued the business at Newton Brook, on the west side of Yonge Street, just south of Steeles Avenue, the original Humberstone site. Aside from his keen interest in the pottery, Simon Thomas was active as a reeve and deputy reeve of York Township. He ran the pottery business for fifty years, during which time the pottery produced stoneware, Rockingham ware and other art wares. Stoneware containers were produced with the impressed mark S.T. HUMBERSTONE/NEWTON BROOK. A stoneware butter crock with this mark is shown in plate 7.1. Plate 7.2 is an example of a piece with the addition of ONT. Although pieces are rare, they are found in private collections and demonstrate the wide

range of pottery made by Simon Thomas Humberstone.

During the years 1872-1902, Simon Thomas Humberstone kept notebooks describing his experiments with different glazes and his efforts to overcome the problem of blistering. He records information about other potteries in the province, especially the glaze formulas reportedly used at the potteries of Brantford and Paris. These notebooks have been microfilmed by the Archives of Ontario and represent the most complete extant documentary record of the operation of a pottery workshop in nineteenth-century Ontario.

The census of 1870-71 reports the extent of the business at the time of S.T. Humberstone's management. The workshop used 300 tons of clay and seventy-five tons of lead a year to produce 900,000 pieces of crockery valued at $8,000. It took eight men to operate the pottery.[2] Simon Thomas Humberstone attempted to adjust to the changing taste of the public, and experimented with Egyptian black, Parian wares and whitewares, but apparently without notable success. In the 1890s, he sold wares without glazing so they could be painted, a favourite pastime of the period.

7.2 *Four-gallon stoneware butter crock. The mark includes the designation ONT.*

7.3 *Remains of Humberstone pottery kiln at Newton Brook in 1919.* Courtesy Mr. Lewis Humberstone.

Potters who worked at the Humberstone pottery included Caleb Saunders, George Saunders, John Pegler, George Stunden, John Hill, and William Bansley.

Simon Thomas Humberstone died in 1915 and his son, Thomas Allan Humberstone, assumed control of the business. The pottery was closed after the First World War, and the vacant building burned down in the fall of 1919. A photograph of the site after the last fire (plate 7.3) shows the shape and construction of the kiln, all that remained of a once-thriving enterprise.

Michael Whitmore

An advertisement in the *Canadian Freeman* of January 18, 1827 (plate 7.4), is the next mention of a pottery in York County. The adver-

tisement appeared several times in 1827. In the *Colonial Advocate* of July 22, 1830, the following advertisement appears:

Yonge St. Pottery. Four miles from York. Wanted, a pedlar to hawk Brown Pottery Ware through the Country. He may either furnish a Waggon or have one furnished him on giving security. He will be required to receive orders for ware to be made at this pottery. Merchants supplied Brown Ware at Wholesale Prices with the usual credit; and their orders will be attended to at the shortest notice. An assortment of crockery is constantly kept on hand. One or two journeymen wanted who will receive liberal wages. Michael Whitmore, April 26, 1830.[3]

The pottery operation was brought to an abrupt end when fire destroyed the business. A report of the tragedy was published in the

TO POTTERS.

GOOD encouragement given by the subscriber, three miles north of York, U. C. on Yonge-Street, for two or three Journeymen POTTERS that understand making Brown Earthenware.

MICHAEL WHITMORE.

February 23, 1826.   35tf

7.4 *Advertisement of Michael Whitmore for potters in* Canadian Freeman, *July 18, 1827. Courtesy Public Archives, Canada.*

Colonial Advocate of Oct. 14, 1830 (plate 7.5). Whitmore's pottery was described as being located between the Yorkville Tollgate and Montgomery's Tavern, probably on Yonge Street north of St. Clair Avenue. It is possible that a description of a pottery owner by the name of John Walmsley, near Whitmore's Mill, refers to the successor to Whitmore in the trade.

John Walmsley
Henry Scadding, in *Toronto of Old*, describes a pottery on Yonge Street north of St. Clair Avenue as follows:

As we reach again the higher land, after crossing the dam of Whitmore's Mill, and returning into the more direct line of the street, some rude pottery works met the eye. Here in the midst of woods the passerby usually saw on one side of the road, a one-horse clay-grinding machine, laboriously in operation; and on the other, displayed in the open air on boards supported by wooden piers driven into the great logs composing the wall of the low windowless building, numerous articles of coarse brown ware, partially glazed pans, crocks, jars, jugs, demijohns . . . primitive products of the plastic art [were] ever pleasant to contemplate. These works were carried on by Mr. John Walmsley. [4]

John Walmsley was born in Lancashire, England, in 1799, and as a young man immigrated to Upper Canada, first to Niagara and then to Yonge Street, the modern Deer Park area. [5]

In 1832 he acquired a piece of land in the

Yonge Street Pottery Burnt.—This valuable and highly useful establishment, the property of Mr. Michael Whitmore, an enterprising and patriotic inhabitant, has been burnt to ashes. It took fire on Saturday last, suddenly, and resisted every attempt to extinguish the flames. The loss of $1500 will fall heavy on the proprietor, but it is said that his neighbours, journeymen and friends intend to give him every aid in their power towards its entire re-establishment.

7.5 *Notice of burning of Whitmore's pottery from* Colonial Advocate *of October 14, 1830.* Courtesy Public Archives, Canada.

area, known as lot 4, in the gore in the west side of Yonge Street.[6] This was followed in 1840 by the purchase of adjacent lots 1, 2, and 3.[7] John Walmsley died in 1846; following his death nothing more is heard of the pottery.

Joseph Walmsley
There were two potters with the name Joseph Walmsley, both operating in York Township at the same time. The first potter with this name is reported in 1850 as working on lot 21, concession 3, which is located between St. Clair and Eglinton Avenues, west of Yonge Street.[8] By 1867 he was living in Sydenham Township, Grey County, where he was listed as potter and farmer.[9]

The second Joseph Walmsley was located on part of the southern half of lot 11, concession 2, York Mills. He purchased the twelve-acre property in 1854.[10] It is located on the east side of Leslie Street, just north of York Mills Road. The 1860-61 census indicates that he had $100 invested in the business.[11] Joseph Walmsley died ca. 1878.

John Burns/Yorkville Pottery
John Burns came to Ontario ca. 1849 and settled on the west side of Yonge Street in the area known as Yorkville. The first record we have of the Yorkville pottery concerns the Provincial Exhibition of 1858, when John Burns won the first prize for the best specimen of pottery and the second prize for the best assortment of pottery.[12] The 1860-61 census returns indicate that he had $800 invested in the business and that he used fifty tons of clay a year; three men were hired to produce the pottery.[13] The business became known as John Burns & Son by 1871.[14] Shortly before the death of John Burns, the son, John Harrison Burns, is listed as operating the business.[15] Samuel R. Burns, a younger son of John Burns, was reported in the 1870-71 census as operating a pottery in Markham Township.

The census of 1870-71 gives a glimpse of the business activity during J.H. Burns' ownership. He hired four men to produce earthenware, valued at $1800 a year and requiring ninety tons of clay (costing $150).[16]

An order form from the 1870s, from the Yorkville Pottery/J. Burns & Son, lists the following types of pottery produced by the firm: cream pots, milk crocks, milk pans, bottles, preserve (jars), butter pots, pitchers, flowerpots and flowerpot saucers.[17]

John H. Burns did not stay at the Yorkville Pottery for long, for by 1871 he has relocated in Albion Township, Peel County.[18]

James McCluskie
The 1860-61 census reports that James McClasky (McCluskie), with the assistance of John and Robert McCluskie (presumably his

brothers), was operating a pottery on a one-acre parcel of land in the northwest part of York Township. The McCluskies were born in Ireland, and probably had arrived in Canada shortly before 1860.[19] McCluskie employed four hands to turn out $800 worth of wares annually.[20] By April, 1864, James McCluskie was in the hamlet of Kilsyth, Grey County, where he operated a pottery in partnership with William Walmsley.

Henry James
Henry James' pottery first appears in the 1851 directory of York Township as located on lot 10, concession 1, on the east side of Yonge Street, York Mills.[21] James came to Canada about 1840. A land-registry office document of 1855 describes a three-and-one-half-acre parcel belonging to James, bounded on the west by Old Yonge Street and on the north by York Mills Road.[22] James is not mentioned in the 1860-61 census. Presumably the pottery had been discontinued before that time.

George Plant
George Plant was born in England in 1849 and it was there he learned the pottery trade. In 1873 he arrived in Canada and two years later began his career with Samuel R. Burns, in Markham Township. He later moved to Toronto Junction where he worked with Mr. Warwood, making sewer pipes, and then with George Townsley.[23] In 1886 he bought two-and-one-half acres in lot 39, concession 3, known as Carleton West, on Weston Road near Keele Street, where he erected a pottery and tile yard. He worked at the business until his retirement in 1905.

Beers describes Plant's business as follows:

While engaged in business he had an annual output of about 500,000 flowerpots for the florists' trade, as well as weeping tile, of which he made about 150,000 . . . He is a skilled designer and worker in clay goods, being able to produce anything in this line.[24]

John Brown
In 1856, John Brown moved from Bowmanville, Durham County, to Todmorden.[25] At the 1858 Provincial Exhibition held in Toronto, he

7.6 Earthenware Staffordshire dog money bank marked J. & W.O. BROWN & CO./PATENTED 1859.

won a first prize for the best specimen of pottery, and an extra prize for a flowerpot vase.[26] He established a pottery at Mount Dennis near Toronto Junction in 1860, on a one-acre piece of land. The 1860-61 census reports that he employed five hands to produce crockery.[27] Three of these workmen were probably his sons, Joseph, William O., and John, who were described as potters in the census.[28]

After Brown's death in 1866, his son Joseph continued the business until 1881.[29] The pottery was located on concession 3, lot 40, Davenport, which is in the area south of Eglinton Avenue and west of Keele Street, between Weston Road and the CPR tracks.[30] Joseph Brown then concentrated on the manufacture of bricks and tile. He retired in 1900, and his sons Joseph W., John A., and Albert E.J., under the business name of Brown Brothers, continued the brick-making enterprise until 1907.[31] An earthenware dog bank (plate 7.6), signed J. & W.O. BROWN & CO./PATENTED 1859, was produced by the Brown Brothers from a clay formula patented by John Brown in 1859.

William Lea
William Lea was born in Lancashire, England,

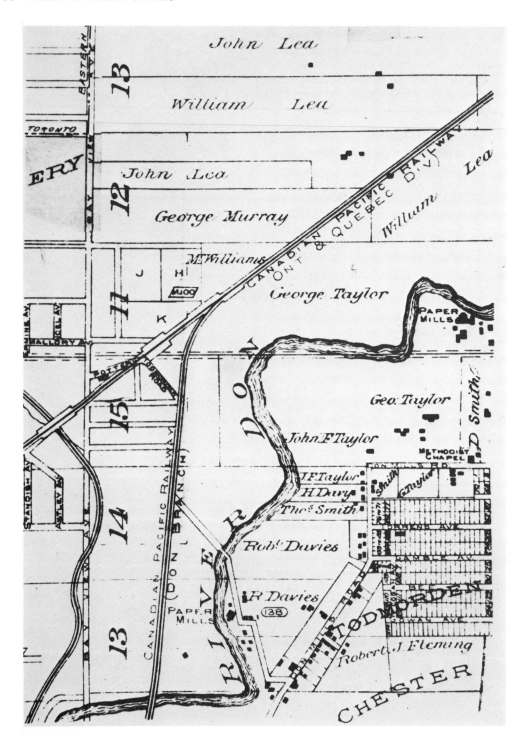

7.7   *Map showing land owned by William Lea and later John Cudmore, at the western part of lot 15, concession 2, York Township. Map is from* Goad's Toronto Atlas of 1890 *(revised to 1893). Courtesy Ontario Archives.*

in 1814. He came to Canada with his parents, John and Mary, by way of the United States ca. 1820. John Lea purchased a farm on lot 13, concession 3. He died in 1854.[32] William Lea had purchased a 130-acre farm on lot 13, concession 3, by 1841 (see plate 7.7). In the 1851-52 census William Lea was listed as a farmer, but in the 1860-61 census he was listed as "farmer and potter."[33] Lea won a second prize for the best specimen of pottery and the best assortment of pottery in 1858.[34] In the 1866 exhibition he won a first prize for a water filter, and a second prize for the best assortment of pottery.[35] The location of Lea's pottery is not known, but it may have been on the fifty acres he purchased in 1856 on the west part of lot 15, concession 2.[36] In 1860 he sold this parcel to George Cudmore, whose sons John and George were later involved in pottery-making. William Lea discontinued his pottery business sometime before 1869 as the business is not mentioned in the 1870-71 census.

John & George Cudmore
By 1869 John and George Cudmore were making pottery on the property they had purchased from William Lea (plate 7.7). Only John Cudmore was potting under the name of Cudmore & Co., in 1870 in a partnership consisting of John Cudmore and William Browne. The 1870-71 census gives information on the pottery operation. Four men were employed making earthenware and flower-pots. Fifty tons of clay for pots and 2500 pounds of lead for making glaze were used. The annual value of the pottery produced at the workshop was $3,400.[37] John Cudmore was reported as a potter as late as 1884, but the pottery does not seem to have continued very long after this date.[38] Potters who worked for Cudmore include Alexander Elliott and John Cranston. Elliott worked for Cudmore in 1871 before moving to Cannifton, Hastings County (q.v.). John Cranston is reported working as a potter in 1883.[39] By 1887 he was working at the stoneware pottery run by James R. Burns on Scadding Avenue, Toronto.[40]

Samuel R. Burns
In the York Township assessment rolls for 1885, Samuel R. Burns is reported as operating a pottery on a part of lot 15, concession 2, land owned by George Cudmore.[41] Burns came to York Township from Markham, where he had operated a pottery, and he worked at Doncaster until 1905.[42] The pottery was located on lot 15 until 1895, when it was moved to a one-acre part of lot 14, concession 2, on the Don Valley Road. In 1906 Burns moved to Bolton, Peel County.

DAVISVILLE

Davisville Pottery
The Davisville pottery was founded by John Davis, who had come to Canada in 1840 and settled in the area north of the city of Toronto, on Yonge Street between the Second and Third concession roads. The community that developed in the area was known as Davisville, named in his honour. In 1845 he began a pottery business. Davis had come to Canada as a teacher or bookkeeper, and had learned the pottery-making trade while in the Toronto area, possibly at the works of either Thomas Humberstone in Newton Brook, or of John Walmsley, west of Yonge Street in the Deer Park area.

The 1860-61 census indicates that the pottery operation had $1500 invested and that two male employees helped Davis produce $500 worth of pottery annually. According to the 1870-71 census the business had grown significantly in a decade. By this time there was $7,000 capital invested and six employees produced $4,000 worth of pottery a year. Clay for the potting was dug from deposits on Eglinton Avenue near the Don Valley, and from a hollow on Millwood Road near Yonge Street on the Davis property.[43]

John Davis had a number of sons who helped in the pottery business, including Alexander John, Frederick H. and Joseph Stanley. Later, William S., a son of Alexander John, worked at the pottery. It was Joseph Stanley, the youngest son of John Davis, who eventually had a leading role in the development of the business. Joseph Stanley was born in 1849. He went to commercial college to study bookkeeping and then returned to the family business.[44] By 1890 the business had become known as John Davis & Son, with Joseph S. taking over the operation of the plant (shown in plates 7.8 and 7.9) in 1891. In

7.8 *Davisville Pottery on Yonge Street, near Millwood Avenue, Davisville, ca. 1892.* Courtesy Toronto Public Library.

the first decade of his management the company enjoyed a good deal of expansion. According to Beers, he replaced the old buildings and installed new machinery for the manufacture of earthenware.[45] Joseph Stanley also found time to become active in local politics. He succeeded his father as postmaster for the community, and was a reeve and deputy reeve of Council, eventually being elected as Mayor of North Toronto in 1898.[46]

In the pottery enterprise Joseph Stanley introduced a green-glazed line of horticultural products, including rose jars and jardinières (see plate 7.10). Advertisements of the firm in the early years of the twentieth century indicate that the business concentrated on producing horticultural wares (plate 7.11). Pottery produced by the company was marked JOHN DAVIS & SON/DAVISVILLE, ONT.

In 1913 the factory moved from its original site at Yonge Street and Millwood Road to 377 Merton Street, although the head office remained on Yonge Street. In 1916 the factory moved again to 601 Merton Street. The firm continued to operate as John Davis & Son until Joseph S. Davis' death. In 1928 the family sold the business to a new corporation formed to purchase it. The new owners, though not family, kept the name and were incorporated as John Davis & Sons, Ltd., with a share capital of $30,000.[47] The corporation never filed an annual return as required by provincial law, and was dissolved by the Government in 1956. Meanwhile, a partnership of Gerald W. Herod and Norman W. Walton was established in 1938 to operated the Davisville Potteries. This partnership was duly registered in the land registry office,[48] but the pottery came to an end the next year when the partnership was dissolved.[49]

TORONTO

There was only one pottery in Toronto in the

7.9 *Davisville Pottery with pottery workers, ca. 1892.* Courtesy Toronto Public Library.

7.10 *Unglazed hanging flowerpot with moulded mark JOHN DAVIS & SON/DAVISVILLE, ONT.*

nineteenth century. It was owned by a succession of potters during its more than thirty years of operation. The history of the pottery is re-

counted here under the different owners, all of whom marked the stonewares with their name.

Warner & Co. (1856-1863)
The business was established in 1856 by William E. Warner, an American potter who immigrated to Toronto sometime between 1852 and 1856. Warner had worked in New Jersey and then at West Troy, New York, from 1829 to 1852.[50] In Toronto, he formed a partnership with J.B. Hayden and J.H. Cornell, known as Warner & Co. The factory was on lots 72, 73, and 74 on the east side of Mill Road (later known as Scadding Street, and now named Broadview Avenue) between Eastern Avenue and Queen Street.

The factory produced a variety of stoneware products, including jugs, spittoons, chamber pots, cream pots and butter pots. An advertisement in Brown's *Toronto Directory* of 1856 (see plate 7.12) shows the wares offered and the price per dozen. An example of the

FLOWER POTS

ROSE JARS and FANCY WARE

MAY | E HAD FROM

DAVISVILLE POTTERIES

John Davis & Sons

Davisville P.O., Ont.

7.11 *Advertisement of Davisville Pottery from Canadian Horticulturalist of January 1905.*

wares produced by the firm, and marked with the impressed name WARNER & CO./ TORONTO, C.W., is shown in plate 7.13.

The partnership of Warner & Co. was short-lived, for by 1857 only Warner and Cornell were listed in assessment rolls as working at the pottery. The following year Warner alone is listed as operating the business, although it continued to be known as Warner & Co.[51]

The pottery property consisted of three lots with three buildings. The main building was a two-storey frame structure, 120 feet by 23 feet. The other two buildings were never described, but presumably were for the kiln and pottery storage.

The business did not prosper and by the time of the 1860-61 census Warner was listed as insolvent.[52] Tax assessment rolls for 1862 and 1863 describe the pottery as "vacant." In

1863 Warner sold the property to John Smith, a farmer. Late in the year the pottery was leased by Smith to Nicholas Eberhardt.

Eberhardt & Halm (1863-1865)
Nicholas Eberhardt was born in France and immigrated to Canada ca. 1860. In 1861 he is working at Paris, Ontario, for either J.H. Ahrens or J.M. Marlatt.[53] The 1864 Toronto assessment rolls report Eberhardt, together with Joseph Halm and Peter W. Heilman, working together at the pottery site.[54] Irving's *Toronto Directory . . . for 1865* lists the firm of Eberhardt & Halm, but there is no other documented evidence of an actual partnership. A piece of stoneware made during this short partnership is shown in plate 7.14.

N. Eberhardt (1865-1879)
There survive two brief records made during the time Nicholas Eberhardt ran the business on his own. Sutherland's *Toronto Directory of 1867* describes the factory as follows:

7.12 *Advertisement of Warner & Co., from* Brown's *Toronto Directory of 1856. Courtesy Metropolitan Toronto Library Board.*

Don Bridge Pottery, established in 1852 (carried on by Nicholas Eberhardt since 1863), manufacturing every description of stoneware such as open creampots, butter pots with covers, jugs, preserve jars, fruit jars with corks, pitchers, flower pots, churns, milk pans, spittoons, etc., employs about five hands, importer and dealer in fireclay and sand.[55]

In the 1870-71 census the pottery is described as employing two persons all year to produce stoneware valued at $3,000. To make this ware, Eberhardt imported 100 tons of stoneware clay, valued at $500.[56] From these figures, this was a small stoneware factory compared with that of Brantford or Picton, Ontario.

Eberhardt decorated the stoneware containers with characteristic cobalt-blue flower designs. Pots were also marked with the impressed name N. EBERHARDT/TORONTO,

7.13 *A four-gallon stoneware crock with cobalt-blue flower. Piece has impressed mark WARNER & CO/TORONTO.*

7.14 *A four-gallon stoneware butter crock with impressed mark of EBERHARDT & HALM/TORONTO, C.W.*

7.15 *Two-gallon stoneware crock with elaborate blue flower and impressed mark N. EBER-HARDT/TORONTO, C.W. Courtesy Sharon Temple Museum.*

7.17 *Jug with cobalt-blue flowers. Piece is marked with impressed name N. EBERHARDT/ TORONTO, C.W. Courtesy Black Creek Pioneer Village, Toronto.*

7.16 *Five-gallon butter crock with cobalt-blue flower design. Piece is marked N. EBER-HARDT/TORONTO ONT. Courtesy Sharon Temple Museum.*

C.W. on those produced before 1867, and with N. EBERHARDT/TORONTO, ONT. on those produced after 1867, although the changeover from one mark to another cannot be assumed to have occurred at the time of Confederation. The containers in plates 7.15 to 7.18 illustrate the wares produced by Eberhardt.

For unknown reasons, Eberhardt gave up his lease on the pottery in 1879. The landowner, John Smith, leased the business in December, 1879, to James Burns and William James Campbell, operating under the name Burns & Campbell.

Burns & Campbell (1879-1881)
James R. Burns was born in County Tyrone, Ireland, where he operated a pottery for fifteen years before coming to Canada in 1879.[57] William J. Campbell, also born in Ireland,

7.18 *Five-gallon stoneware butter crock with impressed name N. EBERHARDT.* Courtesy Black Creek Pioneer Village, Toronto.

7.20 *Stoneware butter crock with the impressed mark J.R.BURNS/TORONTO.*

worked at the Brantford stoneware factory from 1877 to 1879. The two men joined in partnership, but their effort was of short duration, as Campbell relinquished his interest in the business in 1881, returning to work at Brantford.

Because of this partnership's short life-span, pottery with the impressed mark BURNS & CAMPBELL/TORONTO is very rare. An example of a stoneware container is shown in plate 7.19.

James R. Burns (1881-1887)
Burns continued the business until 1887, when the pottery was dismantled and the land redeveloped for housing. Potters who worked for Burns included Thomas J. Fleming, who had earlier worked at Paris, Ontario. Fleming worked in Toronto in 1882 and 1883 before moving to Belleville, Hastings County. John Cranston, who came from Doncaster, worked for Burns in 1887 before going to Weston to work for George Plant. An example of a stoneware butter crock produced during Burns' operation of the business is shown in plate 7.20.

Toronto Pottery Co. (1899-1924)
This company was formed in Toronto in 1899 and was granted letters patent as a corporation

7.19 *A two-gallon butter crock made by BURNS & CAMPBELL/TORONTO.*

STONEWARE

JARS and SPECIALTIES

Packages Made to Order

Quality Guaranteed

T<u>HE</u> **TORONTO POTTERY CO.**

LIMITED

Write for Catalogue — Toronto, Canada

Blue Flemish
Water Keg

7.21 *Advertisement of Toronto Pottery Co., from* Canadian Pottery and Glass Gazette, *of January 1908.*

in 1904.[58] Unlike the Toronto stoneware pottery, the Toronto Pottery Co. never produced any crockery in Canada, but acted as importer of American wares. The Toronto firm was a wholly-owned subsidiary of the Robinson Clay Product Company, Inc., of Akron, Ohio. Pottery with the name of the Toronto corporation was made in Akron and shipped by rail to Toronto.

The Toronto Pottery Co., Ltd., had its head office and warehouse at 75-81 Cottingham Street. In 1912 the head office was moved to 617-618 Dominion Bank Building, and the warehouse was located at 125 Shaftesbury Avenue at the C.P.R. tracks. By 1924 the head office had moved again, this time to the Temple Building, 62 Richmond Street West, Toronto.

From its founding, the company flourished. The *Mercantile Agency Reference Book*, one of the credit-rating manuals issued by Dun, Wiman & Co., reported the pecuniary worth of the corporation at $35,000 in 1914 and $75,000 by 1919. The rapid increase in the company's credit rating is one indication of its ability to capture the Canadian market at a time when the over-all demand for stoneware, Rockingham ware and bristol ware was declin-

ing. A company advertisement from a 1908 magazine is shown in plate 7.21.

In the early 1920s the Robinson Clay Product Co., of Akron, Ohio, decided that all its subsidiaries should carry the name of the parent firm. To accomplish this change, the officers from Akron formed the Robinson Clay Product Company (of Canada) Ltd., on March 24, 1924, to purchase the Toronto Pottery Co., Ltd. Therefore, after 1924 the name Toronto Pottery Co. was no longer used on imported pottery, although the corporation did not formally end until 1935. Blair, writing about Ohio potteries, reports that the Akron company discontinued the production of stoneware, Rockingham ware and yellow ware in 1914.[59] If this is correct, then the Toronto Pottery Co., Ltd., which continued to import large quantities of stoneware as late as 1923, must have bought them from firms other than the Robinson Clay Product Company. It is known that the Toronto firm purchased stoneware from the American Clay Product Company in 1923, but it is unlikely that they continued to have names stencilled on products at that time.

A Toronto Pottery Co., Ltd., catalogue dated ca. 1913 lists several styles of teapot, including Rebecca-at-the-well, trilby and cloverleaf teapots. The company also adver-

7.22 *Flowerpots with bullrush pattern, made for sale in Ontario by Toronto Pottery Co., Ltd.*

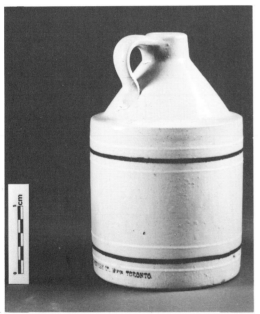

7.23 *Blue and white-banded shoulder jug with printed name TORONTO POTTERY CO., MFG^R TORONTO.* Courtesy Royal Ontario Museum.

tised the Champion teapot, similar in design to those produced by R. Campbell's Sons of Hamilton. Other interesting products included ginger beer bottles, blue Flemish growlers and

steins, glazed flowerpots with embossed bull-rush pattern (see plate 7.22) and blue Flemish water kegs. The complete catalogue with useful illustrations and names for different types of pottery has been published by the present author elsewhere.[60]

A blue-banded shoulder jug is shown in plate 7.23. The stencilled or stamped name TORONTO POTTERY CO. MFG^R, TORONTO is found on the outside of the jug near its base. Other pieces are known, with the addition of the name of a merchant or manufacturer. The company advertised "jugs stamped with customers name, and attractive ad, 2 cents per gallon extra."

The Robinson Clay Product Company (of Canada) Ltd., is still an active Ontario corporation, with its head office in Concord, Ontario.

MARKHAM

Eby/Ensminger/Burns
Early in 1855 William Eby, twenty-three years old, established a pottery business in Markham. Eby, a Mennonite, had moved from Waterloo Township, a Mennonite area, to Markham, where he purchased a half-acre part of the east half of lot 16, concession 7, Markham Township, for £31.5.0.[61] The pottery, according to a plan dated 1885, was on the northwest corner of the lot, on the site of the old Mt. Joy schoolhouse.[62] Eby worked

7.24a, b and c *Slip-decorated jar with Markham/ Pottery/1862. The jar has three panels with slip decorations, two of which are shown here. Simi-* lar motifs are found on Ontario German fractur art from the Markham area.

at Markham until 1856, when he sold the pottery property to John Byer and moved to Conestogo, Waterloo County.[63]

Byer leased the pottery to Philip Ensminger, who had emigrated from France ca. 1840, and settled in New York State for about seven years before moving west to Illinois. Ensminger moved again to Chippewa, Ontario, in 1852 and finally to Markham in 1855.[64] Ensminger rented the property until 1862. The 1860-61 census indicates that the pottery building was a one-and-one-half-storey frame structure.[65]

After 1862, Cyrus Eby, brother of William Eby, began a short tenure at the workshop until 1867 when he went to Conestogo to help his brother, William, in the pottery there.[66] An example of pottery made by either Ensminger or Cyrus Eby is shown in plate 7.24. The final operator of the pottery was Samuel R. Burns, son of John Burns, of Yorkville. Burns arrived

7.25　Bowls produced by S.R. Burns at Markham, Ontario. These unglazed bowls were recovered dur-

ing archaeological excavations at the site in 1968. (Scale runs from one to five centimetres.)

in Markham in 1870 and worked until 1884, when he moved to the Don Valley area of York Township (q.v.).

The 1870-71 census gives details of the pottery operation. Burns employed three men to produce pottery valued at $1,200 a year. He had $900 invested in the business.[67] Archaeological excavations of the site were conducted by Miss Helen Sutermeister of The Royal Ontario Museum, Toronto, in the summer of 1968. She reported finding two distinct deposits of waste pottery on the site, with pottery found north of the schoolhouse representing wares produced by William Eby, and pottery found south of the school representing the later product of Samuel R. Burns.[68]

The Eby materials were limited in number of sherds and types of wares represented. Sutermeister reports that seventy percent of the sherds represents bowls. The style was typical of bowls later produced at Conestogo; small bowls with "convex" rims and a small groove cut into the outside of the bowl, about one and one-half inches below the rim. The bowls were glazed inside and out. The clay burned to a yellow colour, and with the clear lead glaze, a uniform yellow appearance in the finished product resulted.

Along the southern side of the schoolhouse, Sutermeister uncovered the remains of the pottery building and large quantities of pottery. In the probe trench, she located three

cellars used for storage of partially finished biscuit ware and glazed pottery. The wares were apparently stored on shelves in the cellar, as the excavators found wares still stacked one on top of the other. The cellars contained bowls, moulded wares, spittoons, moulded dogs, moulded crock lids, preserve jars, pitchers, bottles, jugs, and milk pans. Birns glazed his wares with a Rockingham glaze or with an olive-green to yellow glaze. Chemical analysis of glaze compound found at the site showed that the glaze contained lead oxide coloured white by the addition of tin oxide, or green or yellow by the addition of copper or iron.[69] Rockingham-glazed wares were rare and this type of glaze was apparently used on pitchers and some types of moulded wares only.

Examples of pottery from the Burns period are shown in plates 7.25-7.29. Two of these were a preserve jar with a flanged rim (plate 7.26 left) and a tomato or fruit jar with a rounded rim (plate 7.26 right). The flanged-rim jar was probably closed with a pottery lid, not unlike a flowerpot saucer, which is inverted over the top. The plain round-rim jar is closed with a cork. An intact molasses jug (plate 7.27) was recovered during the archaeological excavations. It had not been glazed, but small fragments of jugs recovered from the site indicate that they would normally have been finished in yellow or buff-coloured glaze. Bottles were usually ten inches high and with a

7.26 *Preserve jar (left) and tomato or fruit jar (right) recovered from Burns Pottery, Markham.*

7.27 *Intact molasses jug recovered from Burns site, Markham. The jug was found unglazed.*

basal diameter of between three and one-half and four inches. The bottles were finished in white or buff glaze (see plate 7.28).

Fragments of several types of moulded ware were uncovered in the dig, including fluted table bowls, moulded Staffordshire "King Charles" spaniel pottery dogs, and spittoons

with a shell pattern. The most commonly found moulded pieces were lids for crocks, each with an intricate raspberry design (plate 7.29). This pattern is so far unknown

7.28 *Bottles recovered from the Burns site, Markham. Some bottles were found with buff or cream-coloured glaze.*

7.29 *Covers for butter crocks with raspberry fruit pattern. Pieces were recovered from the Burns site at Markham. They have a glaze that has not been fired.*

elsewhere in Ontario.[70] The lids recovered in the dig were unglazed, but they would have been finished in yellow or buff-coloured glaze or in the Rockingham glaze.

Joseph Wideman

A second pottery was operating in Markham Township by 1863. In that year the assessment rolls report that Joseph Wideman was operating a workshop on a one-acre part of lot 31, concession 6.[71] He apparently operated the pottery in conjunction with a farm, for in subsequent years he is also reported as a farmer. In 1871 he is described as a "mouse trap manufacturer" and in 1872 as a "clock cleaner."

In 1876, Wideman is again listed as a potter, now renting one acre, part of lot 21, concession 8.[72] Wideman continued to work at his pottery until 1908. His son Abram N. worked at the business from 1886-97. Throughout the years, the Wideman pottery was a very marginal business. Credit ratings for the pottery indicate that it had very limited resources and a pecuniary worth of less than $500.[73]

Wideman purchased the pottery property in 1891 for $200;[74] after his death in 1912 the property was sold by the administrators of his estate.[75] Wideman, like the Ebys, was a Mennonite, and represents part of their small but interesting cultural influence in the pottery craft of the nineteenth century.

8.
Potters of West Central Ontario

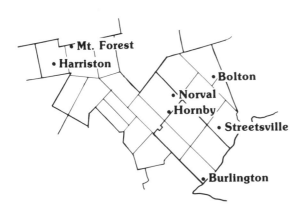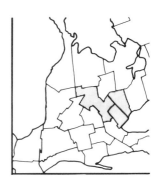

Fig. 8.1 *Map showing the location of potteries in west central Ontario during the nineteenth century.*

The counties of Halton, Peel, Dufferin and Wellington in west central Ontario had potteries established from the late 1840s. The last pottery in the county closed its doors in the 1890s. In all there were eight communities in the region with potteries. The location of these potteries is shown in figure 8.1.

HALTON COUNTY

Burlington
A pottery was established in Burlington (earlier called Wellington Square) sometime between 1847 and 1851 by William Campbell, an Irish immigrant potter.[1] In 1852 his brother Robert came to Canada from New Jersey to join in the business.[2] In May 1854 the two brothers purchased the pottery property, a half-acre parcel known as lot 65, on Brant Street.[3] This is now the site of a post office.

William and Robert Campbell moved in 1859 to Hamilton, where they both continued careers in the pottery trade. No wares with the impressed name of the Campbells is known to have been made in Burlington during these

early years. It is assumed that the firm made earthenware containers, as no record of stoneware products is known from this area.

In the 1851-52 census the potter William Brittain is listed as working for William Campbell. Brittain (Britton) later established a pottery in the hamlet of Waverley, Simcoe County.

Hornby
Henry McCluskie (sometimes spelled McCloskie) worked for Bernard Collins in Streetsville, Peel County in the early 1850s.[4] Sometime before 1860 he moved to Trafalgar Township, Halton County and established a workshop on a one-acre part of the northeast half of lot 14, concession 7, land now occupied by the southwest cloverleaf of the intersection of Highway 401 and Trafalgar Road.[5] He sold this pottery in 1871 and moved a short distance northward to Esquesing Township, where he purchased a six-and-one-half-acre part of lot 1, concession 8.[6] McCluskie continued the business until 1889, when he sold his land and buildings.[7]

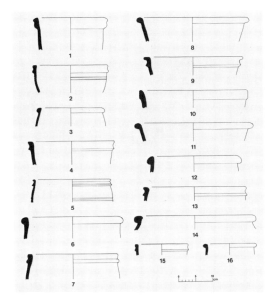

Fig. 8.2 *Profiles of pottery sherds recovered from Collins Pottery in Streetsville, Peel County.*

Norval

George McConnell started a pottery shop in the town of Norval ca. 1857. In the census of 1860-61 we learn that he had come from Ireland and had settled in Canada around 1840.[8] By the time of the census three of his sons were also working in the pottery, George Jr., Adam and John.[9]

The 1870-71 census indicates that the pottery operated for eight months of the year to produce earthenware valued at $1,200.[10] I have not been able to locate the pottery, nor have I found any pottery that was made at the Norval pottery shop.

PEEL COUNTY

Streetsville

There were two potteries in the village of Streetsville during the nineteenth century. The earlier one was established by Bernard Collins ca. 1849, and the later workshop was founded by Robert Irwin in 1854.

Bernard Collins

In the year 1849 Bernard Collins purchased lot 6, on Queen Street in the village of Streetsville, for a pottery shop.[11] Collins had emigrated from Ireland ca. 1840, bringing with him his

wife and his son William. The census of 1851-52 indicates that he employed five men to make pottery ware,[12] but other details of the business are not known. Collins continued to operate his business until 1865, when he moved to the town of Orangeville. His three sons worked as potters: William worked at his father's business and also for Irwin in Streetsville, Barnet J. left Streetsville for a pottery in Hamilton in 1863,[13] and in 1865 Henry J. joined Barnet J. in Hamilton.[14]

During excavation for a house at the Collins lot (now 158 Church Street), thousands of sherds were uncovered. In 1975 the town of Streetsville relaid the sidewalks and again large numbers of sherds were uncovered. These were salvaged by Mr. William Tolton, who gave them to the author for study. Cross-sections of these pot fragments are shown in figure 8.2, illustrating the types of earthenware containers produced by Collins.

Henry McCluskie, listed as working in Streetsville for Collins in the 1851-52 census, later established a pottery in Trafalgar Township, near Hornby.[15]

Robert Irwin

The second pottery in Streetsville was established by Robert Irwin on lot 1, Queen Street. He bought the land in 1854 for £150.[16] We know about the pottery from advertisements that appeared in local newspapers in the early years of the business. An advertisement for the "New Streetsville Pottery" appeared in the July 23, 1857, issue of the local newspaper, and is reproduced here as plate 8.1. Irwin's pottery was small in its production, for in the 1870-71 census he is reported as employing only two persons, one of whom was his eighteen-year-old son. The same census states that Irwin produced $1,200 worth of wares a year, using thirty tons of clay and fourteen quantils of red lead and manganese for glaze.[17] Irwin combined his pottery work with the job of town constable and bailiff. From assessment records it appears that he discontinued his pottery work around 1880, after which he is described as a "bailiff".[18] But in the year 1886 he apparently resumed it, for the assessment rolls again list him as a potter.[19] A note in the January 17, 1889 *Streetsville Review* states:

Or to GEO. HAWKINS,
Land Agent and Anctioneer.
Streetsville, Jan. 23rd, 1857.   136-tf

Streetsville New Pottery !!

THE undersigned, having at great expense errected the best

POTTERY,

In the County, is prepared to manufacture al
kinds of

Superior Earthenware,

AT THE

SHORTEST NOTICE!

And upon the most reasonable terms.

His articles are by admitted judges, pronounced the best that can be found ; and he hopes from
good workmanship and reasonable prices to
merit that patronage industry universally de-
mands.

☞ **Remember the Streetsville New Pottery.** ☜

ROBEET IRWINE.

Streetsville, Oct.16th, 1855.   78-tf

THE CANADA
GROCERY AND TEA STORE

8.1 *Advertisement of Irwin's pottery from* Brampton Standard and County of Peel Conservative
Journal, *July 23, 1857.*

Robert Irwin is getting his pottery in working order, getting a supply of material at which he will soon begin working again.[20]

Irwin moved to Toronto in 1891, although he owned the pottery lot for a few years longer.[21]

Bolton
By 1871 James Harrison Burns had moved from Yorkville to Albion Township and had started the first pottery in the region. His workshop was on a three-acre parcel of the east part of lot 7, concession 7. In 1876 Burns moved the business to the nearby town of Bolton, although he continued to own the land in Albion Township until 1890. Burns located the pottery in Bolton on lot 33 in block 1, land now at the northwest corner of Willow and James Streets.[22]

Burns operated the pot shop until 1887. A later owner of the business was Caleb Saunders, who had earlier worked at Lynden, Wentworth County, before coming to Bolton in 1898. He continued to pot at the workshop until his death in 1904.[23] An example of the Rockingham-glazed wares Saunders produced is shown in plate 8.2. This caramel-

8.2 *Rockingham-glazed spittoon made by Cabel Saunders in Bolton. Piece is marked with impressed name ALBION POTTERY/C. SAUNDERS/BOLTON, ONT. Saunders worked at the pottery from 1898 to 1904.*

brown spittoon is marked with the impressed name ALBION POTTERY/C. SAUNDERS/BOLTON, ONT on its base.

In the spring of 1905 Samuel R. Burns, brother of James Harrison Burns, purchased the pottery, having moved from Todmorden in the Don Valley, York County. He worked at

8.3 *Advertisement from* Historical Atlas of Waterloo & Wellington Counties *of 1877 describing the products of the Orangeville Pottery.*

the business until his death at the age of sixty-five in 1911, when the making of pottery ceased in the town of Bolton.

DUFFERIN COUNTY

Orangeville

The history of the pottery in Orangeville covers the period that the town was part of Wellington County but that history is related here under its later county designation, Dufferin County.

Bernard Collins and his family moved to Orangeville in 1865. He worked as a potter on land owned by Jesse Ketchum. James Gahan, who had also worked for Collins in Streetsville, came to Orangeville at the same time. The tax assessment rolls for the town from 1867 through 1869 indicate that Gahan was a tenant at the pottery. This might mean that he actually rented the pottery and Collins worked for him, or that he merely lived above the pottery workshop, with Collins being in charge of the business. The exact owner of the business, as distinct from the property, is not known, but it might have been John Anderson, a local merchant and entrepreneur, who is listed as the proprietor in the 1870-71 census. The census reports that the pottery produced $3,000 worth of crockery.[24] In March, 1874, the property was sold by Jesse Ketchum to his son Oliver W., and was then described as being located on lot 15, block 1, north of Broadway Avenue.[25] This is now the site of a bank. An advertisement from a county atlas of 1877 (see plate 8.3) describes the products of the pottery, including a patent stoneware. No record of a patent for clay mixture was recorded in Patent Office records. An example of pottery made in Orangeville is the money bank (box) shown in plate 8.4. The Orangeville Pottery continued until 1880, when O. W. Ketchum moved to Toronto. Three years later he gave a local real estate agent power of attorney to sell the land and buildings.[26]

From 1888 to 1890, B. J. Collins, son of Bernard, is listed in Orangeville assessment rolls as a potter at block 3, lot 2, in the east ward of Orangeville.[27] It is not certain if he operated a pottery at this location, or worked at a pottery elsewhere in the region. After 1890 his name disappears from local assessment rolls.

8.4 *Elaborately decorated money bank (box) made at the Orangeville Pottery. The name of the pottery is found on the side of the piece but is difficult to read because of the glaze.* Courtesy Mrs. Robert Bull.

WELLINGTON COUNTY

Harriston

A notice in the Huron Expositor of Seaforth, Ontario, dated April 14, 1876, announces:

Harriston has a pottery just recently established, where they are able to glaze white ware and burn it equal to any stone ware manufactured and it is difficult for experienced persons to detect it from the best stoneware . . . They

HARRISTON POTTERY,

Harriston, *15 Jun* 187*6*

M _____

Terms--Cash on Delivery.
Thirty-three and one-third per
cent off to actual merchants·

Bought of Cadwell & Pegler,

MANUFACTURERS OF STONE ENAMELLED WHITE WARE

DOZ.		PER DOZ.	EACH	$	CTS.
	Cream Pots.				
	6 Gallon	7 20	$0 60	2	40
	3 Gallon	3 60	0 30		
	2 Gallon ·.......	2 40	0 20		
	1 Gallon	1 80	0 15		
	Half Gallon..........	0 96	0 08		
	Milk Crocks.				
	2 Gallon	3 00	0 25		
	1 Gallon	1 80	0 15		
	Half Gallon.........	0 96	0 08		
	Milk Pans.				
	3 Gallon	3 60	0 30		
	2 Gallon	2 64	0 22	5 28	
	1 Gallon	1 80	0 15	10 80	
	Butter Pots.				
	5 Gallon	9 00	0 75	18 48	
	4 Gallon	7 50	0 62½	6 16	
	3 Gallon	6 00	0 50		
	2 Gallon	4 50	0 37½	12 32	
	1 Gallon	3 75	0 31		
	Jugs.				
	3 Gallon	7 20	0 60		
	2 Gallon	4 50	0 37½		
	1 Gallon	3 00	0 25		
	Half Gallon............	2 40	0 20		
	Quart	1 50	0 12½		
	Molasses Jugs.				
	1 Gallon	3 60	0 30		
	Half Gallon...........	2 40	0 20		
	Quart	1 50	0 12½		
	Tomato, or Fruit Jars.				
	WITH CORKS.				
	2 Gallon	4 80	0 40		
	1 Gallon	3 60	0 30		
	Half Gallon............	2 40	0 20		
	Quart	1 50	0 12½		
	Preserve Jars.				
	2 Gallon	4 50	0 37½		
	1 Gallon	3 00	0 25		
	Half Gallon...........	2 40	0 20		
	Quart	1 50	0 12½		
	Chambers.				
	1st Size..............	3 00	0 25		
	2nd Size	2 25	0 18¾		

DOZ.		PER DOZ.	EACH	$	CTS.
	Fancy Flower Pots.				
	1st Size..............	4 50	0 37½		
	2nd Size	3 00	0 25		
	Stove Tubes.				
	1st Size..............	$3 00	$0 25		
	2nd Size	2 40	0 20		
	3rd Size.............	1 80	0 15		
	Flower Pots.				
	12 Inch..............	4 80	0 40		
	10 Inch..............	3 00	0 25		
	8 Inch	1 80	0 15		
	7 Inch	1 20	0 10		
	6 Inch	0 96	0 08		
	5 Inch	0 72	0 06		
	4 Inch..:............	0 60	0 05		
	3 Inch	0 36	0 03		
	2½ Inch	0 25	0 02		
	Saucers one-half the price of the Flower Pots.				
	ROCKINGHAM,				
	OR FLINT ENAMELLED WARE.				
	Water Pitchers.				
	1st Size..............	7 50	0 62½		
	2nd Size	4 50	0 37½		
	3rd Size.............	3 00	0 25		
	4th Size.............	2 25	0 18¾		
	5th Size.............	1 50	0 12½		
	Spittoons.				
	1st Size..............	9 00	0 75		
	2nd Size	7 50	0 62½		
	3rd Size.............	6 00	0 50		
	4th Size.............	4 50	0 37½		
	5th Size.............	3 00	0 25		
	Pie Plates.				
	1st Size..............	0 96	0 08		
	2nd Size	0 75	0 06¼		
	Hanging Flower Pots.				
	1st Size..............	3 60	0 30		
	2nd Size	2 40	0 20		
	Water Filters·				
	Each.............		4 00		

RECEIVED PAYMENT,

The above Ware is made of a very superior material. Orders by mail respectfully solicited, and will be promptly attended to.

8.5 *Price list of Cadwell & Pegler Pottery, of
Harriston.* Courtesy Royal Ontario Museum.

MOUNT FOREST POTTERY.

Mount Forest, Ont., *17th Jany* 187*3*

M Alse, Weikly Jno Ho

Bought of **E. W. BRADWIN,**

Manufacturer of, and Wholesale Dealer in

All Descriptions of Earthenware.

Doz.	CREAM POTS. PER DOZ.	$	cts.	Doz.	AIR-TIGHT JARS.	$	cts.
1½	5 Gallon,......... $6 00	9	00		2 Gallon	4	50
1½	4 Gallon,......... 4 50	6	75		1 Gallon	3	00
1	3 Gallon,......... 3 00	3	00		¾ Gallon	2	25
1	1 Gallon,......... 1 50	1	50		½ Gallon	1	50
1½	½ Gallon,......... 0 75	1	12½		*MOLASSES JUGS.*		
	MILK CROCKS.				1 Gallon	3	00
2	2 Gallon...........	2	25		¾ Gallon	2	25
	1 Gallon........... 1 50	3	00		½ Gallon	1	50
	½ Gallon........... 0 75				*WATER PITCHERS.*		
	MILK PANS,				1 Gallon	3	00
6	2 Gallon........... 2 25	9	00		¾ Gallon	2	25
	1 Gallon 1 50				½ Gallon	1	50
	BUTTER POTS with cover.				*CHAMBERS.*		
	5 Gallon........... 9 00				1st size...	3	00
	4 Gallon........... 7 50				2nd size.............	2	25
	3 Gallon........... 6 00				*STOVE TUBES.*		
	2 Gallon........... 4 50				12 inch	3	00
	JUGS.				9 inch..............	2	25
1½	2 Gallon........... 4 50	6	75		6 inch..............	1	50
2	1 Gallon........... 3 00	6	00		*FLOWER POTS.*		
3	¾ Gallon 2 25	6	75		8 in. Flower Pots, at $8 per 100 net.		
3	½ Gallon........... 1 50	4	50		6 in. do. at 5 do.		
	PRESERVE JARS, 3	59 62	½		5 in. do. at 3.50 do.		
	2 Gallon 4 50	19	87		4 in. do. at 2.50 do.		
	1 Gallon 3 00	39	75		*Saucers one third the price of Flower Pots.*		
	¾ Gallon 2 25						
	½ Gallon 1 50						

The above Ware is made of the very best Clay. A general assortment kept on hand, warranted equal in quality and finish to any manufactured in the Dominion. Orders by mail respectfully solicited and promptly executed.

ADDRESS—Box 122, }
Mt. Forest P.O. }

Received Payment,

E. W. Bradwin

per William Howe

8.6 *Price list from Mount Forest Pottery, owned by Edwin Bradwin.* Courtesy Wellington County Museum, Fergus.

have now a kiln burnt which can be tested by any person calling. This establishment is quite an acquisition to the village, and the future prospects of Messrs. Caldwell & Pegler, the proprietors, are as bright as those of any firm in the village . . .

The partnership was composed of William Cadwell (also spelled Caldwell), who had worked earlier in Waterloo County, and John Pegler, who had worked in London, Middlesex County, in the early 1870s. A price list for the pottery is shown in plate 8.5.

I have been unable to locate the site of the pottery, as assessment rolls for the town were destroyed by fire. The partnership of Cadwell and Pegler did not last beyond 1876, as a second price list of that year had Cadwell's name scratched out. This does not mean that Cadwell ceased potting, for a directory of 1879 lists him as a potter in Harriston.[28] In the July 1883 *Mercantile Agency Reference Book,* he is again reported as owning a pottery in Harriston.[29] Cadwell purchased a half-acre parcel of land in the village in 1880, known as lot 9 on the northeast side of Webb Street.[30] This may have been the location of his pottery, and it could have been the location of the earlier pottery operated under the partnership.

A pottery was operating in the town as late as the first years of the 1890s, as an 1892 directory lists Henry Brittain (also spelled Britton), formerly of Waverley, Simcoe County, as working in Harriston.[31] As Cadwell did not sell his land until 1896, it may be that Brittain was working for him in 1892.

Pottery-making in Harriston probably ended in 1894, when Cadwell's name appears in tax assessment rolls for the Village of New Hamburg, Waterloo County.

Mount Forest

Edwin Bradwin moved from Lynden, Wentworth County, to Mount Forest ca. 1872. Soon afterwards he opened a pottery on part of lot 27 on the west side of Main Street. By 1878 his brother Joseph had joined him in Mount Forest, but Joseph did not work there for long as by 1879 he had opened a pottery in Wingham, Huron County. John Lyons (sometimes spelled Lines), who had worked at the Lynden pottery, joined Bradwin in Mount Forest and worked at the pottery from 1878 until its closure in 1884.

In 1882 Bradwin purchased land north of the town of Mount Forest in Normanby Township, Grey County, where in 1884 he established another pottery. No pottery ware made at the Mount Forest Pottery is known to bear the workshop's identifying mark, but a price list from the Mount Forest Pottery, shown in plate 8.6, indicates the basic items made by Bradwin.

Two other potters are reported in Wellington County in the 1860s, but there is no evidence to suggest they actually operated a pottery workshop. Jesse Hill is listed in an 1864 directory in Salem, Nichol Township[32]; William Spence is listed in an 1865 directory as working in Hollen, Maryborough Township[33].

9.
Kilns of the Georgian Bay–Lake Simcoe Region

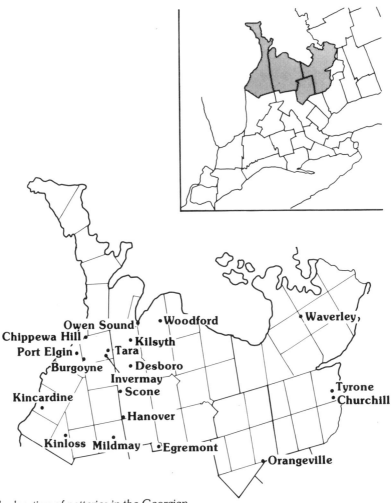

Fig. 9.1 *The location of potteries in the Georgian Bay–Lake Simcoe Region.*

The counties bordering Georgian Bay and the western side of Lake Simcoe were rich in clay, with good material for making pottery and brick. The many red-and buff-brick farmhouses are testimony to the brickmaking, while evidence of the pottery workshops is more fragmentary, with only a small number of crocks and decorative pieces left as a reminder of the potter's work.

The three counties in the region are Simcoe, Grey and Bruce. The location of potteries in these counties is shown in figure 9.1.

SIMCOE COUNTY

Waverley

Henry Brittain, an Irish-born potter, immigrated to Canada around 1858 and settled in Simcoe County on lot 77, concession 2, Tay Township. He cleared five of the 100 acres he had received from the Crown.[1] The 1870-71 census provides us with an account of the pottery operation. He produced 6,000 pieces of "merchantable brown earthenware" a year at a market value of $700. To produce these crocks, Brittain worked eight months and used fifteen tons of clay and sand.[2]

In later years Henry Brittain was assisted by his son, Henry Jr. By the mid-1880s the third generation of the family was busy at the wheel. Robert J. Brittain, son of Henry Jr., was operating the business. The pottery continued until late in the year 1897, when the credit-rating information indicates that the business had been discontinued. No pottery identified as made at this site is known.

Churchill/Tyrone

These two hamlets in Innisfil Township, on the modern-day Highway 11, the main road connecting Simcoe County communities with Toronto, to the south, were the location of active potteries from 1860 until 1875. In 1860 a one-acre plot on the northwest corner of the northern half of lot 16, concession 3, Churchill, was purchased by Edward Helweg, who was at the time listed in the assessment rolls as a potter.[3] Helweg worked at the site until 1863, when the business was sold to August Schultz.[4] Schultz continued to pot at Churchill until ca. 1865, then moved his business north to concession 5, near the village of Tyrone. He made pottery at this second site until ca. 1875. There is no record of Helweg or Schultz marking their wares, nor is there any pottery attributed to their workshops.

GREY COUNTY

With the migration of people into Grey County, new villages and hamlets were established. Small potteries were established in six communities in the county. The history of each of these workshops illustrates the nature of the potter's craft and the range of wares produced in the region.

Kilsyth

The hamlet of Kilsyth, located about eight kilometres south of Owen Sound, was the location of the first pottery in the county. George Smith, of Sullivan Township, arrived in Kilsyth in 1858 and leased the south part of lot 10, concession 7 for $30 a year. The terms of the three-year lease specified that the property was to be used for a pottery only. In 1860 Smith purchased a one-acre tract of lot 9, and established another workshop.[5] In April, 1864, William Walmsley and James McCluskie entered into a partnership in pottery-making, apparently in association with Smith, although documentary sources do not make this fact certain. A county directory for 1865-66 describes the pottery operated by the partnership.

The earthenware manufacture of Walmsley & McCluskie has attained considerable proportions, the pottery having now been in successful operation for several years; and many articles of the more ornamental kinds, as well as those in common use, are now produced at the works.[6]

William Walmsley sold his interest in the partnership to Alexander Brady in 1866; shortly thereafter, James McCluskie sold his interest to George Smith. Brady apparently relinquished his interest to Smith by 1869, for in this year George Smith leased the entire business to Alexander Sinclair for $100 a year. The pottery was at this time known as the Derby Pottery, a name it retained until it closed in the fall of 1909. By 1871 Alexander Sinclair was able to purchase the pottery for $400, while operating the business in conjunction with a small farm.[7] A note in the 1870-71 census indicates the size and importance of the operation. Sinclair had $1,000 and produced wares worth $2,000 a year.[8]

During Sinclair's ownership of the business

DERBY POTTERY
KILSYTH P. O.

190

Bought of **ALEX. SINCLAIR,**

Manufacturer of all Kinds of POTTERYWARE.

TERMS.—33⅓ PER CENT. DISCOUNT FOR CASH ON DELIVERY.

Richardson Printer, Owen Sound.

Doz.		$	C	Doz.		$	C
CREAM POTS.				**Brought forward......$**			
	Per Doz.						
6 Gallon	$6 00			**HANGING BASKETS.**			
4 "	4 20						
3 "	3 00				Per Doz.		
1 "	1 50			½ Gallon	$3 00		
½ "	0 84			¼ "	1 80		
BUTTER POTS (with covers)				**MOLASSES Jugs.**			
4 Gallon	$6 60			2 Gallon	$4 20		
3 "	5 40			1 "	3 00		
2 "	4 20			½ "	1 80		
1 "	2 40			¼ "	1 50		
CHURNS.				**JUGS.**			
6 Gallon	$12 00			2 Gallon	$4 20		
5 "	9 00			1 "	3 00		
3 "	5 00			½ "	1 80		
				¼ "	1 50		
MILK CROCKS.				**WATER PITCHERS.**			
2 Gallon	$2 40			1 Gallon	$3 00		
1 "	1 50			½ "	2 40		
½ "	0 84			¼ "	1 50		
MILK PANS.				**STOVE TUBS.**			
2 Gallon	$2 16			12 inches long	$3 00		
1 "	1 20			8 "	2 40		
				5 "	1 50		
PRESERVE JARS (with corks).				**CHAMBERS.**			
1 Gallon	$2 40			1st size	$3 00		
½ "	1 80			2nd size	1 80		
¼ "	1 20						
TEA POTS.				**SPITTOONS.**			
1st size	$4 50			1st size	$9 00		
2nd size	3 60			2nd size	6 00		
				3rd size	3 60		
FLOWER POTS (with stands).							
1 Gallon	$2 40					$	
½ "	1 80						
¼ "	1 20						
1 pint	0 84						
½ "	0 60						
Carried forward......$				**Discount**			

9.1 *The former Derby Pottery building in the village of Kilsyth, Grey County, being destroyed in* 1971 *to make room for housing.* Courtesy Mrs. Keith Angel, Kilsyth.

a number of potters worked in Kilsyth, including John Horning, later to be in partnership with Samuel Brownscombe in Owen Sound, and Robert Wallace, later to establish a pottery at Millbank, Perth County.

A price list from the Derby Pottery, now in the possession of Sinclair's grandson, is shown in figure 9.2. The type of wares produced demonstrates the utilitarian nature of the pottery. Unlike modern art potteries in Grey County, it did not cater to the tourist trade or decorative art market.

The Derby Pottery building was a two-storey stone structure, set back from the main road of the village. After the pottery was discontinued the building was used for storage of farm tools. This local landmark remained until June of 1971, when the owner of that time had it demolished. A picture taken during the destruction of the building, plate 9.1, is a mute testimony to the loss of what was the last remaining pottery structure in Ontario. The pottery land is now part of the front lawn of a new house.

A second pottery, owned by John Spilka,

Fig. 9.2 (left) *Price list for Derby Pottery, ca. 1900-1909.* Courtesy Mr. Don Witherspoon.

operated in Kilsyth during the nineteenth century. The 1860-61 census indicates that the business was located on a two-acre plot,[9] presumably near the hamlet. Spilka could not have met with much success, as by 1868 he had moved to Owen Sound, where he established another pottery.

Desboro
George Smith left Kilsyth and returned to Desboro, in Sullivan Township, a distance of twenty-one kilometres directly south, to open an inn, store and pottery. The pottery operated from 1870 until 1896. The business was located on the northeast corner of lot 13, concession 7.[10] Pieces of pottery made by Smith are still owned by his granddaughter, but none is marked or stamped with an identifying symbol or name that would verify its relationship to the Desboro site.

Hanover
John Keuhner moved from Waterloo County in 1863 to the Village of Hanover, where he established a business on land leased from Henry Adams, the one-acre site known as lots

9.2 *Picture of the Owen Sound Pottery Co., owned by Horning & Brownscombe, showing pottery wagon, willow crates for shipping, cordwood* *for the kiln, and examples of some of the pottery manufactured.* Courtesy Mrs. Laberta Fralic (née Brownscombe).

10, 11, 12 and 13 on the east side of Victoria Street.[11] After Keuhner's death in 1867, his wife Sophia continued the business with the assistance of her two sons — Conrad and Lewis. In the 1870-71 census the pottery is reported as employing one male hand to produce $450 worth of pottery yearly. The yearly wage of the potter was $200.[12] The Hanover business was discontinued in 1876. No known pottery can be attributed to the Hanover workshop, as the Kuehners did not mark their wares.

Egremont
Edwin Bradwin established a pottery in 1882 on lot 62, concession B, in Normanby Township.[13] He had moved from Mount Forest, where he had a shop; presumably the move was to be closer to the source of clay.

In the summer of 1977 I visited the Egremont site and was able to find the remains of two kilns. The kiln nearest to the present road, Highway 6, had been completely destroyed by grading and re-routing of the highway. The earlier kiln, which was inside the lot, was still visible as remains under the topsoil.

Woodford
In 1867, John and James Lemon established a

Fig. 9.3 (right) *Price list of Owen Sound Pottery, dated January 22, 1900.* Courtesy Messrs. Bruce & Howard Krug.

Owen Sound
Pottery

OWEN SOUND, ONTARIO *Jan* *2* 190

Joseph Dunn
Orillia

Bought of HORNING & BROWNSCOMBE,

—MANUFACTURERS OF—

ORIENTAL VASES, DOUBLE GLAZED AND STONE ENAMELLED WHITE WARE.

TERMS *5 a/o cash in 30 days or 3 months*

J H LITTLE PRINTER OWEN SOUND

LIST OF PRICES.

CREAM POTS.	Each.	Net Per Doz.
6 Gallon	$0 50	$4 00
4	0 40	3 20
3	0 30	2 40
2	0 25	2 00
1	0 12½	1 00
½	0 07	0 60

MILK PANS.		
2 Gallon	0 18	1 44
1 "	0 10	0 80

MILK CROCKS.		
2 Gallon	0 20	1 60
1 "	0 12½	1 00
½ "	0 07	0 60

BUTTER POTS with COVERS.		
5 Gallon	0 65	5 20
4 "	0 55	4 40
3 "	0 45	3 60
2 "	0 35	2 80
1 "	0 20	1 60

BUTTER POTS UNCOVERED		
4 Gallon	0 45	3 60
3 "	0 35	2 91
2 "	0 25	2 00
1 "	12½	1 00

PRESERVE or PICKLE JARS.		
2 Gallon	0 20	2 40
1 "	0 20	1 60
½ "	0 15	1 20
¼ "	0 10	0 80

FRUIT JARS WITH CORKS.		
2 Gallon	0 30	2 40
1 "	0 20	1 60
½ "	0 15	1 20
¼ "	0 10	0 80

JUGS.		
2 Gallon	0 37½	3 00
1 "	0 25	2 00
½ "	0 15	1 20
¼ "	0 10	0 80

MOLASSES JUGS with CORKS		
2 Gallon	0 37½	3 00
1 "	0 25	2 00
½ "	0 20	1 60
¼ "	0 12½	1 00

CHURNS.		
8 Gallon	1 25	10 00
7 "	1 12½	9 00
6 "	1 00	8 00
5 "	0 75	6 00
Churn Dashes	0 15	1 20

FLOWER POTS with SAUCERS		
2 Gallon	0 30	2 40
1 "	0 20	1 60
½ "	0 15	1 20
¼ "	0 10	0 80
1 Pint	0 07	0 60
½ "	0 05	0 40

BELL FLOWER POTS.	Each.	Net Per Doz.
1 Gallon	$0 25	$2 00
½ "	0 20	1 60
¼ "	0 12½	1 00

CRIMPED FLOWER POTS.		
1 Gallon	0 25	2 00
½ "	0 20	1 60
¼ "	0 12½	1 00

HANGING BASKETS.		
1st size	0 20	1 60
2nd "	0 15	1 20
3rd "	0 10	0 80

LAWN VASES.		
6 Gallon, figured, per pair		5 00
4 "		3 50
3 " plain, "		1 50

ROCKINGHAM WARE

PITCHERS.		
1 Gallon	0 25	2 00
½ "	0 20	1 60
¼ "	0 12½	1 00

SPITTOONS.		
1st size	1 00	8 00
2nd "	0 50	4 00
3rd "	0 30	2 40

CUSPADORES.		
1st size	0 40	3 20
2nd "	0 25	2 00
3rd "	0 15	1 20

CHAMBERS.		
1st size	0 25	2 00
2nd "	0 20	1 60

PUDDING DISHES.		
1st size	0 15	1 20
2nd "	0 10	0 80
3rd "	0 07	0 60

BATTER BOWLS.		
1st size	0 15	1 20
2nd "	0 10	0 80
3rd "	0 06	0 48

BOWLS.		
1st size	0 06	0 48
2nd "	0 05	0 40

BEDROOM SET.		
6 Pieces	1 25	10 00

9.3 *Examples of pottery made at the Owen Sound Pottery Co., Owen Sound. Bedroom sets were finished with a white slip and then decorated* *with brushwork in brown. Pieces are finished with a clear glaze.* Courtesy Royal Ontario Museum.

small pottery in the village of Woodford in Sydenham Township. The pottery was on part of lot 3, concession 1, north of the centre line road.[14] A recent local history of Grey County states that the pottery produced milk pans, pitchers, flowerpots and bricks.[15] In 1883 John Lemon purchased land along Georgian Bay, called broken front lot 37.[16] He also obtained lots 7 and 8 on Stephen Street, north of Front Street in the town of Owen Sound, now known as First Avenue West, north of Tenth Street West.[17] The pottery in Owen Sound was in operation until 1896. The Georgian Bay property was owned by John Lemon until late in 1899. I believe that either he operated two potteries, which is very unlikely, or produced pottery at the Georgian Bay site and sold it in Owen Sound. The latter supposition

is partially supported by credit-rating records, which describe John Lemon as owner of a pottery until 1900, the year he sold the Georgian Bay lot.

Owen Sound
The centre of pottery-making in the county was Owen Sound. The first pottery was operated by John Spilka, who had moved from Kilsyth. The exact location of the Spilka workshop in Owen Sound is not known. An 1865 directory locates the pottery on "Park lots, east of Town," while a listing in 1871 places it "off Garafaxa Rd."[18] Both descriptions are too vague to be of help to the field investigator. The 1870-71 census reports that John Spilka had $40 invested in the business, which he

9.4 *"King Charles Spaniel" dog made at the Owen Sound pottery.* Courtesy Royal Ontario Museum.

9.5 *Group of miniatures made by Samuel Brownscombe for his daughter and now in the collection of the Royal Ontario Museum.*

operated for six months a year. He employed three potters at a total yearly wage of $300. During the year 1870, the pottery produced 1800 pieces of crockery at a value of $1,500.[19]

In September, 1895, John Horning, who had also worked in Kilsyth, joined with Samuel Brownscombe, son of John Brownscombe, Jr., to form the partnership of Horning & Brownscombe, owners of the Owen Sound Pottery Co.[20] Brownscombe had previously worked in Kinloss Township, Bruce County. The Owen Sound pottery was located on the south side of Baring Street East, five houses east of Murdock Street, now known as Seventh Street East and Fourth Avenue East. The building is shown in plate 9.2, a late nineteenth-century photograph.

The Owen Sound Pottery Co., produced a wide assortment of household wares, some of which were covered in a cream slip and then decorated with brown flowers. The result was a weak imitation of porcelain, with a definite pioneer flavour. Although the pottery was not marked, the origin of this distinctive ware is known from the information supplied by Brownscombe's daughter, Laberta, who at the age of ninety-four recalled the operation of the business. The pottery produced by Horning & Brownscombe is unique in its decorative

9.6 *Miniature pieces from a wash-stand set.* Courtesy Royal Ontario Museum.

techniques. Of all the potters in Ontario in the nineteenth century, only Horning & Brownscombe produced such highly individualized pieces. A price list from the pottery is shown in figure 9.3. Examples of pottery produced at the workshop are shown in plates 9.3 and 9.4. Samuel Brownscombe produced a number of miniature pieces for his daughter, some of which are illustrated in plates 9.5 and 9.6. These miniatures were, according to Laberta Fralic (née Brownscombe) similar to samples made for the three salesmen the firm employed to sell the pottery.

By 1904 Brownscombe had purchased a grocery business, which he operated while maintaining an interest in the pottery. When the pottery closed in the fall of 1907, he continued his grocery business.[21] Eventually the family moved to Toronto, where Brownscombe became a successful real estate agent.

BRUCE COUNTY

There were nine potteries operating in the county throughout the nineteenth century. The documentary and archaeological evidence is scarce, and it is often possible to ascertain only the existence and possible location of the sites.

Kincardine

Gad Curtis and his son, Moses, migrated from Shakespeare in Perth County to the town of Kincardine, sometime after 1860. Kincardine tax assessment rolls for 1864 locate the pottery on a one-acre lot on East Avenue. The location of this site has not been established. No other record of the pottery has been found. By 1871 Moses Curtis had moved to Invermay, Arran Township, and was operating his own business.

Port Elgin

John Barlett (or Bardeles?), a German-born potter, was making crocks in Saugeen Township by 1860. In the census of 1860-61 he is reported to be operating a pottery on a forty-five-acre lot in the township. He is also listed in an 1867 directory as a potter.[22] No other information on the history or location of the pottery has been found in documentary records.

Burgoyne

A pottery and brickyard was in business near this hamlet from 1884 until about 1895. Isaac Aves conducted the business on a two-acre part of lot 15, concession A, Arran Township.[23] Norman McLeod in a recent history of Bruce County writes, "In olden days it [Burgoyne] boasted . . .a store, several houses, a cheese factory, a crock factory, a brickyard . . ."[24] The hamlet has not grown signifi-

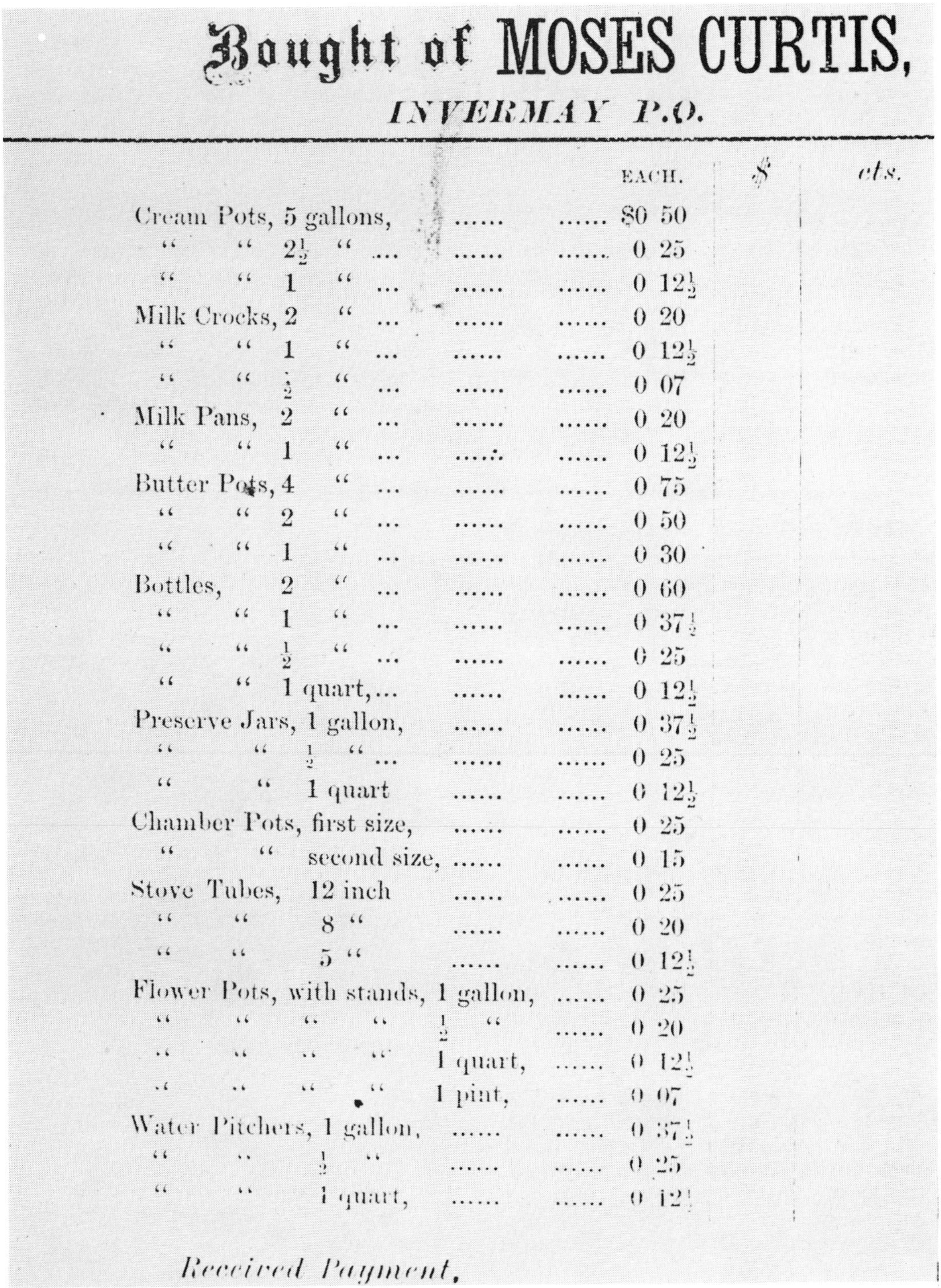

Bought of MOSES CURTIS,

INVERMAY P.O.

	EACH.	$	cts.
Cream Pots, 5 gallons,	$0 50		
" " 2½ "	0 25		
" " 1 "	0 12½		
Milk Crocks, 2 "	0 20		
" " 1 "	0 12½		
" " ½ "	0 07		
Milk Pans, 2 "	0 20		
" " 1 "	0 12½		
Butter Pots, 4 "	0 75		
" " 2 "	0 50		
" " 1 "	0 30		
Bottles, 2 "	0 60		
" " 1 "	0 37½		
" " ½ "	0 25		
" " 1 quart,	0 12½		
Preserve Jars, 1 gallon,	0 37½		
" " ½ "	0 25		
" " 1 quart	0 12½		
Chamber Pots, first size,	0 25		
" " second size,	0 15		
Stove Tubes, 12 inch	0 25		
" " 8 "	0 20		
" " 5 "	0 12½		
Flower Pots, with stands, 1 gallon,	0 25		
" " " " ½ "	0 20		
" " " " 1 quart,	0 12½		
" " " " 1 pint,	0 07		
Water Pitchers, 1 gallon,	0 37½		
" " ½ "	0 25		
" " 1 quart,	0 12½		

Received Payment,

Fig. 9.4 *Price list of Moses Curtis pottery in Invermay, Bruce County.* Courtesy Messrs. Bruce & Howard Krug.

cantly since the end of the nineteenth century. The site of the pottery has been cultivated for many years and the only evidences of the pottery produced at the site are the sherds that can be seen when the crops and grass have been removed.

Chippewa Hill

Cyrus Eby left his brother William Eby's pottery at Conestogo, Waterloo County, and moved to Amabel Township where he obtained Letters Patent for a seventy-nine-acre lot of land, described as lot 49, in the western continuation of the strip of land obtained from the Chippewa Indians.[25] Cyrus Eby continued potting at this site, in conjunction with farming.

Scone

Donald Haines moved from the village of Blyth in Huron County to Scone, and by 1880 had established a pottery on a one-acre lot leased from Thomas Bearmore. The site was described as part of the middle of the south part of lot 34, concession 3, Elderslie Township.[26] Haines did not stay long in the area, and by 1884 he is no longer reported in the township assessment rolls. The site continued as a brickyard, though, for many more years.

Invermay

Moses Curtis established a pot shop in this hamlet beside the Owen Sound stagecoach road. In the 1870-71 census the business was described as employing one hand for six months to produce "pots and pans" valued at $250 a year.[27] The pottery was located on lots 155 and 156 on the east side of Sarah Street at the intersection of Margaret Street. The pottery lots bordered the Sauble River, guaranteeing both a source of clay and a plentiful supply of water. An early price list from the pottery is shown in figure 9.4. Potters known to have worked at Invermay include George A. Brown, Murtoch McLay, Silvester Fox and J. Henderson.

Tara

In 1867 James McCluskie, who had moved from the village of Kilsyth, purchased land for a

pottery on the west side of Massey Terrace, the east side of Yonge Street (now Main Street).[28] By 1878 McCluskie was also operating the British Hotel, located on Main Street. The pottery was operating until 1884. McCluskie died about that year and his wife, Sarah, continued to run the hotel up to the early years of this century.

The pottery is described briefly in the 1870-71 census. McCluskie worked year-round and hired two men to produce $1,600 worth of "pots and pans." The pottery used seventy tons of clay for its wares.[29] A crock marked TARA POTTERY is shown in plate 9.7. Bricks used in a house in the village are also marked with the impressed stamp TARA POTTERY.

Potters known to have worked at Tara include John Horning and George A. Brown.

9.7 *Yellow earthenware crock made at Tara pottery. The piece is covered with a clear lead glaze.*

Mildmay

The early settlers in the area, later known as Mildmay, were a group of people from New Hamburg, Waterloo County. They arrived to assume possession of land laid out by the Waterloo County entrepreneur Samuel Merner, who had purchased a large acreage and sub-divided it for settlers. Among this group of settlers was Ignatz Bitschy, who had previously worked at Xavier Boehler's pottery in New Hamburg. Bitschy purchased fifty acres from Samuel Merner in March of 1866. The northern limit of this acreage was later marked as Ignatz Street. Directories indicate that the pottery continued until 1903, although credit-rating sources suggest that Bitschy was potting only until 1889.

The 1870-71 census returns report that Bitschy worked only four months, suggesting that he probably farmed during the remainder of the time. He hired two men to produce 12,000 pieces of pottery, with a value of $800.[30]

No known pieces can be traced to the Bitschy workshop. Collectors occasionally associate with Bitschy the production of red earthenware with elaborate applied flower decorations, but this cannot be confirmed.

Kinloss

John Brownscombe, Jr., migrated from Hope Township, Durham County, along the northern shore of Lake Ontario westward to Kinloss Township, where in 1870 he purchased a 100-acre farm, known as lots 16 and 17, in the second range south of Durham Road.[31] Brownscombe apparently farmed and potted until his death in a well-digging accident in the 1880s.[32] After John Brownscombe's death his son Samuel continued the pottery; another son, James, also worked there. Samuel purchased the five-acre pottery lot, described as the southwest corner of lot 16, in 1882 and continued the business until about 1892.[33]

9.8 *Miniature jug from Kinloss Township, Bruce County. This piece is attributed to the Browns-combe pottery in that township.* Courtesy Mr. Gil Graham, Kincardine.

After that date he moved to Owen Sound. Only two pieces of pottery are known from the Kinloss Township site. The jug shown in plate 9.8 with the painted J'B is reported to be from the site. A second piece is mentioned in *Ontario Showcase*, July 5, 1971, and is signed James/Kinloss, 1879.

10.
Pottery Shops of Waterloo County

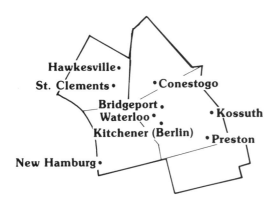
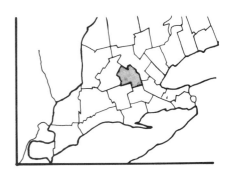

Fig. 10.1 *Map showing Waterloo County communities with potteries in the nineteenth century.*

The researcher tracing the history of potteries is immediately drawn to Waterloo County, where there were potteries operating in ten communities during the nineteenth century (fig. 10.1). There were also more potters of German and French origin here during the period 1851-1861 than in any other county in the province. The potters who described themselves as being of French origin were German-speaking families from the Alsace region, and were in some instances closer to the German pottery-making traditions than the French. One such potter listed as being of French origin in the 1851-52 census for Ontario was working in Waterloo County. In the 1860-61 census, four of the seven potters of French origin in the province were working in the county, and by the 1870-71 census, two of the five potters of the same heritage were working in Waterloo County.

The intermingling of "English" and "German" or "French" cultural traditions, expressed in different pottery shapes and glaze colours, is more pronounced in Waterloo County than anywhere else. An added interest to the historian is that two Waterloo County pottery sites have been excavated, one by the Royal Ontario Museum[1] and the second by Wilfrid Laurier University, Waterloo[2]; each archaeological exploration provides detailed information on the history and wares produced at each site.

The history of the individual potteries follows.

Waterloo Township
The earliest known marked piece of Ontario pottery was produced by Jacob Bock of Waterloo. The potter is known from two moulded red earthenware jars, both decorated with relief portraits of St. Ambrosius, and showing a crowned and bearded man carrying a book in one hand, staff in the other (see plate 10.1). Incised on the base of one of the crocks is "Waterloo the 4 Jan 1825" (plate 10.2). The second piece is marked "Waterloo, Upper Canada, September 17, 1825, Jacob Bock, Potter". No other information is known about this early Waterloo County pottery, and I have not been successful in ascertaining the location

10.1 *Tobacco jar with applied relief portrait of St. Ambrosius, made in Waterloo County.* Courtesy Royal Ontario Museum.

of the workshop from existing documentary sources.

Waterloo

John Jacobi was born in 1816 in Germany, where he learned the pottery trade. Sometime between 1843 and 1847 he, together with his family, immigrated to the town of Waterloo. He had two sons and three daughters in Canada; the second son, Daniel, who was born in 1850, eventually followed in his father's trade.

In 1852 John Jacobi purchased part of lot 4, east of King Street in Elias Snyder's Survey, now the northeast corner of King and Dupont Streets.[3] Here he made pottery until his death ca. 1871-73. In the 1860-61 census John Jacobi is reported as living in a one-storey frame building on a one-fifth acre of land, where he produced pottery valued at $400 annually. Capital invested in his pottery was reported as $1,000.[4] In the 1870-71 census we learn more about the extent of the business, as the reports indicate that he employed three men to produce fifteen kiln loads of pottery annually, with a total of $1,000 worth of

10.2 *View of bottom of tobacco jar of 10.1.* Courtesy Royal Ontario Museum.

crockery being produced.[5] On August 15, 1874, the pottery and residence was purchased by Daniel Jacobi.[6] Daniel continued to work at the site until 1886, when the land was sold to the Waterloo Mutual Fire Insurance Co.

In 1886, Daniel Jacobi purchased lots 10 and 11 in Moses Springer's Survey, located on the southeast corner of the intersection of Duke Street (now Dupont St.) and Queen Street North in Waterloo.[7] In later years, when buildings were numbered, the Jacobi residence became Number 21 Duke Street East. From 1890 until his death in December, 1905, Daniel Jacobi's residence and workshop were assessed at a value of $1,600.[8] The pottery was demolished shortly after 1908. No marked pieces are in museums or private collections.

Berlin (Kitchener)

The pottery in Berlin (now Kitchener) was established by Anselm Wagner sometime between 1840 and 1845. Wagner and his wife, Magdalena, had emigrated from the Alsatian mountains in northern France. In the 1860-61 census for Berlin, he was fifty-six years old, and had a family of nine children, all born in Canada.[9] The children ranged in age from three to twenty years. The family business was located on lot 10 on the north side of King Street, between Cedar and Frederick Streets. The lot was a half-acre and was valued at

10.3 *Spittoon with yellow slip and number decoration. The inside of the spittoon has a mottled glaze. The piece is marked JOSEPH WAGNER/ BERLIN POTTERY.*

10.5 *Earthenware jug with cream-coloured slip. The piece is marked JOSEPH WAGNER/BERLIN POTTERY. (Scale runs from one to five centimetres.)*

10.4 *Jug with applied blue-green colour flower decoration. The jug is marked JOSEPH WAGNER/BERLIN POTTERY. Courtesy Royal Ontario Museum.*

$2,000.[10] He reported to the 1860-61 census taker that he produced 4,000 crocks annually, using twenty-four wagon loads of clay.[11] He employed two hands and paid them each $10 a month.[12]

Joseph Wagner, son of Anselm, took over the pottery sometime between 1867 and 1869. In the 1870-71 census returns he reports that the pottery ran for eight months of the year and produced 3,000 crocks valued at $400.[13] Little more than the above information is known of the business. It was discontinued in the early 1880s and Joseph Wagner moved to Stratford (Perth County) where he worked in a pottery for several years.[14]

Pieces made at the Berlin Pottery are now very rare. Three that are marked with the impressed stamp JOSEPH WAGNER/ BERLIN POTTERY are shown in plates 10.3, 10.4, and 10.5. The pieces are decorated with a greenish-blue flower or other pattern.

Kossuth

In the eastern part of Waterloo Township is the hamlet of Kossuth, now one of the curious "deserted villages" of the county. One of the

10.6 *Open earthenware jug with clear lead glaze and stamped in two places on the base JoHN GROH PR. Private collection.*

original settlers of this small hamlet was Conrad Groh, a German-born potter who settled in Canada around 1845. By the time of the 1851-52 census he is reported as operating a pottery in Kossuth.[15] The assessment rolls for 1853 (the earliest year for which rolls still exist) locates Conrad Groh on a three-quarter-acre parcel of lot 89 in the Upper Block of Waterloo Township.[16] He purchased this parcel in 1856,[17] and worked at the site until 1863, after which time his son, John D. Groh, continued the business.[18] John D. Groh (sometimes reported in directories as T. D. Groh) continued to operate the workshop until the early 1870s. In the years 1872 and 1873 he was listed in the assessment rolls as the village postmaster,[19] but by 1874 he had moved to the hamlet of Little Germany, where he operated an inn.[20] One piece of Groh pottery is known. It is shown in plates 10.6 and 10.7. Made of local clay, it has been finished with a clear lead glaze, giving a reddish-brown colour to the piece.

The Groh pottery soon faded from public notice. The only comment on the former workshop was made in 1930 in the *Eighteenth Annual Report of the Waterloo Historical Society*, where it states, "John Groh, a Pennsylvania Dutchman, made clay crocks and shallow clay pansions for milk also flower pots."[21]

Bridgeport

The pottery in this village was founded in 1853 by Philip Diefenbacher, who in that year purchased lot 4 on the southeast corner of the intersection of Bridge and John Streets for £100.[22] Diefenbacher had settled in Bridgeport by 1851, since by that year his name appears in the 1851-52 census, where he is described as twenty-nine years old, from Germany, and with a one-year-old son, Jacob, who had been born in Canada.[23] We do not know if Diefenbacher had in fact been potting on the lot before 1853, but this possibility cannot be ruled out. In the 1860-61 census, when Philip had owned the business for eight years, he is reported to be making 1,000 crocks and 100,000 bricks a year with an estimated total value of $600.[24] The pottery trade was therefore only a small part of the business, and Diefenbacher was known in the vicinity primarily as a supplier of brick. The business was sold by 1867, this time to the potter Adam Bierenstihl.[25]

Adam Bierenstihl was also an emigrant from Germany. He settled in Canada in 1853. In 1861 we find him living in Lexington, a small village to the northeast of Bridgeport, on a one and one-half-acre parcel, part of lot 61 of the German Company Tract. He had moved to Bridgeport by 1866, probably working with Diefenbacher.[26] The next year he purchased Diefenbacher's business. From 1867 until 1873 he is listed as living at lot 4 in Bridgeport.

10.7 *Close-up of the impressed mark on the crock in plate 10.6.*

In the 1870-71 census returns, Bierenstihl is reported as working six months of the year to produce crockery valued at $300.[27] By 1874 he is listed as both potter and farmer, and is working a twenty-three-acre farm on lot 59 in the German Company Tract. In this same year he sold the village property and continued to rent the farm from its owner.[28] Three years later, in 1878, Bierenstihl bought a part of lot 59.[29] He financed the purchase by obtaining a mortgage for $1,000.[30]

Adam Bierenstihl worked at his craft for the remainder of the nineteenth century. In the years 1874 and 1875 his son Henry was an apprentice in the shop. Henry left in 1876 to establish his own pottery in Milverton, Perth County. In the year 1900, after the death of Adam Bierenstihl, Henry returned to Bridgeport, but does not appear to have continued the business for long. In 1901 he is listed as a "traveller" (i.e. salesman) on the assessment rolls.[31]

In the years since the closing of the pottery shop, people in the Bridgeport area have reminisced about the pottery and have shown visitors jugs and crocks supposedly made by Bierenstihl. Bierenstihl's work was unusual for its use of bright, prominent spotted decoration. A piece made for a relative is shown in plate

10.8 *Interior of deep bowl with cream slip and painted design. The name reads Emilie Bierenstihl/Bridgeport.* Courtesy Mrs. Jack Rock.

10.9 *Small pottery whimsey made by Bierenstihl at his Bridgeport workshop.* Courtesy Mrs. Jack Rock.

10.8. Additional pieces made by him are shown in plates 10.9 and 10.10.

10.10 *Decorative earthenware piece made by Adam Bierenstihl, Bridgeport. Bierenstihl was noted for his use of brightly coloured decorations in reds, greens and blues.* Courtesy Mrs. Jack Rock.

Preston

On January 15, 1833, William Schwab purchased lot 1 on the northeast corner of King and Potter (now Laurel) Streets, Preston, for £70.[32] Schwab did not stay long in this bustling town along the Grand River, for by 1834 he had sold the property and moved to establish another pottery in Beamsville, Lincoln County.[33] Schwab sold the pottery to Michael Steumpfle and William Gady[34] for £85 15s.[35] This partnership was short-lived, and on June 27 of the same year Gady sold his interest in the pottery to Steumpfle.[36] The Steumpfle house and three pottery buildings are shown in plate 10.11. Sometime between 1851 and 1860 Michael's oldest son, Henry, began working with him. In the 1870-71 census the pottery is reported to be working ten months of the year, producing 7,000 crocks valued at $400.[37] Sometime after 1873 Henry Steumpfle took over the business and continued it until ca. 1899.[38]

St. Clements

Joseph Adam and his son Joseph Jr. operated a small workshop in this village. By 1865 they had purchased the first of two parcels of land, a small part of lot 64 according to Funk's Survey.[39] In 1866 the second parcel was purchased, a larger area, part of lot 61 in Funk's Survey.[40] The Adams family did not work long

in this village. By January 19, 1869, they had sold their holdings and are next heard of in the village of Hawkesville, a few kilometres north of St. Clements.

Hawkesville

The Adams are potting in Hawkesville by 1884, because their business is mentioned in credit-rating manuals of that time. They purchased land for the business in 1884.[41] The pottery was on a one and one-half-acre lot, part of village lot B in lot 2, Concession XII, eastern section of Wellesley Township. In 1887 Joseph Adam, Sr., sold the land surrounding the pottery business (but not the pottery building or lot) to Catharina Knittel.[42] The next year, Joseph Adam, Jr., who was by now operating the pottery himself, sold the pottery building and lot to George W. Knittel for $900.[43] During the year 1888 the pottery was operated under the name Knittel Brothers, but the business does not appear to have continued longer than a year.[44]

The firm of Pepler and Winn was reported in a Huron County newspaper as having a pottery in Hawkesville. Issues of the *Mercantile Agency Reference Book* for the mid-1880s describe Jacob Pepler as the operator of a brick and tile yard, but the brickworks might have produced an occasional piece of earthenware.[45] William Cadwell, later to work

10.11 *The Michael Steumpfle Pottery. The wares were made in the basement and fired in the kiln* *located in the building at the rear of the lot.* Courtesy Mrs. V. F. Petersen.

at potteries in Waterloo, Harriston and New Hamburg, is listed as a potter in Hawkesville in 1864-65, but no other reference to Cadwell at this early date can be found in town records.[46]

Conestogo

The pottery at Conestogo is probably the best known rural pottery workshop in Ontario. Archaeological investigations at the pottery, the first industrial dig in Ontario, produced a wealth of material evidence for the business.[47] In the published report of the archaeological explorations, Webster suggests that either William Eby, the second potter, purchased a defunct pottery with little archaeological evidence of its early period, or that the original owner, Burton Curtis, made pottery elsewhere.[48] Although this view may help to explain the apparent lack of pottery that could be assigned to the Curtis period, it obscures the fact that Burton Curtis was described as a potter in 1843, when he purchased the pottery land, part of lot 32 in the German Company Tract, Woolwich Township[49]; he is still listed as a potter in the 1856 and 1857 assessment

rolls. The 1854 roll, the only other early one extant, does not list Curtis, but this might have been an error. The absence of any further assessment rolls for this early period cannot be used as evidence against Curtis' working as a potter. Curtis sold the pottery to Eby in 1857 and moved to Elkhart County, Indiana, where he established the first pottery in that region.[50] There is no evidence which proves that Curtis was not potting during the years for which no records remain.

William Eby purchased the ten-acre pottery on July 2, 1857, for £250.[51] He operated the

10.12 *Pie plates with fruit decorations.* Courtesy Royal Ontario Museum.

Conestogo Pottery, _____ *189*

M _____

Bought of # WILLIAM EBY,

MANUFACTURER OF AND WHOLESALE DEALER IN

❧ EVERY DESCRIPTION OF COMMON EARTHENWARE. ❧

❧ ❧ 33⅓ PER CENT. OFF FOR CASH ON DELIVERY. ❧ ❧

DOZEN	CREAM POTS.	PER DOZ.	EACH.	$	CTS.	DOZEN	UNGLAZED. FLOWER POTS.	PER DOZ.	EACH.	$	CTS.
	6 Gallon..........	$6 00	0 50				10 Inch	$3 00	0 25		
	4 Gallon..........	4 50	0 37½				8 Inch	1 80	0 15		
	2 Gallon..........	3 00	0 25				7 Inch	1 20	0 10		
	1 Gallon..........	1 50	0 12½				6 Inch	0 96	0 08		
	½ Gallon..........	0 75	0 06¼				5 Inch	0 75	0 06¼		
	MILK CROCKS.						4 Inch	0 60	0 05		
	2 Gallon..........	2 40	0 20				3 Inch	0 36	0 03		
	1½ Gallon..........	1 50	0 12½				2½ Inch............	0 24	0 02		
	½ Gallon..........	0 75	0 06¼				SAUCERS INCLUDED.				
	1½ Pint...........	0 48	0 04				GLAZED FLOWER POTS.				
	MILK PANS.						1st Size............	1 20	0 10		
	2 Gallon..........	2 40	0 20				2nd Size............	1 00	0 08		
	1½ Gallon..........	1 50	0 12½				GLAZED HANGING FLOWER POTS.				
	JUGS.						1st Size............	1 80	0 15		
	2 Gallon..........	4 50	0 37½				2nd Size............	1 50	0 12½		
	1 Gallon..........	3 00	0 25				3rd Size............	1 20	0 10		
	½ Gallon..........	2 40	0 20				**CHAMBER POTS.**				
	¼ Gallon..........	1 50	0 12½				1st Size............	2 40	0 20		
	MOLASSES JUGS,						2nd Size............	1 50	0 12½		
	1 gallon	3 00	0 25				**SPITTOONS.**				
	½ gallon	2 40	0 20				1st Size............	3 00			
	¼ gallon	1 50	0 12½				2nd Size............	2 40			
	WATER PITCHERS						**PIE PLATES.**				
	1 gallon	3 00	0 25				1st Size............	0 96	0 08		
	½ gallon	2 40	0 20				2nd Size............	0 75	0 06¼		
	¼ gallon	1 50	0 12½				3rd Size............	0 50	0 04		
	STOVE TUBES.										
	12 Inch	3 00									
	8 Inch	2 40									
	4 Inch	1 50									

Received Payment.

≈ The above Ware is made of the Best Material. ≈

☞ Orders by mail respectfully solicited, and will be promptly executed.

PRINTED BY HY. DELION, CONESTOGO, ONT.

Fig. 10.2 *Price list for Conestogo Pottery, showing various kinds of pottery made by William Eby, and their cost.*

10.13 *Salt container with blue-green decoration on the outside rim.* Courtesy Royal Ontario Museum.

Fig. 10.3 *An 1854 plan of New Hamburg shows the location of Boehler Pottery on Lot 21 on the east side (top of photo) of Peel Street.*

business until about 1900, when his son, William Jr., assisted in the workshop. William Eby died in 1905, and the next year the property was sold.[52] The Eby pottery was never very large physically. An 1870 directory describes the building as "built of brick, 30 × 22 [feet], two stories high. . ."[53]

The variety of wares produced by Eby is shown in the price list in fig. 10.2. A characteristic of Eby's earthenware pottery is the twin-stem cherry decoration placed on pie plates and other table wares. Three decorated pieces are shown in plates 10.12 and 10.13. Much of the ware produced by Eby used local red clay and had a clear lead glaze finish. The pottery shapes were similar to those used by other contemporary Ontario potteries. Recent excavations at the Boehler pottery in New Hamburg (q.v.) illustrate this similarity, and caution against ascribing unmarked pieces found in the region to the Curtis-Eby pottery, without careful scrutiny.

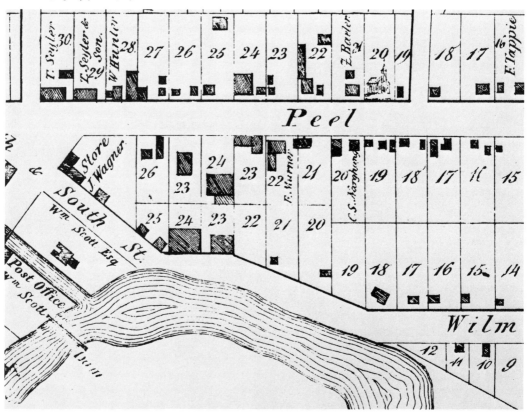

New Hamburg

There were two potteries in this village in Wilmot Township. The earliest known shop was established by John Wallace. He is listed as a potter in the 1851-52 census, but does not actually purchase land (presumably the site of the pottery) until March 15, 1853, when he acquires the northern half of lot 9, and lots 10, 11 and 12 on the east side of Peel Street.[54] The pottery did not exist long, for Wallace sold the property on August 11, 1856.[55] The *Canada Directory* for 1857 describes the partnership of Matheson & Wallace, potters.[56] A James P. Matheson purchased lot 8 and part of lot 9 on the same side of the street in August 1858.[57] It is possible that after Wallace closed the business, it was purchased by Matheson, who might have continued to operate the shop under a partnership. Nothing more is known about the partnership. Wallace lived in New Hamburg until 1865.

The second and more significant pottery in the village was founded by Xavier Boehler, a German-speaking immigrant from Alsace, France. The first documentary evidence of Xavier Boehler's residence in the village is the census of 1851-52, where he is listed as a potter. An 1854 plan of the village (fig. 10.3) shows the pottery on the east side of Peel Street, even though Boehler did not actually purchase the lot until 1856.[58] In the earliest assessment roll of the town, dated 1858, his business has an assessed value of $650, a moderate value for the time. Xavier Boehler worked at the pottery until 1881. During those years, he had many assistants who later became known for the products of their own workshops. In 1860 Ignatz Bitschy worked at the New Hamburg pottery; he later established his own business in Mildmay, Bruce County. In 1862 Abraham Marlatt worked with Boehler; he later owned a pottery in the village of Colborne, Norfolk County. Henry Schuler, who later took over the John M. Marlatt pottery in Paris, Ontario, learned the pottery business under Xavier Boehler's watchful eyes. From 1869 to 1874, Boehler apparently worked alone in the shop, and he is the only potter listed in the town's assessment rolls. By 1874 his son, Joseph, then twenty-three years old, joined him in producing earthenware. In 1877 another son, Henry, also began an as-

sociation with the pottery. Father and sons continued to operate the business until Xavier Boehler retired in 1881, at which time Joseph Boehler took over the business.

The only known marked piece of pottery from the site is shown in plate 10.14. A close-up of the impressed mark JOSEPH BOEHLER/NEW HAMBURG is shown in plate 10.15.

Beginning in 1894 the pottery was operated by William Cadwell (also spelled Kadwell and Caldwell), an elderly potter with years of experience from the Jacobi pottery in Waterloo, Ontario. He continued the pottery, first under the partnership of Cadwell and Staples (1894-1896), and then as sole proprietor from late 1896 until mid-1910, when the business again changed hands, this time being taken over by W. J. Hulse, of the Hulse & Son firm of potters of London, Ontario. Throughout this time the pottery remained a very marginal enterprise. W. J. Hulse operated the pottery during the years 1911-1913, and was followed by John

10.14 *A large preserve jar with olive green glaze, the only known marked piece from the New Hamburg pottery.*

10.15 *A close-up of the impressed mark on the piece in Plate 10.15.*

Monk, who ran the business until early in 1916, when the pottery closed its doors.

Further details on the history and archaeology of the pottery have been published elsewhere.[59]

Other Potters in Waterloo County
Potters are reported from three county towns, but there is no documentary or achaeological evidence at this time proving that potteries were in operation in Heidelberg, New Aberdeen, nor in Wellesley. John Waltz is listed as a potter in Heidelberg in the assessment roll of 1857. No other details are known of the potter.[60]

Henry Fait (or Fade) is reported as a potter in the hamlet of New Aberdeen in W. H. Smith's *Canada: Past, Present and Future*.[61] He purchased lot 99 in 1856 in New Aberdeen for £167.10p.[62] Using the 1851-52 census report of Henry Fade we learn that the potter had emigrated from Germany and settled in Canada sometime between 1845 and 1849. He is listed in the census reports as a farmer, indicating that his potting might have been a sideline, perhaps part of his winter work. He apparently moved away from New Aberdeen during the decline of the village, precipitated in part by the railway being built closer to Berlin (Kitchener) than had been expected.

The potter Jacob Henry Ahrens emigrated from Germany to the village of Wellesley in the early 1850s. He purchased a small parcel of land on lot 7 on the south side of William Street, now the main street of the town, and owned it from August, 1854, until November, 1855.[63] Ahrens is listed as a potter in the land office records, and apparently settled in this village before moving to Berlin (Kitchener). Ahrens was a Swedenborgian, and both Wellesley and Berlin had very active Swedenborgian congregations at the time.

11.
Pottery Shops of Perth & Huron Counties

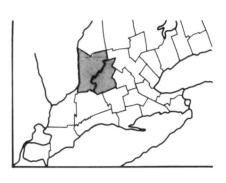

Fig. 11.1 *Location of potteries in Perth and Huron counties in the nineteenth century.*

The settlement of Western Ontario followed along colonization roads such as the Huron Road, intended to lead immigrants into the Huron Tract. Small hamlets sprang up on the highway, often as a result of deliberate planning by the Canada Company. Early potteries were among the craft industries that were established along the Huron Road, now Highway 8; in Perth County there were four potteries established in these communities, and two potteries established in the northern part of the county.

Huron County was an active area of pottery-making. Workshops were established in six widely separated communities. Figure 11.1 shows the location of the potteries in Perth & Huron Counties.

PERTH COUNTY

Shakespeare
Gad Curtis and his son, Moses, moved from the Toronto area sometime after the late 1830s and started a pottery in the small community of Shakespeare. In 1855, the business was located on village lots 8, 9 and 151, the southwest corner of the intersection of the Huron Road and Regent Street.[1] The 1860-61 census indicates that Gad Curtis had $600 invested in the business. He produced 50,000 crocks annually with a value of $6,000[2]; Moses Curtis earned $12 a month for his labour.[3] The Curtis family moved from Shakespeare to Kincardine sometime before 1864.

Stratford
There were two potteries in the town of Stratford in the nineteenth century. The earlier pottery was begun by Baptist Halbling in 1871 on lots 409 and 470 on the north side of Hibernia Street.[4] Halbling continued to produce pottery at this location until 1883, when the business was rented to David B. Burritt & W. B. Knox.[5] Burritt was a court clerk and Knox a printer, and presumably their interest in pottery-

making was primarily financial. At this time Joseph Wagner, son of Anselm Wagner (the potter of Berlin, later Kitchener), was working in Stratford. Wagner may have been the trained craftsman for the Hibernia Street workshop.

In 1884 Burritt & Knox relocated their pottery-making activities at lot 113 on the east side of Erie Street, today not far from the centre of town. At the Erie Street location they made pottery, brick and drain pipes.[6] In the last year of operation of the Hibernia Street site, 1885, Joseph Wagner rented the business.

The Burritt & Knox operation on Erie Street lasted until 1884, when Burritt continued on his own. An advertisement in the September 5, 1883, issue of the Stratford *Weekly Herald* reads: "Glazed drain tile . . . all kinds of earthenware — at the Stratford Pottery." A later advertisement under Burritt's name only in the July 17, 1885 issue of the Stratford *Beacon* states: "Drain pipe, fire brick, fire clay, etc. — Earthenware of all sorts, Stratford Pottery . . ." In 1886 William Wells rented the Erie Street pottery. The next year Burritt sold the property and evidently moved his brickmaking and tile yard to a new location, as credit ratings on his business continue until 1907.

Mitchell

Gottlieb Kreuch, a German-born farmer-potter, purchased thirty-six acres of land in the vicinity of Mitchell in 1859.[7] The land was known as lot 17, concession 1, Fullarton Township. In the 1860-61 census Gottlieb's son, Robert, is listed as a potter, while his father is listed as a farmer.

Dublin (Carron Brook)

A directory for 1871 lists John Myers as an "earthenware manufacturer" in this small hamlet.[8] The same gazetteer lauds Dublin as a thriving village with a saw and planing mill, starch factory, soap and candle factory, sash factory and pottery.[9]

A check of land ownership in the hamlet indicates that Myers did not own land and in the absence of assessment rolls for the village it has been impossible to locate his site.

Millbank

The potter Robert W. Wallace moved from New Hamburg to this village sometime before 1892. Wallace and his son, Robert Jr., rented land from Robert Large in lot 24, concession 3, Mornington Township. Vera McNicol, a Millbank poet, described the oral tradition about the pottery:

"A man by the name of Fraser
Was a saddler by trade.
He sold his shop to Mr. Wallace
And here fine pottery was made."[10]

The exact location of the pottery is not now known, but it is reported to have been near the Anglican Church, and was in operation until 1897.

Milverton

Henry Bierenstihl left his father's pottery in Bridgeport, Waterloo County, in 1876 to establish his own pottery at Milverton. He returned to Bridgeport in 1900 after the death of his father, and apparently continued the Waterloo County workshop for a year.

The location of the Milverton pottery was the southeastern corner of lot 6, concession 4 (now known as city lot 15 at the corner of Main and Albert Streets), which he purchased in 1884.[11] No pottery can be attributed to the site.

Tavistock

An earthenware pottery was reported operating in Tavistock from ca. 1878 to 1885. In the *Perth County Gazetteer & Business Directory for 1878-79,* Wendlin Schuler, who had previously worked in Paris, was reported producing "flint-enamelled and common earthenware." By the year 1881 John Jarvis, a brickmaker, had taken over the business, according to the 1881 *Oxford County Directory.* He continued to make pottery until about 1885. Little is known about the pottery, although there are still sherds on the site.

HURON COUNTY

Egmondville

The Huron Pottery was one of the longest-

11.1 *Base of water container inscribed Boeh-* *29th/ 1874. This is the only known marked piece*
ler & Weber/Makers/Egmondville/November the *dating to this short partnership.*

operating earthenware potteries in early Ontario. For more than sixty years the works
operated in Egmondville, a small hamlet in
Tuckersmith Township.

The first potter at Egmondville was Valentine Boehler, who emigrated from Germany in
1850. His family had been potters in Alsace,
his native province. When he arrived in
Canada he stayed with his brother, Xavier
Boehler, in New Hamburg, Ontario. In the
summer of 1852, Valentine Boehler established the pottery at Egmondville on lots 2 and
3, on the north side of Stanley Street, which he
purchased for £20 from C. L. VanEgmond.[12]

The 1870-71 census gives us a glimpse of
the size and value of the pottery. Valentine
Boehler had $300 invested in the business. He
worked at the wheel for six months with the

help of one male hand, to produce 4,000
crocks.[13]

Boehler continued to operate the pottery for
twenty-one years until he formed a partnership in 1873 with his son-in-law, Jacob
Weber.[14] The partnership ended three years
later, when Jacob Weber became sole proprietor of the works,[15] although Boehler continued to hold a mortgage for $1,000 on the
pottery. During this short alliance the *Mercantile Agency Reference Book* lists the pottery as
valued at $1,000-$2,000, with a "fair" credit
rating.[16] A stand for a water container made
during the partnership and inscribed with the
potters' names is shown in plate 11.1.

Following Boehler's retirement, Jacob
Weber expanded the production capacity of
the pottery and encouraged its reputation so

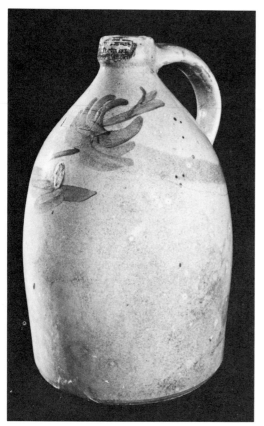

11.2 *Jug with cobalt-blue flower decoration. Piece is stamped in two places with JB WEBER/ HURON POTTERY/EGMONDVILLE, ONT.* Courtesy Royal Ontario Museum.

that it could be announced in the *Huron Expositor* of April 14, 1882, that "Mr. Jacob Webber [sic] of the Egmondville pottery shipped a carload of pottery to Manitoba. It was sold before shipment."

During the 1880s the pottery works had, according to the local newspaper, "four or five hands. . .a man being almost always on the road, distributing to the business centres of Huron and Perth counties." A price list from this time is shown in figure 11.2. There were fourteen different types of pottery produced, in a total of forty-eight different sizes. This list does not include the special pieces that were occasionally produced to order. A rare example of a marked piece from the Weber days is shown in plate 11.2. The jug is marked with an impressed stamp J.B. WEBER/HURON

POTTERY/EGMONDVILLE, ONT. The piece is decorated with blue flowers, making the jug resemble the more sought-after stoneware.

A picture of the pottery building during this decade was first published in a Government of Ontario report on the clay industry. The pottery building is long and narrow, with a kiln in the far end (west) of the board-and-batten structure. There are cream pots drying in the sun in front of the building, shown in plate 11.3, one of very few contemporary pictures of Ontario potteries during the nineteenth century.

In the early years of the business, both Boehler and Weber developed elaborate decorations for their wares. A flowerpot vase, shown in plate 11.4, is one example of the use of applied decorations. During archaeological excavations under the leadership of the author, the site of the pottery yielded a large number of intact pots, pot lids (over three hundred in number), and, most importantly, some of the potter's tools. There were over twenty sprig moulds used to make applied decorative reliefs, including the motifs shown in the flowerpot vase of plate 11.4. The basement of the pottery also produced plaster-of-Paris forms for slip-moulding of lids and jelly moulds, a coggle-wheel for making decorative bands on the outside of rims of flowerpots, and finally, the glaze-grinding wheels.

Five of the sprig moulds were signed and dated 1877. An example of a sprig mould and piece of pottery with the applied sprigging is shown in plate 11.5.

In 1897 Jacob Weber rented the pottery to his brother, Joseph. For the next three years Joseph Weber continued the business, with the assistance of John Allan and Ferdinand Burgard. The *Huron Expositor* of May 4, 1900, reports: "Mr. John Allan who has rented the Huron Pottery from Mr. Joseph Weber intends moving into the house recently vacated by Mr. Weber." Allan's management of the business did not last beyond November of the same year, when Ferdinand Burgard purchased the shop from Joseph Weber.[17]

Ferdinand Burgard was the nephew of the first potter, Valentine Boehler. Born in Alsace, Burgard immigrated to Canada in 1870, probably with the prospect of helping his uncle in the pottery business. Burgard was a skilled

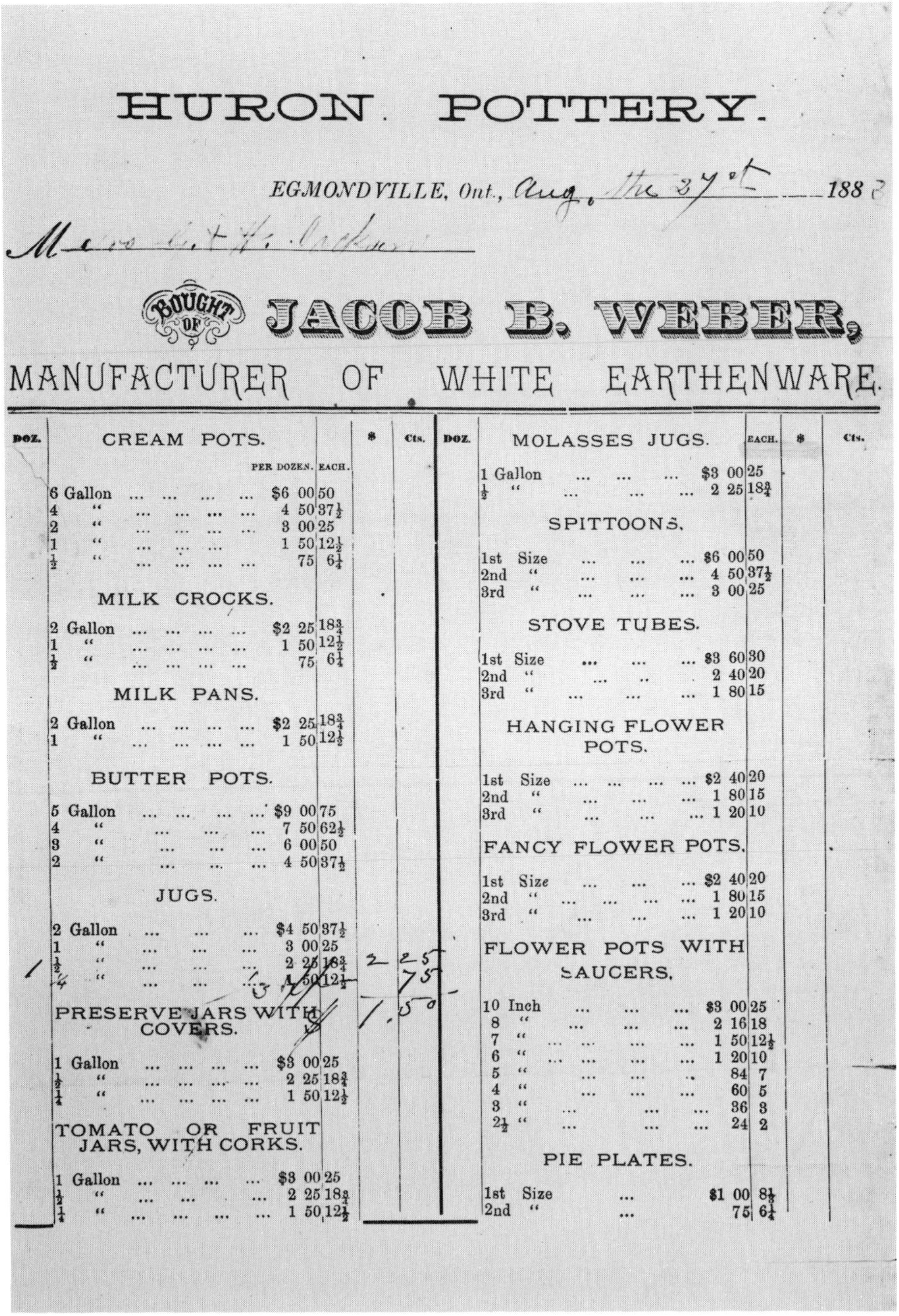

HURON POTTERY.

EGMONDVILLE, Ont., Aug. the 27th 188

BOUGHT OF JACOB B. WEBER,

MANUFACTURER OF WHITE EARTHENWARE.

DOZ.	CREAM POTS.	PER DOZEN.	EACH.	$	Cts.
	6 Gallon	$6 00	50		
	4 "	4 50	37½		
	2 "	3 00	25		
	1 "	1 50	12½		
	½ "	75	6¼		
	MILK CROCKS.				
	2 Gallon	$2 25	18¾		
	1 "	1 50	12½		
	½ "	75	6¼		
	MILK PANS.				
	2 Gallon	$2 25	18¾		
	1 "	1 50	12½		
	BUTTER POTS.				
	5 Gallon	$9 00	75		
	4 "	7 50	62½		
	3 "	6 00	50		
	2 "	4 50	37½		
	JUGS.				
	2 Gallon	$4 50	37½		
	1 "	3 00	25		
1	½ "	2 25	18¾	2	25
	¼ "	1 50	12½		75
				1	50
	PRESERVE JARS WITH COVERS.				
	1 Gallon	$3 00	25		
	½ "	2 25	18¾		
	¼ "	1 50	12½		
	TOMATO OR FRUIT JARS, WITH CORKS.				
	1 Gallon	$3 00	25		
	½ "	2 25	18¾		
	¼ "	1 50	12½		

DOZ.	MOLASSES JUGS.		EACH.	$	Cts.
	1 Gallon	$3 00	25		
	½ "	2 25	18¾		
	SPITTOONS.				
	1st Size	$6 00	50		
	2nd "	4 50	37½		
	3rd "	3 00	25		
	STOVE TUBES.				
	1st Size	$3 60	30		
	2nd "	2 40	20		
	3rd "	1 80	15		
	HANGING FLOWER POTS.				
	1st Size	$2 40	20		
	2nd "	1 80	15		
	3rd "	1 20	10		
	FANCY FLOWER POTS.				
	1st Size	$2 40	20		
	2nd "	1 80	15		
	3rd "	1 20	10		
	FLOWER POTS WITH SAUCERS.				
	10 Inch	$3 00	25		
	8 "	2 16	18		
	7 "	1 50	12½		
	6 "	1 20	10		
	5 "	84	7		
	4 "	60	5		
	3 "	36	3		
	2½ "	24	2		
	PIE PLATES.				
	1st Size	$1 00	8⅓		
	2nd "	75	6¼		

Fig. 11.2 *Price list of Huron Pottery, dated 1883, showing different types of pottery made during the time Jacob Weber owned the business.* Courtesy Royal Ontario Museum.

11.3 *Picture of Huron Pottery building ca. 1905
showing butter crocks drying in the sun. The potter,
Ferdinand Burgard, is standing in front (left) by the
water pump.* Courtesy Ontario Ministry of Natural
Resources.

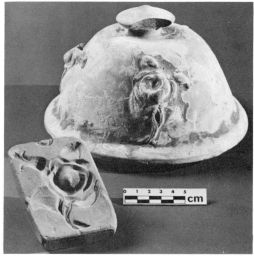

11.5 *Examples of sprig moulds used to make
applied decorations on pottery. The sprig mould
on the left was used to make the sprigging on the
unglazed lid on the right. Both were recovered
during archaeological excavations at the Huron
Pottery site.*

11.4 *(at left) Flowerpot vase decorated with
applied spriggings. The piece is finished with a
bright-yellow glaze and brown sponge work along
the top. Elaborately decorated pieces were produced at the Huron Pottery from the 1870s onward.*

potter, and in the year 1871 he began his long association with the works, first as a salesman, distributing the wares to businesses in the region, and then as joint manager of the pottery with Weber and Allan. In 1900 Burgard took over the business, which became known as F. Burgard & Son (Philip).[18]

Plate 11.6, a photo dating from around 1905, shows Burgard (right) and his assistant, Remley, by a display of the various types of wares produced at the shop. Pottery manufactured there includes various types of jugs (plate 11.7) and cream pots (plate 11.8). These pieces were finished in the characteristic yellow glaze of the pottery.

During the archaeological excavations at the site I was able to examine several examples of

11.6 *Picture of wares produced at the Huron Pottery ca. 1905. Ferdinand Burgard, the potter, is standing on the right and his assistant, Remley, is on the left.* Courtesy Royal Ontario Museum.

miniature jugs (*whimseys*) produced by Burgard. A number of these jugs have been signed by the potter. Four of them are shown in plate 11.9. The potter, according to old-timers who remember the business, made the miniatures as gifts or to commemorate special events in the community. Three whimseys still in private collections read: Have a drink with Jimmy Dick/Seaforth/Ontario; Mrs. Ann Modeland./Egmondville./Ontario./by F. Burgard; John Modeland./Egmondville./Ontario./by F. Burgard.

The pottery closed in 1910. A notice in the *Huron Expositor* dated November 18 announced the sale of the pottery fixtures and the adjoining residence in the following words: "On Saturday, November 27th at the Egmondville Pottery, the plant together with all fixtures, also the dwelling house." The pottery lot was not disposed of at the time, as ownership records indicate Burgard sold it on

11.7 *Examples of the various sizes and shapes of jugs produced at the Huron Pottery.* Courtesy Royal Ontario Museum.

11.8 *Examples of the different sizes of cream pots produced at the pottery. The shape and finish of the cream pot is one of the most characteristic features of wares produced at the Huron Pottery.* Courtesy Royal Ontario Museum.

October 7, 1919, to Arthur Routledge, a butcher.[19]

Ferdinand Burgard died in 1922 at his daughter's home in Hamilton, Ontario. The *Huron Expositor* of October 21 of that year reminisced at the passing of the last potter of Huron County who, "had admitted defeat,

but to the end . . . remained captain of his soul, for he refused ever to capitulate with the machine age."

The pottery building was moved to Brucefield, Ontario, in 1931. The cellar was filled with the remains of the kiln, unsold pottery and refuse from local homes. In the spring of 1974 the remains of the pottery, visible as contours in the land, were brought to the attention of the Royal Ontario Museum, Toronto. Three seasons of excavations at the site have yielded the most complete collection of pottery and pottery-making tools in Ontario (plate 11.10). Several reports on the excavations are now available and give details of the archaeological work and the finds.[20]

Zurich

The first potter in this community was Jonas Beck, a German immigrant, who first appears in the 1860-61 census for Hay Township.[21] Beck lived on a one-fifth-acre lot, the size of a village lot, but the land's location is not certain.

In 1869 Christian Hess arrived at Zurich and began potting. Two years after his arrival, he purchased a pottery lot, lot 11 in Brown's Survey.[22] Hess worked at his wheel until his death in 1900. The workshop was always very small,

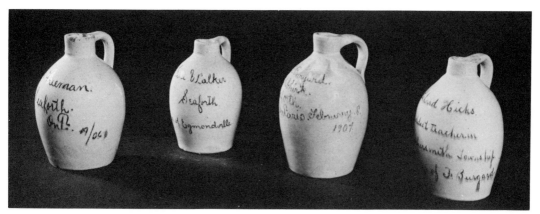

11.9 *Examples of miniature jugs (whimseys) produced by Ferdinand Burgard to commemorate spe-* *cial events or for individuals in the local community.* Courtesy Royal Ontario Museum.

11.10 *Archaeological excavations at the pottery during the years 1974-76 uncovered the most complete collection of pottery and potter's tools known from any Ontario workshop. Here a field* *worker is uncovering a layer of debris from the cellar. Note the pieces of pottery at various levels in the cellar.*

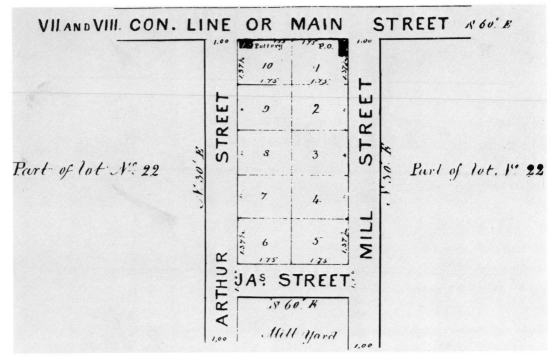

Fig. 11.3 *A plan of Ethel, dated February 1869, showing the location of the pottery building at the intersection of Main and Arthur Streets.*

providing employment only for Hess. In the 1870-71 census he is reported to be producing 3,000 crocks with a value of $300.[23] There are no pieces known to have been marked by Hess.

Ethel
In 1869 William Spence purchased lots 9 and 10 at the southeastern corner of the intersection of Main and Arthur Streets in the Village of Ethel[24] (fig. 11.3). Spence is reported to have continued in the pottery business until 1881.[25] After that date he was the village postmaster. Nothing more is known at this time about Spence or the pottery he produced at his workshop.

Blyth
Even more apocryphal is the location and wares of the pottery of Donald Haines and his son Robert, during their residence in the village of Blyth in 1890-91.[26]

Wingham
Joseph E. Bradwin moved from Mt. Forest in 1879 to settle in Wingham, Turnberry Township. He purchased lots 36 and 37 in Scott's Survey, bordering on the intersection of Josephine and Scott Streets, in March, 1881.[27] Bradwin operated the pottery until 1887, when he sold it to become an "electrician." The following year Ignatz Bitschy of Mildmay purchased the pottery, presumably for his son Albert, as it was deeded to Albert the same year.[28] Albert Bitschy continued to make pottery in Wingham until 1890, by which time he also operated a furniture business.[29]

Holmesville
David William Burns arrived in Goderich Township about 1860 to work a pottery for Bernard Evans on land along the Maitland River that Evans had obtained from the Canada Company. The site, known as lot 46, Maitland Concession, was about four kilometres north of the nearest post office at the village of Holmesville.

Burns was twenty-one years old when he

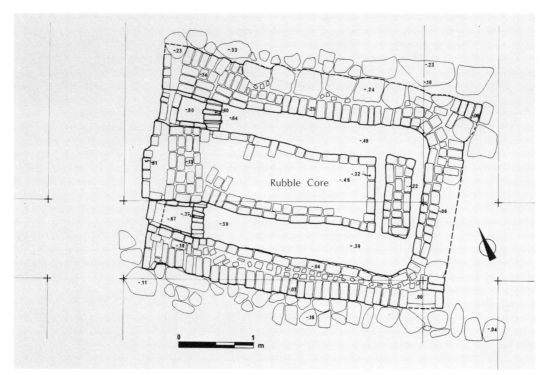

Fig. 11.4 *Drawing of the remains of a kiln found at the site of David W. Burns Pottery, Holmesville. The kiln was rectangular and had two parallel flues (left) and a door for loading pottery (no longer present) on the right.*

came to set up the pottery business on a plot along the southern edge of the nine and one-half-acre lot. Burns later married Evans' daughter in 1865. By 1900 Burns had discontinued the pottery. He died of pneumonia on March 3, 1907. Since his son was not interested in continuing the business, the pottery was abandoned and the building eventually disappeared.

According to Daisy Torrence, a relative of Evans, David Burns had a brother who worked at a pottery in Bolton, Peel County. This could have been either James Harrison Burns or Samuel R. Burns. The connection between David Burns and one of the Bolton Burns has not been established without some doubt.

Daisy Torrence recalls her visits to the pottery. She writes, "My younger brother and I used to help carry the unbaked pots to place in the bake oven [kiln], which was built in a small knoll." Another person who remembers the

11.11 *Examples of bowls produced by David Burns. Glaze colours range from clear (right) to pink (top) to green (left). (Scale runs from one to five centimetres.)*

11.12 *Example of the very simple jug produced in great numbers by David Burns. The flecked appearance of the jug is due to iron impurities in the clay.*

11.13 *Stove tube from David Burns pottery. These sleeves for stove pipes helped to prevent wooden houses from burning by separating the hot metal stove pipe from the wooden frame of the house. Stove tubes could also be used to line chimneys and occasionally were used as drain pipes around houses.*

pottery in operation is Clifford Lobb, of Clinton, Ontario, who recollects watching as a boy and seeing Burns throw his pots on a foot-operated wheel. Lobb recalls that during his visits in the late 1890s, the potter used the kiln by the roadside; his only recollection of the first kiln (which Daisy Torrence had mentioned) was an abandoned building located further back on the property in a small depression.

Lobb remembers Burns loading the kiln (figure 11.4) from a doorway on the east. Burns would load the wood through the two fire doors on the west of the kiln and remark to his youthful admirer, "Well, I'm going to burn some pottery!" The kiln was, according to Lobb, about eight feet high, with a domed roof. Immediately to the east of it was a small

wooden shed, about fifteen by twenty feet in dimension, used by Burns as a workshop. Clifford Lobb points out that the building was built on a beaten earth floor.

The author conducted extensive archaeological work at the Burns site, and retrieved some 9,000 sherds, or broken pieces of pottery.[30] A number of pottery forms were reconstructed from these sherds. These include plain crocks (plate 11.11) with clear glaze finish, jugs of various sizes (one of which is shown in plate 11.12), again with a thin clear lead glaze covering, and stove tubes (plate 11.13). Only one piece of pottery was marked by Burns. This was the base of a candle holder, which he inscribed with D. Burns/Maker (plate 11.14).

11.14   *Base of candle holder inscribed D. Burns/*
Maker. This is the only known piece that was
marked by David Burns.

12.
Potteries and Potters of Brant County

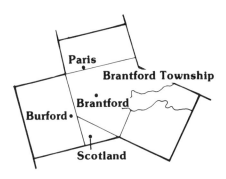

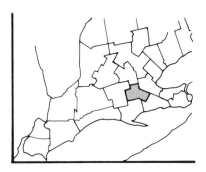

Fig. 12.1 *Map of Brant County showing communities with potteries in the nineteenth century.*

The county of Brant, in south central Ontario, was well endowed with natural features for the development of industry. It had two navigable rivers, the Grand and Nith, where boats could ship raw materials from the Great Lakes to the factories in Brantford and Paris. By the mid-nineteenth century, Brantford had become a railroad terminus, thus guaranteeing the uninterrupted development of industry. Among the early entrepreneurs in the county were pottery manufacturers, specializing in the production of both earthenware and stoneware containers. Potteries were established in four communities (see fig. 12.1): Burford, Scotland, Paris and Brantford.

Burford

The first pottery in the county was established by John Yeigh, whose name appears in the land registry records of Burford Township on July 11, 1803, when he purchased a tract of 200 acres from David Palmer, on land described as lot 8, concession 6.[1] Yeigh had

learned the pottery trade in Pennsylvania before immigrating to Upper Canada. After clearing brush on his farm he established a small earthenware pottery, which he operated until the start of the war of 1812. At the outbreak of the war, he left his business to fight against the American invaders in Captain Mallory's Militia Company.[2] After the war Yeigh returned to the potter's wheel, but did not continue the business beyond the late 1820s.

A simple earthenware crock with a clear lead glaze was found several years ago on the site of Yeigh's pottery. This artifact is shown in plate 12.1, while examples of kiln furniture found with the pottery remains are shown in plate 12.2.

Scotland

A small earthenware pottery was operated by John Mills Marlatt in this village in Oakland Township from 1857 to 1859. The pottery was described as being on village lot 5, on the east side of Simcoe Street and the south side of Oakland Street and the adjoining lot 5, on the east side of Simcoe Street and the north side of

12.1 *Red earthenware crock with clear lead glaze recovered from the site of the John Yeigh pottery, Burford.*

12.3 *Two stoneware jugs decorated with cobalt-blue flower motif, from J.M. Marlatt pottery, Paris.*

12.2 *Kiln furniture recovered from Yeigh pottery site, Burford.*

Elgin Street.[3] Marlatt had potted in conjunction with a "temperance inn." His business was of considerable size as he employed three men.[4]

Marlatt moved to Paris, Ontario, in 1859, perhaps to be closer to the railways and navigable waters of the Grand River.

Paris

The first pottery in the village of Paris was established by Lyman Gleason in the late 1840s. Gleason had emigrated from Genesee County, New York State, and had learned pottery-making at the Charles Gleason Pottery in Morganville, New York.

We know little about Gleason's pottery business, due in part to the loss of important Paris records in a 1900 fire. We do have some information on the pottery though, from the 1851-52 census returns. It reports that the works is "new in this place" and employed five persons.[5] The census taker was interested in the pottery wares, as a comment on the returns reads, "what the cause (is) I do not know, but the ware has not the finish on it that imported goods have."[6] Gleason's pottery was located on lot 10 on the west side of Broadway Street. He continued to operate the business until 1857, when a directory lists him as "innkeeper" at Paris Station.[7] The town of Paris was the junction of the Grand Trunk and Buffalo-Lake Huron Railways, and an important centre for commercial trade.

There are no known pots that can be attributed to the Gleason works as he did not mark his wares.

The next pottery to be established in Paris was begun by John Mills Marlatt in 1859, when he moved from Scotland, Ontario (q.v.). He established his pottery shop on lot 6 on the east side of West River Street. Marlatt continued to produce both earthenware and stoneware containers until his death on January 6, 1868.[8]

During the 1860s the Marlatt pottery was mentioned frequently in directories and gazetteers. The *Brant County Directory of 1865* describes Marlatt as a "manufacturer of and wholesale dealer in flint, enamelled, stone and common earthenware, of every description."[9] Wares produced by Marlatt include stoneware jugs, butter crocks and bottles. These vessels were either undecorated or decorated with a very simple cobalt-blue painted design of flowers. The pottery is marked with the impressed stamps of J. M. MARLATT/PARIS, CW or J. M. MARLATT & CO./PARIS, CW (plate 12.3.)

The 1860-61 census states that Marlatt produced goods valued at $800 a year, using forty-eight tons of clay. Nine part-time persons were employed at an annual average cost of $26 per labourer.[10]

Marlatt entered his pottery in the Provincial Exhibition of 1860 and won three prizes: a first prize in the category for the best assortment of pottery, a second prize for the category of the best assortment of stoneware, and an extra prize for a display of earthenware. His prize money totalled $17.[11]

After his death in 1868, the firm of Schuler & McGlade (sometimes listed as McGlade & Schuler) rented the pottery works from Marlatt's widow. Initially, the new firm restricted its production to earthenware, but later it concentrated exclusively on manufacturing stoneware containers. An 1869 advertisement from a county directory describes the firm and its wares: "Messrs. Schuler & McGlade employ six hands in this business . . . this firm is doing a large trade, and manufacture every description of earthen, flint and enamelled ware"[12] (plate 12.4). During the partnership the firm also traded under the Paris Pottery.

The leading figure of the partnership, Henry Schuler, was born in Illinois, on September 25, 1842, the son of Wendlin and Susanna Schuler. The family immigrated to Canada, settling in the village of New Hamburg, Waterloo County.[13] Henry Schuler's father was a school teacher and later operated an inn.[14] His death in 1856 left Henry with a reasonable schooling but no trade or profession. Susanna Schuler married Herman Schmidt, who was then a carpenter, ca. 1857. Later Schmidt worked as a potter at the Boehler pottery in New Hamburg.[15] It was at New Hamburg that Henry Schuler began his long career as an Ontario potter of distinction.

12.4 *Advertisement for Schuler & McGlade pottery from* County of Brant Gazetteer and Directory *for 1869-70.*

12.5 *A rare example of pottery made during partnership of Henry Schuler and Peter McGlade. Note the reversal of the partnership names.*

In 1867, at the age of twenty-five, Henry Schuler moved to Paris to work for J. M. Marlatt.[16] After Marlatt's death, he formed the

12.6 *Henry Schuler when he worked in Paris.*

partnership with Peter McGlade, which lasted until 1873.

We first learn about Peter McGlade from an 1867 directory, and from the Town of Brantford assessment rolls, where he is described as a potter, probably then working for F. P. Goold.[17] In 1869 he moved to Paris, a distance of some eight kilometres, to work in the former Marlatt business. After the dissolution of the partnership with Schuler, McGlade operated a furniture business in St. Catharines, Ontario, then in 1882 joined Bernard A. Fitzmaurice (who had been a potter in Paris during the time of McGlade's work there) to form McGlade & Fitzmaurice, of London, Ontario.

Pottery with the impressed mark of Schuler & McGlade is rare. An unusual piece is shown in plate 12.5, where the impressed stamping is McGLADE & SCHULER/PARIS, ONT. Pottery made during this period appears similar

12.7 *Price list for Henry Schuler pottery in Paris, dated 1880s. The list was found glued to the inside top of a desk.*

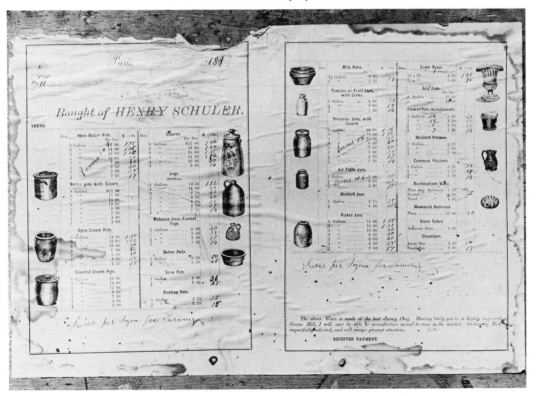

in shape and decoration to the wares known from the Marlatt days.

Henry Schuler (shown in plate 12.6) continued in the pottery business under his own name until 1884. Then he and his brother Wendlin moved to Brantford and began a long association with the Brantford stoneware factory.

A price list from the Schuler years in Paris (plate 12.7) lists the types of wares that were in demand at this time, including butter crocks, preserve jars, fruit jars, and jugs, to name but a few of the forms that were sold to local stores and individuals. The wares were frequently marked with the impression stamp H. SCHULER/PARIS, ONT. Examples of pottery produced by Schuler are shown in plates 12.8, and 12.9.

12.9 A cream pot with blue flower decoration. Private collection.

12.8 A six-gallon stoneware crock with elaborate floral motif in cobalt blue.

Schuler exhibited his wares as part of the Canadian Exhibition at the Paris (France) Universal Exhibition of 1878. His display included butter pots, preserve jars, cream pots, jugs, tomato jars, churns, common pitchers, spittoons, molasses jugs and flower pots.[18]

The third pottery in Paris was owned by Jacob Henry Ahrens, who purchased lots 1 and 2 and part of lot 3 on the west side of West River Street, along the banks of the Nith River in 1860. It was here that he built his pottery shop and operated it until the disastrous flood of August, 1883. A contemporary photograph of the business is shown in plate 12.10. After the flood he continued to sell pottery and operate a wine and spirits business until shortly before his death on June 17, 1905.

We get a glimpse of Ahrens' pottery business from Sutherland's County of Brant Gazetteer and Directory for 1869-70, which reports, ". . . six hands are here employed, and goods to the value of about six thousand dollars are turned out per annum, consisting of flint, enamelled and common earthenwares."[19]

An advertisement from this 1869-70 directory is shown in plate 12.11.

Ahrens produced a wide assortment of pottery at his factory. A price list for 1874 (plate 12.12) shows the types of containers produced and the costs of the various sizes. In

12.10 *Photo of J. H. Ahrens pottery, Paris, ca. 1880, showing pottery plant, delivery wagon and* storage of cord wood for firing kiln. Courtesy Brant County Museum, Brantford.

I. H. AHRENS,

POTTER,

WEST RIVER STREET, PARIS, ONTARIO,

Manufacturer of Flint, Enamelled and every description of

COMMON & FINE EARTHENWARE.

PROMPTEST ATTENTION PAID TO ALL ORDERS.

12.11 *Advertisement for Ahrens pottery in* Sutherland's *County of Brant Gazetteer for 1869-70. (Note initial "I" in name, instead of "J".)*

addition he produced a number of special decorative pieces which are not shown in the price list, such as the earthenware spaniel dog (plate 12.13), an intricately cut picture frame (plate 12.14), a blue mottled picture frame (plate 12.15), and a Rockingham-glazed water jug (plate 12.16).

From 1868 to 1878 Ahrens was reported in the *Mercantile Agency Reference Book* as

being worth $2,000 to $5,000 with a "fair" credit rating. Beginning in July, 1878, and continuing until 1883, the value of his pottery business was estimated at $5,000 to $10,000, and his credit rating was described as "good," but the 1883 flood reduced Ahrens' credit rating to its earlier level.

During the 1860s and 1870s, the pottery business was profitable enough to enable Ahrens to purchase a number of parcels of land. In March, 1865, he purchased the westerly half of lots 3 and 4 on the east side of West River Street.[20] This was opposite the pottery works, and was the site of Ahrens' home, still standing today, a large and comfortable brick house of imposing dignity, overlooking Mechanic Street. Later the same year he purchased lot 6 on the west side of West River Street, for $100.[21] This eventually became the location of his barn, used for the storage and display of finished pottery. In 1885 he purchased lot 6 on the east side of West River Street, the site of the former Marlatt, Schuler and McGlade and Henry Schuler pottery.

PARIS POTTERY,

Paris, Ont., 27th Feby 1874

M [illegible handwriting]

BOUGHT OF **J. H. AHRENS,**

POTTER.

Manufacturer of Flint, Enamelled & Common Earthenware.

List of Prices adopted by the Earthenware Manufacturers' Association, held at Hamilton, 21st November, 1872.

33 1-3 per cent. off for Cash on Delivery.

Cream Pots.

DOZ.		PER DOZ.	EACH.	$	CTS.
1	6 Gallon	7 20	0 60	7	20
½	4 Gallon	5 40	0 45	2	70
½	2 Gallon	3 60	0 30	1	80
1	1 Gallon	1 80	0 15	1	80
1	½ Gallon	0 96	0 08		96

Milk Crocks.

DOZ.		PER DOZ.	EACH.	$	CTS.
2	2 Gallon	3 00	0 25	6	00
3	1 Gallon	1 80	0 15	5	40
4	½ Gallon	0 96	0 08	3	84

Milk Pans.

DOZ.		PER DOZ.	EACH.	$	CTS.
	3 Gallon	3 60	0 30		
3	2 Gallon	2 64	0 22	7	92
10	1 Gallon	1 80	0 15	18	00
				$55	62

Butter Pots.

	PER DOZ.	EACH.
5 Gallon	9 00	0 75
4 Gallon	7 50	0 62
3 Gallon	6 00	0 50
2 Gallon	4 50	0 37½
1 Gallon	3 75	0 31

Jugs.

	PER DOZ.	EACH.
2 Gallon	4 50	0 37½
1 Gallon	3 00	0 25
½ Gallon	2 40	0 20
¼ Gallon	1 50	0 12½

Molasses Jugs.

	PER DOZ.	EACH.
1 Gallon	3 60	0 30
½ Gallon	2 40	0 20
¼ Gallon	1 50	0 12½

Tomato, or Fruit Jars, with Corks.

	PER DOZ.	EACH.
2 Gallon	4 80	0 40
1 Gallon	3 60	0 30
½ Gallon	2 40	0 20
¼ Gallon	1 50	0 12

Preserve Jars.

	PER DOZ.	EACH.
2 Gallon	4 50	0 37½
1 Gallon	3 00	0 25
½ Gallon	2 40	0 20
¼ Gallon	1 50	0 12½

Fancy Flower Pots.

	PER DOZ.	EACH.
1st Size	4 50	0 37½
2nd Size	3 00	0 25

Stove Tubes.

DOZ.		PER DOZ	EACH.	$	CTS.
	1st Size	3 00	0 25	55	62
	2nd Size	2 40	0 20		
	3rd Size	1 80	0 15		

Chambers.

	PER DOZ	EACH.
1st Size	3 00	0 25
2nd Size	2 25	0 18¾

Flower Pots.

	PER DOZ	EACH.
12 Inch	4 80	0 40
10 Inch	3 00	0 25
8 Inch	1 80	0 15
7 Inch	1 20	0 10
6 Inch	0 96	0 08
5 Inch	0 72	0 06
4 Inch	0 60	0 05
3 Inch	0 36	0 03
2½ Inch	0 24	0 02

Saucers, one-half the price of the Flower Pots.

ROCKINGHAM,

Or Flint Enamelled Ware

Water Pitchers.

	PER DOZ	EACH.
1st Size	7 50	0 62½
2nd Size	4 50	0 37½
3rd Size	3 00	0 25
4th Size	2 25	0 18¾
5th Size	1 50	0 12½

Tea Pots.

DOZ.		PER DOZ	EACH.	$	CTS.
½	1st Size	6 00	0 50	3	00
1	2nd Size	4 50	0 37½	4	50
½	3rd Size	3 00	0 25	1	50

Spittoons.

DOZ.		PER DOZ	EACH.	$	CTS.
	1st Size	9 00	0 75		
	2nd Size	7 50	0 62½		
1/6	3rd Size	6 00	0 50	1	00
1/6	4th Size	4 50	0 37½		75
	5th Size	3 00	0 25		
				66	37
				22	12
				$44	15

Pie Plates.

	PER DOZ	EACH.
1st Size	0 96	0 08
2nd Size	0 75	0 06¼

Hanging Flower Pots

	PER DOZ	EACH.
1st Size	3 60	0 30
2nd Size	2 40	0 20

March 26/74

Received Payment, [illegible] Jacobson

12.13 *Earthenware "King Charles Spaniel" dog with dark chocolate-brown glaze. Attributed to J. H. Ahrens.*

12.15 *A picture frame with cream slip and blue-mottled decoration. The piece was made at Ahrens's pottery.*

12.14 *An intricately cut picture frame made by Ahrens, reportedly for the Paris (France) Universal Exhibition of 1878.*

12.12 *(opposite) Price list for Ahrens pottery, 1864.* Courtesy Royal Ontario Museum.

12.16 *Water jug with Rockingham glaze and marked with impressed stamp J-H-AHRENS.* Courtesy Brant County Museum, Brantford.

12.17 *Certificate of Merit presented to Ahrens for his contribution to the Canadian exhibit at the Paris* (France) *Universal Exhibition of 1878.* Courtesy Brant County Museum, Brantford.

Ahrens was a frequent competitor at International and Provincial exhibitions. He displayed his pottery at the American Centennial Exhibition of 1876 and the Paris (France) Universal Exhibition of 1878. A certificate presented to Ahrens for the 1878 exhibition is shown in plate 12.17. At the Provincial Exhibition of 1864 Ahrens won a first prize for the best water filter and a second prize for the best assortment of pottery. He won a second prize in both categories in the 1865 exhibition.

Ahrens and his workmen produced in a skillful manner a number of interesting, even exceptional, pieces of earthenware. He marked some, but by no means all, of the pieces he produced. The most frequent mark is the stamped J. H. AHRENS, placed on the side or base of the ware. His red earthenware products had either a chocolate-brown coloured glaze, a Rockingham glaze (plate 12.18), or a deep-brown mottled gaze (plate 12.19).

12.18 *Rockingham-glazed spittoon marked J. H. AHRENS.*

The location of Ahrens' pottery at the edge of the Nith River enabled him to ship his wares by boat, or to transport the wares by wagon.[22]

12.19 *Jelly mould with dark-brown glaze. The piece was made at Ahrens's pottery.*

But the Nith and Grand Rivers have a long history of flooding. In the late nineteenth century the flooding of the Nith was controlled by a dam, located less than a mile upstream from the pottery. In 1869 the dam broke and par-

12.20 *The Ahrens pottery after the disastrous flood of August, 1883. Ahrens stands in the centre, looking at the ruins of the workshop.* Courtesy Brant County Museum, Brantford.

tially destroyed the pottery, with a loss to Ahrens of $2,558. The flash flood of August 20, 1883, completely destroyed the pottery and cost Ahrens $7,500.[23] The results of the disaster are shown in plate 12.20.

Following the flood, a motion was introduced into the Town Council to "have a by-law prepared to submit to the ratepayers, granting a bonus of two thousand dollars to Mr. Ahrens on condition of his building a pottery and carrying on that business in Paris."[24] The motion was dropped when it became apparent that some councillors objected. A second motion was made, "that the charity committee . . . ascertain what assistance those who have suffered by the late flood require, and if they think advisable, to give them that assistance or report to the town council."[25] However, reports of the charity committee to the town council do not mention any assistance having been granted to victims of the flood.

In the late 1880s Ahrens opened a wine and liquor shop near the intersection of Mechanic and Grand River Streets. It has been assumed that he discontinued the pottery business, but, further research, starting with the *Mercantile Agency Reference Book* for the years 1887-

12.21   *Early map of Brantford showing location of Morton & Co., stoneware pottery at the corner of Clarence & Dalhousie Streets.*

1891 reveals two credit references for Ahrens: one for J. H. Ahrens & Co., pottery; and a second for J. H. Ahrens liquors.[26] By January, 1892, the listing for the pottery had been dropped but the liquor listing continues until 1904. The end of the pottery listing corresponds with the sale in November, 1892, of the pottery lots. A directory listing in 1889 indicates that the firm J. H. Ahrens & Co., pottery, was located near the Paris railway station.[27] Is

it possible that Ahrens re-activated a pottery founded by Gleason decades before?

Brantford

Few Ontario potteries are as well known as the stoneware factory established by Justus Morton in Brantford in 1849. The fame of the potter is due, in part, to the large number of marked pieces in private and public collections, and the long period during which the firm was producing wares, under a succession of familiar names. As each owner, or group of

12.22   *Examples of stoneware containers made at Brantford during the time of Justus Morton.*

owners, identified by an impressed mark some or all of the wares they produced, it is possible to trace the history of the factory by the names of the successive owners.

Morton & Co. (1849-1856)
The pottery in Brantford was founded early in 1849 by Justus Morton, who had emigrated from Lyons, New York, a year earlier.[28] Morton established his business in a leased factory on lots 32 and 33, at the northeast corner of the intersection of Dalhousie and Clarence Streets, as indicated on an early map of Brantford showing the buildings (plate 12.21).

The first mention of the pottery in municipal records is in 1851, when the tax assessment rolls give an assessed value of $150 for land and buildings, and $250 for stock.[29] From these humble beginnings the business grew and flourished during the 1850s. By 1853

Morton was in a financial position to purchase the property, which he obtained for £125.[30] In the same year he employed about six men and produced wares estimated at $8,000 per year.[31]

During the eight years that Morton operated the pottery, he produced a variety of forms, many of which were decorated with cobalt-blue flower designs and marked MORTON & CO./BRANTFORD, C. W., impressed below the rim and directly above the blue design (see plates 12.22, 12.23, and 12.24 a and b).

The quality of Morton's work was recognized at the Provincial Exhibition of 1852, when the firm was awarded a first and second prize for the best specimen of pottery.[32]

The firm continued under Morton's leadership until 1856, when he entered into a partnership with A. B. Bennett, of Goold & Bennett foundry.

Morton & Bennett (1856-1857)
This partnership did not survive beyond the

12.23 *Small stoneware butter crock with blue flower. The crock is lined with Albany slip.*

12.24b *Reverse of container shown in 12.24a. The decorations were applied to the piece before firing. Notice how some of the appliqués have chipped off at the bottom.*

12.24a *Elaborately decorated water container made during the time of Justus Morton. This piece is very similar to pieces produced at the Lyons, New York pottery during the same period, indicating a direct influence of that pottery on the early products of Brantford.*

spring of 1857. The purpose of the partnership might have been to obtain additional capitalization for the business, as Bennett was a well-known and prosperous entrepreneur in Brantford. Although there was a demand for crocks, the costs of producing them must have been high, as the clay had to be shipped from northern New Jersey to Brantford. The freight costs accounted for over half the final cost of the raw material when it was delivered to the factory door.[33]

The basic shapes and decorative techniques of the crocks produced by Morton & Bennett did not differ from those of the earlier period, as an examination of typical products will demonstrate (plate 12.25).

At the dissolution of the partnership, the property was leasted to James Woodyatt, a former tailor.[34] Woodyatt's interest in the business may have been prompted by William E. Welding, then a salesman for the pottery who resided at the Woodyatt home.

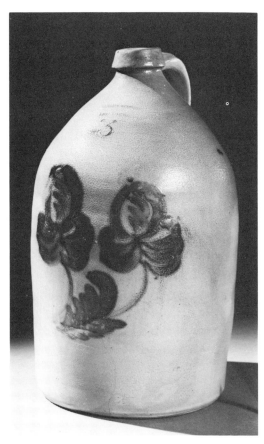

12.25   *Three-gallon jug made at Brantford during the period of Morton & Bennett.*

12.26   *A rare example of a Woodyatt period butter churn.*

James Woodyatt & Co. (1857-1859)
Woodyatt's lack of pottery-making experience was probably compensated for by Welding's practical business knowledge of the stoneware industry. The Brantford *Expositor* wrote about the pottery operation shortly after Woodyatt assumed control:

The main structure is built of wood, and is 90 feet long by 40 feet wide. Besides other buildings there are two kiln sheds, each 50 feet long by 30 wide. The kilns, of which there are two, are of circular form, 45 feet in circumference, and are the largest in Canada . . .15 operatives are constantly employed, the product of whose labour is over $20,000 annually. About 900 cords of wood are consumed each year in the kilns and drying rooms, and over 400 tons of clay are imported . . . among the articles

manufactured at this pottery are jugs, churns, milk pans, wash bowls, beer bottles, stove tubes, fire brick, stove linings, etc . . . besides a variety of beautiful fancy articles of moulded spittoons and pitchers . . . [35]

An example of an article made during the Woodyatt period is shown in plate 12.26.

In the same issue of the Brantford *Expositor* quoted above, there appears another, shorter note, which reads:

Holmedale Pottery . . . on the Grand River near the precincts of town . . . Messrs. Woodyatt & Co., proprietors.

The article continues:

. . . it is not yet in operation, though a supply of wood and clay is already to be seen upon the

12.27 *Only a few pieces of pottery are known to have been produced during the brief time that the partnership of Morton, Goold & Co., owned the pottery. This five-gallon butter churn is one of three known pieces.*

premises. The main building is of wood, two storeys high, and 110 feet long by 50 feet wide. It has one large kiln built of fire brick, at a cost of $1,400 . . . the various machinery used in forming and fashioning the ware will be driven by water, instead of by the foot . . .[36]

This venture seemingly disappears, as no further mention is made of it in contemporary historical records available to the author. It is not known if the pottery ever produced crocks, but it is possible to speak of a second Woodyatt pottery building. If the pottery did indeed produce wares, they were probably marked in the same way as those produced at the main plant at Dalhousie and Clarence Streets.

Woodyatt continued to operate the pottery

until the year 1859, when he began a long and distinguished career as Brantford's town clerk.

Morton, Goold & Co. (1859)
Woodyatt gave up his lease in February, 1859, and the business was taken up again by Justus Morton, this time in partnership with Franklin P. Goold. This new arrangement was dissolved before the summer had ended. Justus Morton was the partner with the pottery-making experience, while Goold was probably the financial backer of the enterprise. We have no information to explain the short life of this partnership.

There are very few pieces known to be marked with the impressed stamp of MORTON, GOOLD & CO./BRANTFORD, C. W. One piece is shown in plate 12.27.

On August 20, 1859, Morton sold the pottery to Franklin P. Goold and Charles H. Waterous,[37] who continued to produce stoneware under the name of F. P. Goold & Co.

12.28 *A Rockingham-glazed picture frame with inscribed signature of George Beech, a potter at Brantford in the 1860s.* Courtesy Royal Ontario Museum.

12.29   *An intricately decorated three-gallon preserve jar with cover made during the time of F. P. Goold.*

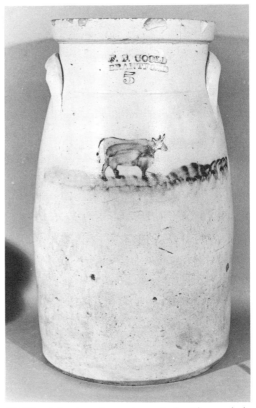

12.30   *A butter churn decorated with a cobalt-blue picture of a cow.*

F. P. Goold & Co. (1859-1867)

Neither Goold nor Waterous are known to have had pottery-making experience sufficient to manage the technical part of the business. To meet this need, Goold hired additional skilled potters, including Rufus Smith, Oliver Smith, John Marks, Peter McGlade, Thomas Martin and George Beech.[38] A moulded picture frame with the inscribed signature of Beech is shown in plate 12.28. The increase in the number of skilled potters in the firm may explain the apparent sophistication and refinement of the applied slip designs on the stoneware produced during his ownership. An example of this skill is a crock with a delicately executed design of a bird in cobalt blue (plate 12.29), a churn with a cow (plate 12.30), and a

12.31   *(at right) Large open crock with inscribed pair of birds. The use of inscribed lines for decoration is not common in Ontario, but may reflect the more common practice in New York State. Courtesy Royal Ontario Museum.*

crock with an incised pair of birds (plate 12.31).

Goold's products did not go unnoticed among the entries in the Provincial Exhibition of 1860. He was awarded the first prize for the best assortment of stoneware. On this occasion the judges commented:

There were several assortments of pottery of an excellent and very complete character, among which we particularly noticed those of Messrs. Goold & Co., of Brantford . . .[39]

In the 1862 Provincial Exhibition held at Toronto, Goold won $10 for the best assortment of stoneware and a second prize of $6 for the best stoneware sewage pipes.[40] Prizes were also won at the Provincial Exhibitions of 1864 and 1865.[41]

From all outward appearances the business was prospering in the year 1867. The town's tax assessment rolls report the assessed value of the pottery property at $1,800, up from the small sum of $300, the assessed value when Goold took over the business. In spite of the growth in the business and the continued demand for stoneware crocks, Goold had difficulty meeting mortgage payments on the property. The Bank of British North America foreclosed on a mortgage which was finally discharged and the property conveyed back to Goold to be sold to William Erastus Welding.[42]

Welding & Belding (1867-1872)
On October 29, 1867, Welding, together with W.W. Belding, purchased the pottery for $3,200 from F. P. Goold.[43] Welding had an intimate, thorough knowledge of the pottery business, having previously worked as salesman, agent, and then manager of the works. Belding was the financial backer of Welding, and was respected in the town of Brantford as a successful lumber dealer. During the six years of the partnership the business showed an impressive record of growth. In July, 1868, the *Mercantile Agency Reference Book* lists the business as worth between $2,000 and $5,000 and having a "fair" credit rating. By February, 1873 (information for this manual was gathered in late 1872), the business was estimated as worth $10,000 to $25,000, with a "good" credit rating.

12.32 *A large four-gallon open crock with elaborate decoration in cobalt blue. Such elaborate decorating was characteristic of the Welding & Belding period.*

During the period that the ownership changed from Goold to Welding & Belding, there was no major turnover in factory staff. Skilled potters such as John Marks, George Beech, Oliver Smith, William Waller, and Thomas Martin all continued to work under the new owners. In light of this stability it is no wonder that the basic products of the factory resembled those of the Goold days. An example of the stoneware made during this period is shown in plate 12.32.

The partnership of Welding & Belding was dissolved after a disastrous fire on the morning of December 1, 1872. It took but two hours for the wooden pottery building, the nearby wooden tenements, and part of the large supply of dry cord wood stored in the pottery yard to become a smouldering ruin. Contemporary accounts indicate that nearly $9,000 worth of pottery had been destroyed, including pottery-making tools. At the dissolution of the partnership Belding assumed an outstanding mortgage on the property for $2,500.[44] In March, 1873, Welding repurchased the pottery for $1,000, leaving Belding with an outstanding liability of $1,500.[45] The loss of the factory was duly recorded in the credit-rating

12.33 *A picture of the Welding pottery from the* Brantford Expositor *of December 8, 1891. Welding is seated in the carriage.* Courtesy Brantford Public Library.

agency in New York City and credit references during 1873 and early 1874 give no pecuniary worth for the pottery. By January, 1875, the credit-rating books indicate that the pottery had been rebuilt and the manufacture of stoneware resumed. In January, 1875, the credit rating for Welding is listed as "good" and the business worth $5,000 to $10,000.

W. E. Welding (1873-1894)
Welding rebuilt the factory on a larger scale, making the building two storeys high and of buff-coloured brick. By August, 1873, work had recommenced in the factory, shown in plate 12.33. Welding was a keen businessman who saw the need to diversify the pottery's products. Although the grey stoneware containers with cobalt-blue floral decoration were in steady demand, there was a growing interest

in fancier wares for the home, including teapots, bowls, bake pans, jardinières, and other domestic containers in the Rockingham and yellow glazes then popular in America. As an example of new products, Welding produced the well-known "Beaver" and "Rachel-at-the-Well" teapots. Evidently, Welding considered his own profile as worthy of honour, and it too became a source of decoration for the ever-popular teapot (plate 12.34).

Another exceptional piece of pottery produced during Welding's time at the pottery is an unusually large Rockingham-glazed picture frame. On the back of the frame, and at the bottom, is the signature of Welding with Brantford, C.W. impressed beneath. At the top of the frame are the initials I.H.A. ("I" is the German "J") for Jacob Henry Ahrens (plates 12.35, 12.36, 12.37). Because of its size, inscriptions and excellent condition, this picture frame must be one of the finest pieces from the Brantford pottery. We do not know the occasion that prompted Welding to make

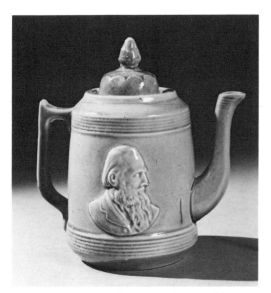

12.34 *Yellow-glazed teapot with applied likeness of W. E. Welding.* Courtesy Brant County Museum, Brantford.

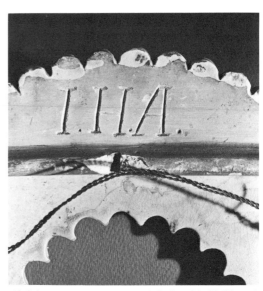

12.36 *Inscribed initials of I.(Jacob) H.(Henry) A.(Ahrens) at top back of the picture frame shown in 12.35.*

12.35 *A large (eighteen inches high) Rockingham-glazed picture frame made by Welding as a presentation piece to J. H. Ahrens of Paris.*

this presentation piece for Ahrens. Other examples of wares produced during Welding's time are shown in plates 12.38, 12.39, 12.40.

12.37 *Signature of Welding at bottom back of the picture frame of plate 12.35.*

During Welding's ownership of the business the assessed value of the buildings and stock increased from $2,000 to a high level of over $11,000 in the early 1890s.[46]

The pottery business was interrupted again in late July, 1883, when another fire destroyed the interior of the building and the pottery stock. The loss was estimated at $10,000.[47] This time the shell of the building was saved, and it was only necessary to rebuild the in-

12.38 *Large quantities of stoneware jugs and crocks were produced during Welding's many years at the pottery. This jug is one of the more elaborate examples of decoration on stoneware.*

12.40 *An unusual shape for an Ontario stoneware container; this jug was produced at the Brantford stoneware factory during Welding's time.*

12.39 *A miniature produced during Welding's ownership.*

terior. The new building, similar in appearance to the one destroyed in the fire, was completed sometime in late 1883 or early 1884.

By 1894 Welding was ready to retire. With the increase in the volume of the pottery business had come increased sophistication in pottery technology. What was necessary for the continued success of the business was a potter with a thorough knowledge of the trade. The obvious choice was Henry Schuler.

Brantford Stoneware Manufacturing Co., Ltd. (1894-1905)
On August 11, 1894, letters patent were issued under the Ontario Joint Stock Companies' Letters Patent Act, incorporating the Brantford Stoneware Manufacturing Co., Ltd. A report of stockholders of the new company made to

12.41 *A collection of milk pitchers in honey yellows and pinks. The production of more artistic* *pieces began at Brantford during Welding's time and continued until the factory closed in 1906.*

the Provincial Secretary's Office lists ten persons, of whom only one, Henry Schuler, was a potter. The corporation was authorized to issue stock up to $50,000, although only $30,200 of stock was ever subscribed, and of this only $10,200 worth of stock actually paid for by 1895.

In spite of the obvious financial strain on the Brantford Pottery, the business prospered in the early part of the twentieth century. Wares produced during this period were marked BRANTFORD STONEWARE MFG. CO. /BRANTFORD, ONT. or B.S. MFG. CO., LTD./BRANTFORD. The marks BRANT-FORD/CANADA and BRANTFORD were also impressed on wares, but usually restricted to the fancier art wares. During the 1894-1906 period, the company manufactured Rockingham, caneware, majolica, stove linings, firebrick, and wares for chemical and sanitary purposes. There was also a line of art wares, decorated with glazes in bright blue, copper-green, and iron-red colours. Some pieces had several colours of glaze, from blue to green to honey yellow, in a wash effect (plates 12.41, 12.42, 12.43). Probably the most outstanding piece produced during these

years is a presentation tobacco holder (plate 12.44). This is a large piece (eleven inches high) and is covered in a dark-green glaze. In the centre among the group of tree stumps (the largest stump opens to hold tobacco) sits a figure of an Indian leaning on his lacrosse stick. The inscription reads "Othello's Occupations Gone." When the lid of the largest stump is removed, there is the hand-written inscription, "By T. O'Brien, November 26, 1904." O'Brien first worked in London, Ontario, when John Marks was operating a pottery there, but by 1900 he was in Brantford, where he resided until 1905.[48]

A picture of the moulding room of the Brantford Pottery, taken sometime between 1900 and 1905, is shown in plate 12.45. On the left is John Marks, and at the rear centre is Lincoln Schuler, son of Henry Schuler, at the time the foreman of the shipping department. Of special interest are the pieces of pottery being made on the workbench, including a piece similar to the presentation tobacco holder of plate 12.44, and a tall vase, similar in shape to the one in plate 12.42, but with a floral decoration.

The Brantford Stoneware Manufacturing

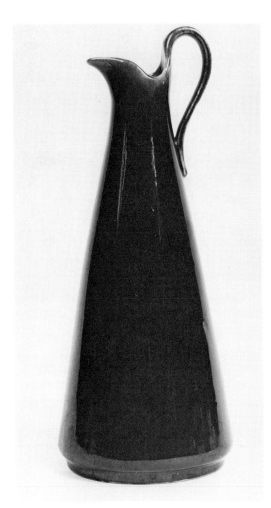

12.42 *Tall flower vase in warm brown colour.*
Courtesy Brant County Museum, Brantford.

12.43 *Jardinière with leaf motif and marked BRANTFORD. Such decorative pieces were finished in a variety of colours, including green, blue and brown.*

12.44 *Unusual presentation piece with inscription "Othello's Occupation's Gone" and "Albert." The piece is finished in dark green glaze. The lid for the largest tree trunk can be removed for storage of tobacco. The inside of this lid is inscribed with the name of the potter who made the piece in 1904.* Courtesy Brant County Museum, Brantford.

Co. had a short period of prosperity from late 1897 to early 1904, but for reasons still not fully known this prosperity came to an abrupt end. Perhaps it was the under-capitalization of the enterprise, as it wasn't until 1904 that the $20,000 of outstanding stock (with the exception of $550 of stock that one investor was unable to pay for) was actually paid in full. The annual report of the corporation for the year 1905 indicates that there was no secretary-treasurer. The next report on the business to the Provincial Secretary's office is a letter from Henry Schuler, dated November 8, 1907, which reads:

I beg to advise that about two years ago the

12.45 *Picture of moulding-room of the Brantford
Stoneware Manufacturing Co., Ltd., ca. 1905.*
Courtesy Paris Public Library, Paris, Ontario.

*above company found it necessary to go out of
business owing to losses, and the factory and
other assets were sold to pay the debts of the
concern . . . as the company has no funds it
could not take steps to cancel its charter . . .*[49]

On January 26, 1907, the plant and the land
had been sold by the company for $9,000 to
the Brantford Rag and Metal Company.[50] The
once bustling pottery had come to an end.

A second pottery business operated in
Brantford from 1889 to 1897. Its owners had a
close connection with the Brantford Stoneware firm. The founder of the business, John

A. Kennedy, is first reported as working in
Brantford in 1871, probably as an employee
of Welding & Belding.[51] By 1889 he was
operating a pottery at 159 Darling Street, one
street north of the stoneware factory.[52] References in Brantford city directories indicate that
Kennedy owned the pottery until 1895.[53] The
next year Wendlin Schuler, brother of Henry
Schuler, had taken over the small pottery on
Darling Street. An advertisement in a directory
of that period reads, "W. B. Schuler, manufacturer of flower pots, hanging baskets, seed
pans, lily pots, lawn vases, glazed ware, etc."[54]
From the Brantford Assessment rolls and
credit-rating information it appears that
Wendlin Schuler worked only a year or so at
the pottery,[55] since by 1903 he was the town's
first letter carrier.[56] A miniature jug, produced
by Kennedy and made of unglazed redware, is

shown in plate 12.46. The pottery was not a threat to the nearby stoneware factory.

BRANTFORD TOWNSHIP

A small pottery was reported to be operating in Brantford Township in the late 1850s at Strawberry Hill. The name of its owners and its precise location have not been determined. An advertisement in the *Daily Globe* of April 24, 1858, reads:

STRAWBERRY HILL POTTERY
To merchants. Tin and dark glazed ware being great conductors of heat, the subscriber has succeeded in getting a white glaze, producing a great deal more butter . . . ''

Two years later in the May 22 issue of the *Daily Globe*, there appeared an advertisement of the sale of the pottery.

. . . that valuable property known as 'Straw-berry Hill', in the township of Brantford, con-taining about 60 acres of land.

Presumably, this marked the end of the pottery business.

12.46 *Miniature jug with impressed name J.A. KENNEDY/Brantford, Ont. The jug is unglazed and is made of terra cotta-colour clay.*

13.
Factories of the City of Hamilton–Wentworth County Region

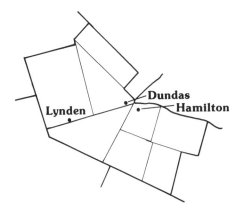

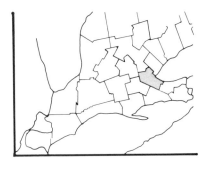

Fig. 13.1   *Map showing location of potteries of the City of Hamilton and Wentworth County Region.*

This region is a thriving centre of industrial activity in the heartland of southern Ontario. In the nineteenth century there were industries of every description, including the major pottery factories. Today Hamilton is an important centre of the steel industry. Few people would be aware of its historical significance with regard to the Ontario pottery trade of the last quarter of the nineteenth and the first half of the twentieth centuries, but Hamilton during this long period was the location of six potteries, two of which operated under various names, and four of which became large factories that produced restaurant, household and garden products. In surrounding Wentworth County, there were two smaller potteries, one in the village of Lynden and the second in the town of Dundas. The locations of the nineteenth-century potteries are shown in figure 13.1.

City of Hamilton

Frederick Ashbaugh
The earliest known pottery in the region was established by Frederick Ashbaugh, Jr. The 1816 Ancaster assessment roll indicates that by that year he had established a pottery in conjunction with his farm, which was located in the area now bounded by Main Street West and Stroud Road, on land presently occupied by McMaster University. Miss G. L Buttrum, writing on the Ashbaugh family, mentions that the farm became the site of several brickyards in the latter part of the nineteenth century.[1]

Joseph Shearsmith
The next pottery to be established in Hamilton was operated by Joseph Shearsmith, on lot 28 on the east side of Catherine Street. Shearsmith was in business from 1848 to 1866. Tax assessment rolls report that the business con-

S. P. FOSTER & CO.

— MANUFACTURERS OF —

Florists' Supplies

Gas Logs, Etc.

MAIN STREET, WEST OF GARTH,

HAMILTON, - - - - **ONTARIO·**

13.1 *Advertisement from* Might's Ontario Directory of 1905 *for S. P. Foster, describing the horticultural wares produced at the Foster Pottery.*

sisted of a brick building and a pottery shed.[2] Little else is known about Shearsmith's works, either from existing records or artifacts.

W & R Campbell (1860-1866)/
Wm. Campbell & Son (1866-1882)
William & Robert Campbell moved from Burlington to Hamilton around 1860, when they opened a pottery on lots 9 and 10 on Garth Street, bounded by Concession & Main. In the 1864 Provincial Exhibition this partnership was awarded a first prize for the best assortment of pottery and a second prize for the best water filters, and was commended for an assortment of lawn vases and hanging flower pots.[3] Again the next year, the firm received a first prize for the best assortment of pottery and an extra prize for lawn vases.[4] The partnership was dissolved by 1866, and William Campbell continued to operate a pottery with his son Robert Campbell, Jr.[5] From 1866 until 1877, William Campbell's business was operated under the trade name William Campbell & Son, a partnership recorded in the registry office in 1872.[6]

The 1870-71 census gives some details of the pottery during the ownership of William Campbell. The firm produced earthenware and sewage pipes valued at $12,000 annually. The factory employed sixteen male hands and used 500 tons of clay and 500 cords of wood

annually.[7] By 1872 William Campbell & Son began to specialize in sewage pipes, apparently more profitable than other lines of pottery, because of the rapid expansion of urban utilities. William Campbell died around 1875, for in the next year his two sons, Robert Campbell, Jr., and Joseph D. Campbell, are the only persons listed as operating the business or living in the Campbell household.[8] In 1882 the company became known as the Campbell Sewer Pipe Company Ltd.

Campbell Sewer Pipe Company Ltd.
(1882-1888)/Hamilton & Toronto Sewer
Pipe Company (1888-1940)
Pipes produced during this long period of steady growth were marked HAMILTON, and street crews still find the stoneware pipes when digging in roads in southern Ontario. In 1888 the company was merged with two others to form the Hamilton & Toronto Sewer Pipe Company, with a factory on Wentworth Street at the Grand Trunk Railway crossing. As demand for stoneware pipes slackened, the business began to decline. The corporation was officially dissolved in 1940.[9]

Foster Pottery Company
A fire on November 24, 1974, brought to an end the historic Foster pottery on Frid Street in Hamilton. The business was started in 1878 by Leonard Foster, on lot 3 on the south side of Main Street at Frid, and remained at that location until the fire. Leonard Foster operated

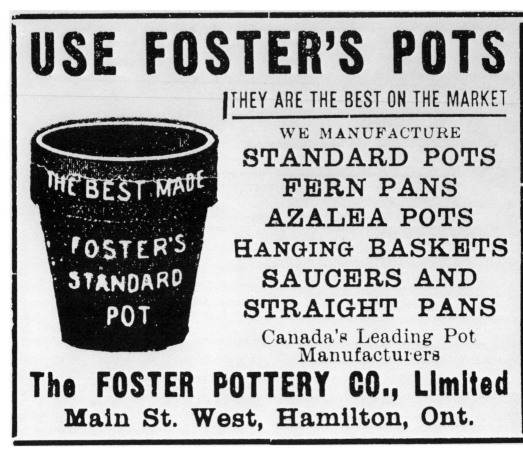

USE FOSTER'S POTS

THEY ARE THE BEST ON THE MARKET

WE MANUFACTURE

STANDARD POTS
FERN PANS
AZALEA POTS
HANGING BASKETS
SAUCERS AND
STRAIGHT PANS

Canada's Leading Pot
Manufacturers

The FOSTER POTTERY CO., Limited
Main St. West, Hamilton, Ont.

THE BEST MADE
FOSTER'S
STANDARD
POT

13.2   *Advertisement of Foster Pottery from Cana-*
dian Horticulturalist *of September, 1911. This was
a standard advertisement of the pottery for many
years.*

the business for fourteen years, specializing in
flowerpots and novelty items for the horticultural trade. He died in 1892 or 1893 and his
son Sidney P. Foster took over the works. An
advertisement from this period is shown in
plate 13.1.

In 1902 Elizabeth Foster (widow of Leonard
Foster) and Fred L. Foster obtained letters
patent for the Foster Pottery Co., Ltd.[10] For
reasons not known, the corporation was dissolved in March, 1912.[11] A statement of assets
and liabilities dated July 29, 1911, indicates
the extent of the business operations. Pottery
sales for the previous year were $16,590; of
this amount, $5,871 was spent on wages
and salaries, and $1,123 was spent for coal
for firing the kilns. The firm regularly adver-

tised in horticultural publications. A frequently
repeated advertisement from this period is
shown in plate 13.2.

The business continued after 1912, with
Stanley Foster and Fred L. Foster as owners.
Various members of the family were involved
in the business during the succeeding years.
An Ontario government report in 1930 states
that the business was making 20,000 flowerpots a day. Surface clay was cleaned in an
open-top pugmill and stored from three to six
weeks before being pugged a second time. A
Baird auger machine produced clay blanks
for four semi-automatic presses, which were
designed and patented by Stanley and Fred
L. Foster. (Details of this machine are given
on page 9.) Four round down-draft kilns, each
eighteen feet in diameter, were kept busy firing
the flowerpots.[12] In plate 13.3 a workman is
stacking flowerpots in a kiln prior to firing.
Flowerpots were dried on wooden planks

placed on steel racks (plate 13.4) on the second floor of the building above the kilns.[13] A fire insurance plan (plate 13.5) gives a detailed description of the floor plan of the factory, including the location of the kilns and storage areas.

The business continued in the Foster family, with little change in the machinery or method of producing the flowerpots, until 1972, when Edwin Foster, grandson of the founder, sold the business to George & Donald Harrison, who formed the Foster Pottery (1972) Ltd. The company was busy turning out about 100,000 flowerpots a week when the disastrous fire of 1974 brought the enterprise to an end.

The end of the business signalled a shortage of clay flowerpots in Canada, as the Foster Pottery was the last major producer. To fill the

immediate need, pots were imported from Germany and Italy, and this new source continues to supply a large part of the present market. Foster's original semi-automatic machines were recovered from the fire and are now in use in Burlington, where an enterprising Canadian is again trying to sell Canadian-made flowerpots to Ontario horticulturalists.

Hamilton Pottery (Robert Campbell) (1866-1898)/
R. Campbell's Sons (1898-1928)
Robert Campbell, Sr., moved with his brother from Wellington Square (now Burlington) in Halton County in 1859 and established the partnership of W. & R. Campbell, already discussed in this chapter. In 1872 Robert Campbell, Sr., founded the largest pottery in the city of Hamilton. Located at Maiden Lane, between Poulette and Garth Streets, it was first

13.3 *Loading a kiln with flowerpots at the Foster Pottery.*

13.4 *Flowerpots drying on wooden planks prior to being fired in the kiln at the Foster Pottery.*

known as the Hamilton West Pottery (1872-74), but soon changed its name to the Hamilton Pottery (1874-1928). In the 1880s it moved to Locke Street, where it remained during the rest of its history. Later names for the business were Canada Potteries Ltd. (1928-29), and finally Hamilton Potteries Ltd. (1929-   ). The business is of special interest because of the survival of photographs and other documentary information that can give us an accurate insight into the manufacturing techniques used in a factory pottery of the period, as well as a record of the types of ware that were produced, especially during the 1890-1947 period. During the 1890s the company was the major Canadian producer of restaurant, kitchen and sanitary ware. A

photograph of the plant, taken around 1929, is shown in plate 13.6.

Robert Campbell, Sr., drew up his will in November, 1897, a few months before his death on January 3, 1898. In it, he stated his wish that his three sons should continue the pottery business.[14] His sons, the first of whom had joined the business as early as 1892, formed the partnership known as R. Campbell's Sons on January 1, 1898, two days before their father's death.[15] One measure of the success of the business prior to this date is the probated will of Robert Campbell, Sr. His estate was valued at over $95,000. His real estate included the pottery building, which was valued at $11,585.[16] The pottery was located on lots 29, 30, 31 and 32, on the south side of Jackson Street, and lots 59 and 60, on the north side of Canada Street. This remained

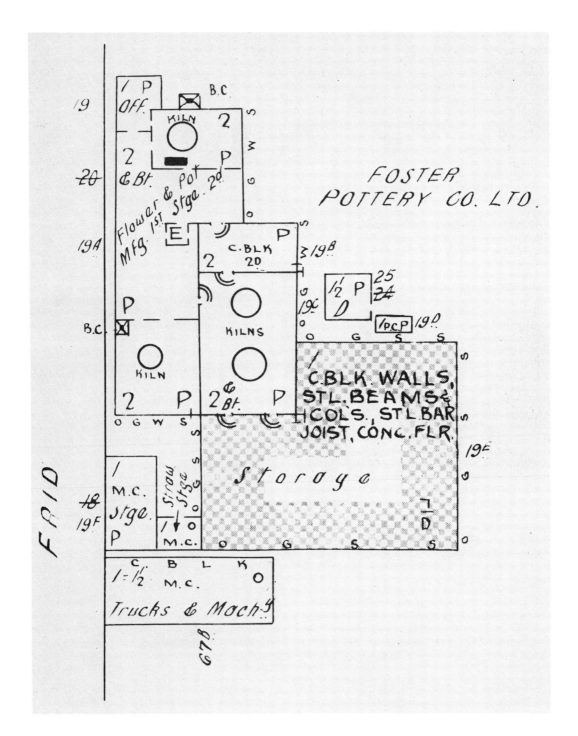

13.5 *Fire insurance plan of the Foster Pottery showing the location of kilns, storage areas. Courtesy Ontario Archives.*

13.6 *R. Campbell's Sons pottery ca. 1929. The building was located on Locke Street, Hamilton. Courtesy Ontario Archives.*

the location of the factory until it was destroyed by fire in 1947. The importance of R. Campbell's Sons can be summarized from a 1906 report of the Ontario Department of Mines:

The firm manufactures many varieties of pottery and stoneware. Tea-pots, coffee-pots, stove mouldings, stove linings, and all classes of ordinary stoneware, such as crocks, cuspidors, etc. including stone mugs, jugs, and water tanks . . . are made by this firm.[17]

The report emphasized that the success of the business (from the viewpoint of the geologist who wrote it) was in the use of imported clays from New Jersey and Pennsylvania, enabling the firm to produce wares of superior quality. This allowed them to compete, as other Canadian firms had been unable

to do, with imported goods from the United States.[18] The company also carried a complete line of imported Japanese china, thus maintaining their dominance in the wholesale crockery business. An advertisement from the R. Campbell's Sons period is shown in plate 13.7.

The process used to make pottery in the plant contrasts with traditional country workshops, where most of the work was done by hand-turning wares made of local clays. The firm's advantage was not only its closeness to markets, but the use of finer quality clays that could be fired at a higher temperature, about 2400° F. to produce oven-ware.

The manufacturing techniques used in ca. 1930 were described by Montgomery:

The pottery is made from a blend of clays which is blunged, filter pressed, pugged and hand-pressed or jiggered in plaster moulds . . . after drying on steam racks the pieces are then

Hamilton Pottery

ESTABLISHED
──1852──

Manufacturers of the Celebrated CHAMPION Tea Pots, also the best lines of Rockingham, Yellow and Yellow White lined ware, made in America, consisting of Tea Pots, Pitchers, Spittoons, Bakers, Bowls, Bed Pans, etc.

Also Direct Importers of **Japanese China**

Personal attention given to all Mail Orders

Champion

Address   96 to 118 South Locke Street

R. Campbell's Sons, Hamilton

13.7 *Hamilton Pottery Advertisement indicating the wares produced in the pottery. A line of Japanese porcelain was also sold by the company.* Courtesy Ontario Archives.

13.8 *Pottery store room at R. Campbell's Sons, Hamilton.* Courtesy Ontario Archives.

13.9, 10, and 11 *Pages from the Canada Potteries Ltd. catalogue ca. 1928-29 show that traditional Rockingham wares in well-established types were still being produced in Canada.*

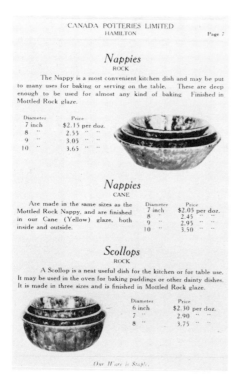

given a first burn at a low temperature. The ware is then glazed and reburned to the maturing temperature of the body and glaze.[19]

The fired ware was stored on shelves (plate 13.8) and then packed in barrels or willow crates when shipped to customers.

The three Campbell sons did not operate the business together for very long. John Dilworth Campbell died in 1901, and Colin C. and Robert Wesley were left to operate the business.[20] By 1912, only Colin C. Campbell was listed in directories as working at the firm, now in association with Andrew J. Taylor.[21] In October of 1916 the partnership was composed solely of Agnes Maud Campbell, widow of Colin C. Campbell, and this fact was recorded in a partnership declaration filed in the Wentworth County Registry Office.[22] The business continued under the name R. Campbell's Sons Hamilton Pottery until May 19, 1928, when it was sold and renamed Canada Potteries Ltd. Eighteen months later, on November 6, 1929, the name was officially changed yet again, this time to Hamilton Potteries Ltd., as the previous name had been pre-empted by another pottery in Trenton, Ontario.[23]

Canada Potteries Ltd. (1928-1929)/ Hamilton Potteries Ltd. (1929-)

Since many of the company's products were not marked, two early known catalogues are useful guides for identifying shapes and sizes of wares, if not the exact pieces, produced at the Hamilton factory. The earliest known catalogue is dated from the 1912-16 period. It is thirty-two pages long and contains a large assortment of wares for sale to stores and businesses. A later catalogue, dating to the 1928-1929 period, and headed Canada Potteries Ltd., is shorter and advertises a smaller selection of wares, but the basic types and sizes have not changed. Three pages from the 1928-1929 catalogue are illustrated in plates 13.9, 13.10 and 13.11. The characteristic Rockingham and yellow-glazed wares, so popular in the last half of the nineteenth century, were still in demand in Hamilton as late as 1929; the shapes so frequently used to date pottery to that century are also still available from the pottery at this later period. This should suggest some caution in dating Ontario Rockingham bowls and jugs!

13.12 *Three examples of yellow-glazed bowls. The middle bowl is marked CANADA POTTERIES; the other two are marked HAMILTON POTTERIES.*

The basic similarity of items marketed by the company over a period of fifty or more years was demonstrated to me when I examined a private collection, where identical shapes and glaze colours were found on pieces marked either Canada Potteries or Hamilton Potteries. The bowls illustrated on the left and right in

13.13 *Straight-sided teapot marked on its base CAMPBELL/CANADA.*

plate 13.12 are marked HAMILTON POTTERIES, while the middle bowl is marked CANADA POTTERIES. The straight-sided teapot of plate 13.13 is marked CAMPBELL/ CANADA and is advertised in the R. Campbell's Sons 1912-1916 catalogue, and again in the Canada Potteries Ltd., catalogue of 1928-29. The glazed flowerpots in plate 13.14 are marked HAMILTON POTTERIES and are not shown in the catalogues, suggesting that they were a new product after 1929.

During the Canada Potteries Ltd., and Hamilton Potteries Ltd., periods, the wares were glazed in the traditional Rockingham or "Rock" glaze, as well as cane (yellow) glaze. Some of the domestic wares were lined with white glaze inside. Many of the household items were produced in brightly coloured glazes, including bright yellows, greens and blues. For example, the flowerpots in plate 13.14 are in mottled purple glaze (left) and light green glaze (right), while the bowls in plate 13.12 have a bright yellow glaze. Another common mark from this pottery is shown on the bright yellow baking dishes in plate 13.15. These are marked HAMILTON POTTERIES/ CANADA/OVEN/PROOF.

The decline in demand for pottery in the 1930s saw a shift from crockery to the manufacture of electrical porcelains and refractories, porcelain bathroom fittings and insulated pads. The production of oven-proof pottery, including porcelain baking dishes, was not entirely discontinued, though.

13.14 *Two flowerpots produced at the Hamilton Potteries after 1930. The flowerpot on the left has a deep mottled purple glaze, and the flowerpot on the right has a light green glaze.*

The manufacture of pottery at the plant came to an abrupt end shortly before midnight on September 21, 1947 when a spectacular fire — reported by the *Hamilton Spectator* to have started in an area over the top of one of the four kilns — completely destroyed the building and its contents. The damage to the building and stock was estimated to exceed $75,000.[24] About one hundred employees were put out of work, as the business never reopened in Hamilton. The corporation moved to Brantford, Ontario, where they con-

tinued to produce porcelain products under the name Hamilton Porcelains Ltd. A letter to the Ministry of Consumer and Commercial Relations, dated July 7, 1969, reports, "Hamilton Potteries Ltd. is not currently actively engaged in any business and is now acting solely as a holding company for the shares of Hamilton Porcelains Ltd., an associate company."[25]

John Cranston & Son
John Cranston and his son George moved to Hamilton from Toronto, where they had worked at the stoneware factory on Broadview Avenue. On July 1, 1894, they formed the partnership of John Cranston & Son.[26] The business continued until ca. 1920.

The pottery was located at 210 Garth Street and was known as the Wentworth Pottery. In the early years they advertised assorted types of earthenware (plate 13.16), but in the twentieth century their advertisements concentrated on flowerpots and other items for the horticultural trade (plate 13.17).

WENTWORTH COUNTY
Lynden
The pottery in this small village was on two lots, totalling a quarter-acre in the village. The

13.15 *Three sizes of household baking dishes; each one is marked HAMILTON/CANADA/ OVEN/PROOF*

13.16 *Advertisement from* Lovell's Directory
for the Dominion of Canada 1896-97 *for the
Wentworth Pottery in 1896 shows the variety of
wares produced at the factory. Courtesy Ontario
Archives.*

village was never very large, and consisted of
part of lot 12, concession 1, Beverley Township. Very little is known of the wares produced at the site, but there is a well-known
sequence of potters who operated the busi-

13.17 *An advertisement from the* Canadian Horticulturalist *for Wentworth Pottery indicates that by
1910, the factory was producing mainly florist
supplies. Courtesy Ontario Archives.*

ness during the forty years the workshop was
making pottery. These included:

Charles Lyons (Lines)	ca. 1854-65
John P. Smith	1866-68
Joseph & Edwin Bradwin	1868-72
Joseph Bradwin	1873-77
John Cranston	1877-82
Marx & Hoehn	1884-86
John Marx	1887-90
John Humberstone	1890-93
James E. Tait	1894- ca. 1899

John P. Smith purchased the pottery site for
eighty dollars on October 1, 1867, from Be-
noni Van Sickle.[27] Smith sold the land and
pottery building for $650 in 1868 to Joseph &
Edwin Bradwin.[28] The Bradwin brothers were
from Paris, Ontario, where they had learned
the pottery trade at either the Ahrens or Marlatt
pottery. Their father had died when they were
teenagers and they apprenticed as potters to
support their mother and her large family.
Their first venture as independent potters was

WENTWORTH POTTERY

Standard Flower Pots, Fern Pans, Hanging Baskets, Cut Flower Jars and all Florists Supplies.

Mail orders given prompt attention.

John Cranston & Son,
Hamilton, Can.

here at Lynden. The 1870-71 census describes the pottery business during their partnership. They hired four male hands who worked twelve months of the year to produce 5,000 crocks with a value of $2,000.[29] Bradwin's employees were S. Page, John Lines, Robert Kerr and Samuel Haines. Edwin Bradwin left for Mount Forest, Wellington County in 1872, leaving the business in the hands of Joseph. Joseph continued the workshop until 1877, when he moved to Mount Forest. The business was sold on June 30, 1877, to John Cranston.[30] Cranston operated the business for five years, before moving to Toronto.

The pottery remained unused until 1884, when John Marx and Frederick Hoehn formed a partnership to make earthenware.[31] They purchased the pottery on March 1, 1884, paying $350.[32] Marx had come to Lynden from the Ahrens pottery in Paris, Ontario, which had been destroyed by a flood the previous year. Hoehn had worked with Marx in 1871-72 in London, Ontario. These two potters therefore had a long association and were familiar with the requirements for the operation of a small workshop. For unknown reasons, the partnership was dissolved in 1886, when Hoehn sold his interest to Marx for $300.[33] Despite hard work and good craftsmanship, qualities that Marx had shown

in Paris, the business did not succeed, and Marx went bankrupt in 1890. The pottery was assigned to his creditors.[34] The next owner of the business was John S. Humberstone, of the well-known York County pottery-making family. He continued the business until 1893. The business was taken over by James E. Tait but his work came to an end on November 16, 1894, when fire destroyed the building.[35] The loss of stock was over $500. It appears that Tait never reopened the shop. In 1899 he sold the property back to Benoni Van Sickle, the local mill owner who had sold the property to John Smith some thirty-three years earlier.[36]

Dundas

In 1847 a pottery was established by Robert Swindle on the north side of Park Street in the town of Dundas.[37] In 1859 he leased the business to Robert Hollingshead, who had come the previous year to work for Swindle. The 1860-61 census indicates that the business employed three hands at an average monthly wage of $17.50 each.[38] Robert Hollingshead, with the assistance of his son William, operated the business until 1868. The exact location of the pottery is not certain, but I believe it was on the northwest corner of Park and Cross Streets.[39]

14.
Workshops of the Niagara Peninsula

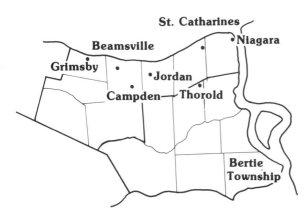

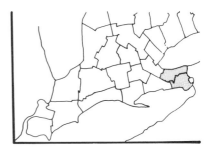

Fig. 14.1 *Location of potteries in the Niagara Peninsula during the nineteenth century.*

The Niagara Peninsula, comprising Lincoln and Welland Counties, was one of the earliest areas in the province settled by potters. The peninsula was a natural land-bridge between the United States and the backwoods of Upper Canada, and many potters immigrated through the Peninsula area during the early part of the nineteenth century.

We may never know the total number of potteries in the area, or the names of many of the earliest craftsmen, because most documentary records are dated to the second half of that century.

The locations of the potteries that have been found in the region are shown in figure 14.1.

WELLAND COUNTY

Bertie Township
George W. Brehms, a German-born potter, purchased a half-acre part of the west half of lot 11, concession 11, Bertie Township, in 1848.[1] He is reported in the 1851-52 census as living in a one-storey log house with an attached shop.[2] Brehms sold the property in 1856, at which time he was living in Crowland Township.[3]

Thorold
A pottery was begun in the town of Thorold around 1851 by William Ramsey, on lots 31 and 32 on the east side of Canal Street (now Ormond Street South), north of Lyndon Street East. Ramsey purchased the property in 1854, and the deed indicates that Ramsey had already erected a pottery on the site.[4] The 1851-52 census report notes that Ramsey's Thorold Pottery employed five persons.[5] Two of these were James McCluskie, later active in the Derby Pottery, Kilsyth, Grey County, and Robert Wallace, later working in New Hamburg, Waterloo County. In 1855 Nicholas Eberhardt purchased a nearby lot and presumably worked at Ramsey's workshop.[6] Eberhardt sold his one-fifth-acre lot in 1859 before going to work at a pottery in Paris, Brant County.[7]

161

Ramsey had a number of financial interests in Thorold, including a temperance hotel.[8] He sold the pottery business in 1869 to Orin Bemiss, who had held a mortgage on the property. The same year Bemiss sold the property to Samuel Briddon,[9] who was in the pottery business with John Booth, under the partnership of Briddon & Booth.[10] The partnership did not last for long, as the 1870-71 census reports Samuel Briddon as the sole proprietor of the business. In the census year the pottery operated nine months and produced 10,000 crocks valued at $1,000.[11] Associated with the business from 1859 until 1869 was Henry Baker, reported in the 1870-71 census as working in Peterborough, Peterborough County.[12]

Samuel Briddon sold the pottery in 1873 to his son Walter, then twenty-one years old.[13] Samuel Briddon regained control of the property in 1875 after legal action in Chancery Court. The next year he sold lots 31 and 32 to John Pendergast, a blacksmith, for $300.[14] Soon afterwards, Walter Briddon purchased the pottery site, but leased it to Matthew Booth, son of John Booth, for a year. A directory published in 1878 reports, "The Thorold Pottery employs six hands in the manufacture

14.1 *Advertisement of John Martindale for potters from the* Niagara Gleaner & Niagara Newspaper, *April 10, 1824. Courtesy Public Archives.*

of earthenware and sewer pipe."[15] Although Walter Briddon owned the pottery until 1898, it appears from town assessment rolls that John & Matthew Booth had leased the business for a number of years.

LINCOLN COUNTY

Niagara
John Martindale advertised in 1824 for potters for his business in Niagara (see plate 14.1). The only other record of Martindale in the area was a crown patent for lot 131 in the town of Niagara, granted to him in 1842.[16] At the same time, he also purchased the west half of the adjoining lot 132. He died in 1847 and his wife sold the properties on July 2, 1849, for £50.[17]

St. Catharines
Lyman Parsons and his wife Achsah were potting in the town of St. Catharines in 1818, and in the May 28 issue of the *Niagara Spectator* newspaper, a short note announced, "L. & A. Parsons recently established a pottery business at St. Catharines . . . ." The business was located on Ontario Street. Marcus Smith's 1852 map of the town shows Parsons' land on the west side of Ontario Street, south of Cherry Alley, now the southwest corner of Ontario and Trafalgar Streets. Although Parsons was

WANTED,

ONE or two POTTERS, to whom liberal wages will be given—stability and sobriety are looked for. Apply to

JOHN MARTINDALE.

Niagara, Feb. 20. 1824. 14.

14.2 *Close-up of B.LENT/UC impressed stamp on sherd from excavations at Jordan, Ontario.* Courtesy David Rupp, St. Catharines.

14.3 *Close-up of B. LENT/UC impressed stamp on sherd from excavations at Jordan, Ontario.* Courtesy David Rupp, St. Catharines.

potting in the town by 1818, he did not purchase the pottery property on Ontario Street until 1823.[18] He continued his business until the late 1850s.

Jordan

B. Lent operated an earthenware pottery on part of lot 18, concession 5, Louth Township, during the late 1820s. Lent may have come from New Jersey, where a potter with the same

name worked in the 1820s.[19] During the years 1976 and 1977 a team of archaeologists under the sponsorship of the Jordan Pottery Study Project uncovered a rectangular updraft kiln and an associated waster dump.[20] A number of sherds with B. LENT/U.C. (see plates 14.2 and 14.3) were uncovered. Decorative motifs used at the pottery include: a rosette stamp, below the shoulder on jars, or on the shoulder below the neck on bottles, or on a lid above the rim; a plain circular stamp on jars in association with rosette stamps; a diamond-shaped stamp made of nine small diamonds on one large crock below the rim. In one instance the rosettes were alternately coloured with a greenish and whitish slip. An earthenware milk pitcher with a clear lead glaze, marked B. LENT, exists in a private collection.

Beamsville

There were three potteries in Beamsville in the nineteenth century. William Schwab moved from Preston, Waterloo County, sometime after 1834, and settled in Beamsville, Clinton Township, where he established a shop on a quarter-acre piece of land at the northwest corner of King & Ontario Streets. Schwab purchased the land in 1853 for £125.[21] A jug produced by Schwab is shown in plate 14.4. It has a clear lead glaze over a buff earthenware clay. The 1860-61 census indicates that the shop employed two hands to make 10,000 jugs, crocks, etc., per year. Fifteen tons of clay were used.[22] Beginning ca. 1863 Schwab's son, William Jr., joined the business.[23] In the 1870-71 census the business is reported to be operating for eight months of the year, producing 8400 pieces of earthenware pottery valued at $700.[24] The pottery was discontinued ca. 1875.

The second pottery in Beamsville was operated by Cyrus Little, who was born in the United States in 1799, and who came to Canada around 1833. In the 1842 census of the Niagara District, he is listed as a potter working in Beamsville.[25] The earliest record of land owned by Little is from the year 1857, when he bought two pieces of land, part of block B on King Street. He purchased the land for £150 from Jacob Beam.[26] The 1860-61

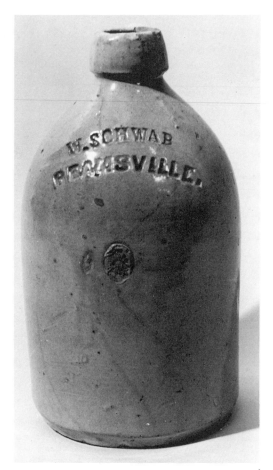

14.4 *Jug with cream slip and clear glaze and impressed mark W. SCHWAB/BEAMSVILLE. Courtesy Jordan Historical Museum of the Twenty, Jordan.*

14.5 *Earthenware dog with D. ORTH/1892 inscribed on base. Courtesy Mrs. Elizabeth Collard.*

census reports that Little employed three hands to produce 20,000 pieces of pottery a year. The goods were valued at $800.[27] Two of the workmen were his sons Julius and Augustus, both listed as potters in the same census. In the next decade the pottery became known as Little & Son (Augustus), and was reported in directories of the time as a "pottery and tile manufactory." It appears that the business was only slightly dependent on brickmaking, for the 1870-71 census indicates that the value of bricks was $1,675, while pottery wares produced were valued at $4,500.[28] In the year 1870 Little worked the pottery for eight months and employed four men at a total

annual yearly wage of $250.[29] The last documentary reference to the pottery was in the year 1872,[30] by which time the business had been closed. The property was sold by Augustus Little in 1872.[31] There is no pottery ware known to have been marked with Little's name.

The third pottery in Beamsville was operated by Lewis Cornwall on lot 6 on the south side of King Street, east of Academy. His pottery shop is reported in the 1851-52 census, but no details of the operation are supplied.[32] Cornwall discontinued his business before 1860 and turned to the trade of blacksmithing. The pottery property was sold in 1866.[33]

Campden
Daniel Orth began potting sometime before

14.6 *Miniature red earthenware spittoon with Campden/D. Orth/1878 incribed on base.* Courtesy Jordan Historical Museum of the Twenty, Jordan.

14.7 *Red earthenware storage jar with clear lead glaze.* Courtesy Royal Ontario Museum.

1851, on land owned by his brother John. The site was known as lot 11, concession 7, Clinton Township, near the town of Campden. In the 1851-52 census Daniel Orth, then thirty-four years old, is listed as a potter.[34] In 1854 he purchased the east half of the lot, comprising fifty acres, for £150.[35] For the next four decades Orth was both a farmer and potter. For example, in the 1870-71 census he was listed as a farmer in the nominal census, but as a pottery owner in the schedule of industrial establishments. In the latter listing he is reported to be working five months of the year. During this short period he produced 600 pieces of crockery valued at $800.[36] Two pieces made by Orth and inscribed with his name and the date are shown in plates 14.5 and 14.6. The earthenware dog in plate 14.5 is inscribed on the base with D. ORTH/1892. The miniature spittoon in plate 14.6 is signed Campden/D. Orth/1878. Both pieces are of red earthenware with a clear lead glaze. The 1890-91 census indicates that the Orth shop was the only remaining pottery in the Niagara area at that time. In the year 1890 Orth produced $325 worth of pottery.[37] He continued to operate his small pottery shop until shortly before his death on May 3, 1902.

Grimsby

John Kulp, born in Pennsylvania in 1799, established a pottery in Grimsby in 1829. Although he is often described as a Mennonite, census records indicate that he took little interest in institutional religion, despite the fact that his wife and children were associated with the Wesleyan Methodists. Kulp purchased two adjoining one-acre parcels in 1829, known as the southeast corner of lot 1, concession 6, East Gore of Grimsby Township.[38]

Kulp moved to Bayham Township, Elgin County, with his son William H., in 1868. In the 1870-71 census William Kulp is reported as a farmer and potter. John Kulp, then seventy-two, was living with his son.[39]

The only known signed piece made by Kulp is shown in plates 14.7 and 14.8. The red earthenware storage jar has two strap-handles and is covered with a clear lead glaze.

Kulp returned to Lincoln County sometime after 1870 and reportedly lived with his daughter in Caistor Township. He died on March 26, 1874.[40] The Grimsby pottery land and buildings were sold for $169 in 1877.[41]

14.8 *Close-up of inscription on base of jar in plate 14.7. Inscription reads John Kulp/Grimsby/August 19/1843.*

In 1966 a group of archaeologists, with the help of the Jordan Historical Museum of the Twenty, excavated the remains of two kilns, one reported as circular in shape, on the Kulp pottery site in Grimsby. The diggers also uncovered a large waster dump.

15.
Pot Shops of the North Shore of Lake Erie

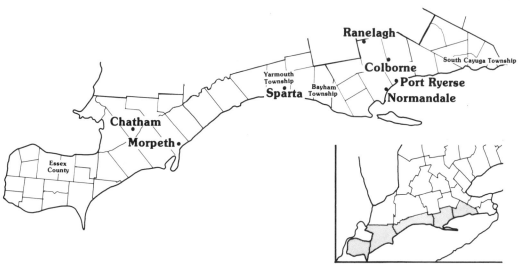

Fig. 15.1 *Location of potteries along the north shore of Lake Erie during the nineteenth century.*

The counties that border the north shore of Lake Erie had large areas of fertile land and a number of good ports for commercial trade, both of which combined to encourage settlements and the beginning of local industry, including several potteries. The pot shops in the region never developed beyond the size of small family workshops, due in part to the rapid development of potteries in the city of London to the west and in the city of Hamilton to the east. The locations of the potteries along the north shore of Lake Erie during the nineteenth century are shown in figure 15.1.

HALDIMAND COUNTY
Early records of the county indicate there was a pottery in South Cayuga Township, and a potter living in the village of Canboro.

James Hodgkins, a thirty-one-year-old Canadian-born potter, is listed in the 1851-52 census as operating an earthenware pottery "of very recent establishment." The value of ware produced in his pottery amounted to between $300 and $400.[1] There is no record of Hodgkins owning land in the township, and the exact location of the workshop is not known. The business had been discontinued by the time of the 1860-61 census.

An 1865 directory lists John Bennett as a potter in Canboro.[2] A year earlier he was listed as a "hotel-keeper."[3] No further information indicates whether Bennett operated a pottery in the village.

NORFOLK COUNTY

Normandale
A pottery was reported in documentary sources as operating in the village of Norman-

15.1 *Red earthenware spittoon with impressed mark EBAN T. GILBERT/PORT. RYERSE.*

dale in 1810. The owner was reported to be Samuel Long. The only other evidence of the pottery is the name of the local creek, which is still called "Potter's Creek."[4]

15.2 *Red earthenware mixing bowl with clear lead glaze. The piece is marked EBAN T. GIL-BERT/PORT. RYERSE.*

Ranelagh

G. Alfred Carter was listed as a potter in Ranelagh, Windham Township, from 1885 to 1903.[5] In an 1888 directory he is described as a "flower pot manufacturer."[6] Carter did not own the land where he worked, and it is therefore difficult to locate the site of his business.

Port Ryerse

Two families, the Marlatts and Gilberts, were active in pottery-making in the Port Ryerse area. Abraham Marlatt was working in the village as early as 1864.[7] By the time of the 1870-71 census the shop was working all year and employed three men, in 1870 producing 24,000 pieces of crockery, valued at $2,000.[8] The pottery was always a marginal enterprise, with credit ratings indicating a pecuniary worth of less than $500.[9] In the 1870s, Abraham Marlatt's son, Clayton, worked at the shop. The business was discontinued in 1898.[10] Abraham Marlatt also had an interest in a pottery originally owned by Ebenezer T. Gilbert.

Abraham Marlatt married Nancy Gilbert in 1857. Their daughter Eliza Jane Marlatt married Ebenezer Gilbert in 1884. These marriages established links between the two pottery-making families.

15.3 *Earthenware crock with clear lead glaze and impressed name EBAN T. GILBERT.*

Ebenezer T. Gilbert is listed as a "farmer" in the census of 1860-61 and again in 1870-71. It was after 1872 that he turned to making pots on a one-and-three-quarter-acre parcel in the centre part of the westerly division of broken front lot 4, Woodhouse Township. This land was sold in 1874 to Abraham Marlatt and his wife Nancy.[11] In 1886 the Marlatts sold the plot back to Ebenezer Gilbert for $400.[12] Gilbert continued to make earthenware pottery, some of which he marked with his own name. It seems likely that Abraham Marlatt had trained the younger Ebenezer Gilbert in the trade. This Ebenezer Gilbert continued the business until 1900, when the property was sold.[13] He marked his pottery with the impressed name EBAN T. GILBERT/PORT RYERSE. Three examples of earthenware made by him are shown in plates 15.1, 15.2 and 15.3.

In the summer of 1968 the Royal Ontario Museum sponsored an excavation at the Marlatt/Gilbert site in Woodhouse Township.[14] Stone foundations of the kiln were all that remained of former structures. A large number of pot sherds were collected, with some being reconstructed. Examples of pottery recovered in the dig are shown in plate 15.4 (a and b).

Colborne

James Garland (Gladden) moved from the village of Scotland, Brant County, in late 1851 and settled on a one-fifth-acre lot on the west side of Main Street, known locally as the tin shop, in the village of Colborne.[15] Nothing further is known of the daily operation of the pot shop. The business was sold by his heirs in 1874.[16]

Benjamin Cole was working as a potter in Colborne as early as 1851, but it was not until 1866 that he purchased land for a pot shop. His holding was known as lot 8 on the east side of Main Street.[17] The lot was adjacent to the Beemer Creek on the east and the Waterford and Simcoe Road on the west, giving it a favourable position for distribution of the wares. Cole made red earthenware containers with a clear lead-glaze coating. Examples of pottery attributed to him are in the Eva Brook Donly Museum, Simcoe, Ontario. In later years Cole's children moved away from the

village, occasionally visiting their parents, but never developing an interest in pottery making. Cole died in 1899 at the age of seventy and left his property to his wife, Mary Ann.[18]

ELGIN COUNTY

Sparta

Three potters were reported in directories as working in Sparta, Yarmouth Township. Darius Burt was listed in 1864 as a "brickmaker and potter."[19] Five years later he is reported as a brickmaker only. Adam Haight and Jordan Minor were also described as potters in Sparta in 1864, presumably working at the same place as Burt.[20]

Yarmouth Township

The 1842 census lists John Harvey as residing in Yarmouth Township between the third and fourth concessions.[21] Harvey purchased a five-acre part of lot 8, concession 4, in 1832.[22] In succeeding years he purchased additional lots. In 1850 he sold all his land, totalling thirty-six acres, and moved to Delaware Township, Middlesex County.[23]

Bayham Township

William Henry Kulp was a potter and farmer in Bayham Township, on lots 19 and 20 in the Gore, south of Talbot Road, and on part of lot 127, south of Talbot Road. He purchased parcels of land in 1868.[24] Eight years later he purchased an adjacent farm of 100 acres.[25] William H. Kulp was the son of John Kulp, the potter of Grimsby, Lincoln County. John Kulp was living with his son at the time of the 1870-71 census. The pottery and farm were sold in 1898.[26]

The 1870-71 census indicates that Kulp was potting for only four months of the year, probably during the winter, when farming chores were not as numerous. He employed two men to produce "crocks, jugs and milk pans" valued at $400.[27] The aggregate returns for the census of 1880-81 and 1890-91 indicate that one pottery was in operation in the district, probably that of Kulp, who was living in the township throughout this period. In the 1880-81 period the workshop employed only one person and produced articles valued at $250 a year, a very modest production for the time.[28]

15.4a *Earthenware crock reassembled from sherds recovered during excavations at the Gilbert Pottery. The yellow glaze has blistered during firing.* Courtesy Royal Ontario Museum.

15.4b *The bowl on the right shows that the glaze has run, which made the piece unsaleable. The example on the left is intact.* Courtesy Royal Ontario Museum.

KENT COUNTY

Morpeth

Jonathan Bills was making pottery in Morpeth, Howard Township by the year 1852, as reported in tax assessment rolls for the area.[29] Since Bills rented the site for his shop, described as part of lot 92 on the north side of Talbot Road, he could have been working in Morpeth as early as the late 1840s.

In the year 1864 James Cullis purchased park lot 14 on the west side of Main Street in Morpeth, and here began a pottery business.[30] Four years later he purchased an additional seventeen acres of lot 197 on the north side of Talbot Road.[31] This latter location was the site of the pottery from 1873 until 1878. The only information we have about the operation of the pottery is the report in the 1870-71 census, that potting was carried out for eight months of the year and produced wares worth $600 annually.[32] The business was discontinued ca. 1878.

Chatham

James Cornhill (Cornell) was reportedly operating a pottery and brickyard in 1896 in the town of Chatham.[33] He is listed at the time as producing brick at the corner of Louise & Emma Streets. He continued in business until 1907. In a government report on the clay industry, published in 1906, it is reported, "at present he (Cornhill) produces a large number of bricks."[34]

ESSEX COUNTY

Two potteries were reported in the 1890-91 census as operating in Essex County, but an examination of documentary sources and a field survey have failed to determine the locations. The two pot shops employed eight men in 1890 and produced articles valued at $5,000.[35]

16.
Potteries of Southwestern Ontario

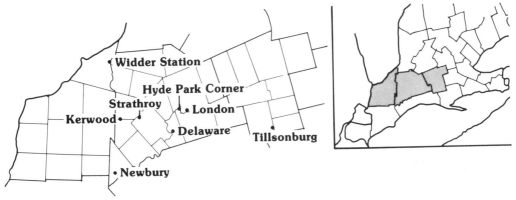

Fig. 16.1 *Location of potteries in southwestern Ontario during the nineteenth and early twentieth century.*

The city of London in Middlesex County was a major centre of the pottery industry during the late nineteenth century. This is illustrated by the census returns for 1880-81, which indicate that two potteries in the city produced about $112,000 worth of pottery.[1] There were six other potteries in Middlesex County, one pottery in Oxford County and one pottery in Lambton County.

The locations of potteries in southwestern Ontario in the last century are shown in figure 16.1.

OXFORD COUNTY

Tillsonburg
The first pottery in Tillsonburg was established in the 1880s by Fred B. Tillson. He apparently operated the business as an investment and was not himself trained as a potter. A note in the *Huron Expositor* from Seaforth, Ontario, indicates both his enterprise and his philanthropy:

Mr. Fred B. Tillson, proprietor of the Tillsonburg Stoneware Works, has made the town a present of five spittoons for use in the council chambers. Now the users of fine cut chewing who sit around the council board need not look out of the corners of their eyes after this to see if the caretaker is looking. . .[2]

Two examples of pottery made during this time and marked F.B. TILLSON/TILLSONBURG, ONT. are shown in plates 16.1 and 16.2. An impressed oval mark with TILSONBURG POTTERY CO./ONTARIO may be from this period or associated with later owners. A mustard jar with this mark is shown in plate 16.3.

The stoneware business was taken over in the fall of 1883 by William Gray, Jr., and Spence H. Betts.[3] The firm exhibited their wares at the Universal Exhibition in Antwerp, Belgium in 1885, and the exhibition catalogue states:

16.1 A Rockingham-glazed spittoon with impressed mark F.B. TILLSON/TILSONBURG, ONT. on base.

16.2 Decorated two-gallon stoneware jug with maker's impressed mark.

16.3 Stoneware preserve jar with impressed mark TILSONBURG/ONT./POTTERY CO.

William Gray and S.H. Betts, who had been only a short time in business together as 'manufacturers of stone, Rockingham and Bristol ware' showed bowls, spittoons, teapots, pie plates, and soap drainers in Rockingham. In salt-glazed stoneware their assortment included 'Dutch pots', fruit jars, butter pots, and oil and water kegs. In 'Bristol ware', or stoneware coated with a liquid glaze, they had sent over ink and beer bottles, jars for pickles, and mustard jars.[4]

Two examples of stoneware jugs made by this firm are shown in plates 16.4 and 16.5. In both illustrations the pieces are marked with the impressed name GRAY & BETTS/TILSONBURG, ONT. This partnership was dis-

16.4 *A five-gallon jug with cobalt-blue flower decoration. The piece is marked GRAY & BETTS/ TILSONBURG ONT.*

16.5 *A second example of a decorated stoneware jug made by GRAY & BETTS of Tillsonburg.*

solved in the spring of 1886, duly recorded in the county land registry office.[5]

Samuel Glass, an entrepreneur from London East, became involved in the potter trade in Tillsonburg, probably because of his former acquaintance with a pottery in the Ealing area of London East, where at least four potteries operated during the nineteenth century. In the spring of 1886 the new partnership of Gray & Glass was formed in Tillsonburg.[6]

The stoneware business continued to be plagued by the high cost of raw materials and intense competition from imported finished wares from the United States. In a letter dated March 20, 1886, Samuel Glass pleads his case to the Hon. John Carling, Minister of Agriculture, and friend of the Glass family:

We are only one pottery out of a dozen or more who have keenly felt the competition of inferior American goods during the past 18 months. And unless we can claim the indulgence of the government and obtain some assistance our potteries now employing fifty hands will have to close down. But on the contrary if the Hon. the Minister of Finance will consider favourably our request we hope to be able to conclude arrangements for the enlargement of our works to three times their present capacity. We are about forming a company to establish [a] large pottery in either London or St. Thomas.[7]

Pottery marked with the name of Gray & Glass is rare, as the business was only operating from March to August of 1886. An example of a piece is shown in plate 16.6. On August 4, 1886, fire struck and completely destroyed the plant. This no doubt hastened the planned move, which was to be to London. A brief announcement of the new venture appeared in the *London Advertiser:*

The London Crockery Ware Manufacturing Company have purchased fourteen acres of land in London East on which is a brick building 50 x 125 feet and three stories high, which will be at once fitted for the crockery ware business, and large kilns erected. . .[8]

MIDDLESEX COUNTY

Ealing (London Township)

John Pegler, Sr., was operating a pottery on

16.6 *A rare example of stoneware pottery marked GRAY & GLASS/TILSONBURG.*

Hamilton Road at Ealing, London Township, as early as 1864. The shop was on part of lot 11, Concession B. In the 1870-71 census he is reported as operating his workshop all year and employing four men to produce 125,000 pieces of pottery valued at $5,000.[9] It is reported that it took sixty tons of clay and sand and 8400 pounds of lead and other chemicals to produce the wares.[10] The pottery was taken over in 1879 by his son, Richard, who continued the business, described as being located at 461 Hamilton Road.

Richard Pegler joined with William Hulse on October 1, 1879, forming the partnership of Pegler & Hulse. This was dissolved the next year and a new partnership established, when Thomas Brown joined to form Pegler, Hulse and Brown.[11] The pottery continued until 1890. At this time Thomas Brown moved back to Strathroy and William J. Hulse joined with his father Joseph to form Hulse & Son, at 95 Rectory Street.[12] It is quite likely that this address represents the same location as the 461 Hamilton Road address.

The partnership of Hulse & Son continued until 1892. In that year John Pegler, Jr., brother of Richard, had become proprietor and it was renamed the Star Pottery. John Pegler, Jr., produced earthenware and "ovenproof" kitchen ware. A miniature pot from the pottery works is shown in plate 16.7. It is marked on the base and has a "star" decorative motif as part of the moulded body. In 1904 John Pegler, Jr., took as a partner James E. Tait, who had earlier operated a small pottery in the village of Lynden, Wentworth County.[13] The Star Pottery now became known as Pegler & Co. and was to continue as such until 1905.[14] By 1907 the pottery was owned by Alexander Ferguson, a former employee of Glass Bros. & Co., and the pottery changed its name to the London Pottery Manufacturing Co.[15] The workshop was very small in size and had a limited credit rating, with a pecuniary worth of less than $500.[16] The business was listed in credit-rating manuals until 1933, but it appears to have been inactive for part of the time.[17]

Another pottery in London Township was Totten & Co., founded by Henry Totten, Jr. In 1880-81 he joined with Hiram Shain, a hotel

16.7 *Miniature pot with wire handle. Made by Star Pottery, London.*

owner, to form Totten & Co., at concession B, lot 11, Ealing, described as being on the south side of Hamilton Road, east of Trafalgar Rd.[18] Henry Totten, Jr., had been listed in the 1870-71 census as an apprentice at the James Elliott pottery. Hiram Shain was probably restricted to being a financial backer of the enterprise.[19] The pottery continued until 1883.[20] In 1886 Henry Totten, Jr., is listed in a directory as working at Abraham Parkinson's pottery on Hamilton Road.[21]

A third pottery in London East was operated by James Elliott. The 1870-71 census reports that he was working with his brother Alexander, with Henry Totten, Jr., and John Nelles, Jr., described as apprentices.[22] The pottery was located on lot 8, concession B, London Township, described as 341 Hamilton Road in an 1884 directory.[23] The 1870-71 census reports that James Elliott hired three men to produce 60,000 pieces of "earthenware of all kinds," valued at $2,000.[24] The business continued until ca. 1887. There are no known pieces of earthenware marked by Elliott, and further details of the business are not known.

R. Jackway and Diem are listed in an 1863 directory as operating a pottery on William Street between Gray and Hamilton Road, London East.[25] Nothing else is known about the business, or its precise location, but it apparently was short-lived, as it is not mentioned again in the 1870-71 census for the area.

Pottersburg
The establishment of the London Crockery

Manufacturing Company in London East on sub-lots 5, 6 and 7 of lot 8, concession C, was watched with great interest by the local press. The *London Advertiser* of September 7, 1886, reports:

The building on the ground will be enlarged, and two large kilns will be constructed at a joint cost of about $5,000. The company will manufacture all sorts and descriptions of majolica, stoneware, Rockingham and Bristol ware, clay ware, clay pipes, etc. This establishment is the only one that manufactures Bristol ware in North America and the only one in Canada which makes majolica, Bristol or clay pipes. . .

The company received its letters patent in November, 1886.[26] Initial shareholders of the firm included William Glass, father of S. F. Glass, William Gray and Frank H. Butler, and Charles S. Hyman.[27] An engraving of the works when completed is shown in plate 16.8. The business employed some seventy-five men and cost over $70,000 to build. Grand Trunk and Canadian Pacific spur lines at the plant enabled the direct unloading of clay and coal and permitted easy shipment of the finished goods. The cluster of workmen's houses with its own post office was appropriately called Pottersburg. A report in the *London Advertiser* of February 10, 1887 states:

. . .This is the largest Rockingham and stoneware pottery in Canada . . . we ship largely to Montreal and Ottawa and intend to go into the farthest Eastern market. We expect to do considerable business in British Columbia when the C.P.R. connection has been established in London.

The business produced many types of pottery including 100-gallon acid receivers and stoneware filters to a capacity of twenty gallons. In ordinary stoneware the company manufactured butter pots, cream pots, churns, jugs, fruit and preserve jars, pitchers and bottles, mustard jars, ale bottles, ink and varnish bottles. In Rockingham ware they produced tea pots, pitchers, saucepans, baking pans and sick room containers.[28]

16.8 *Engraving of factory of London Crockery Manufacturing Company. The engraving dates to the year 1887.*

Examples of Rockingham-glazed wares are the jardinière in plate 16.9 and the soap drainer in plate 16.10. Both pieces are marked with the impressed stamp, LONDON CROCKERY MFG. CO LONDON ONT.

Despite the aggressive salesmanship of the new firm, which manufactured wares for shipment as far as Winnipeg and British Columbia, the competition from U.S. imports still made the feasibility of the manufacture of

16.9 *Rockingham-glazed jardinière made by the London Crockery Manufacturing Co. (1886-1888). The piece is marked with the company name on its base.*

16.10 *Soap drainer made by London Crockery Mfg. Co. (1886-1888).*

stoneware in Ontario uncertain. Correspondence of William Glass, father of S. F. Glass, to the Hon. John Carling vividly states the problem:

...We cannot compete in stoneware with American manufacturers for reasons given in my son's letter — The Americans have the clay and coal at their very doors, while we have to haul our clay from New Jersey 700 miles which at the rate now being charged under the new American Interstate Commerce bill is fully double former rates and the cost of coal to us as you know is three times that paid at the pit . . . I cannot speak too strongly on the subject of increased protection, the very existence of our company depends on it.[29]

16.11 *Two stoneware storage crocks with stencilled G B & Co/London. This is one of a number of different identifying marks of the Glass Bros. & Co. firm.*

Clay was imported by the firm from New Jersey and Devonshire, England, and sulfur-free coal was shipped from Canton, Ohio. The introduction of higher rates in the United States had raised the freight charges on clay, according to S. F. Glass, from $3.25 to $6.40 a ton. Such changes boded ill for Canadian manufacturers dependent on imported raw materials.[30]

The London Crockery Manufacturing Company was liquidated by public auction on March 22, 1888. The firm was under-capitalized and was deeply in debt. Samuel Glass repurchased the business for $21,500[31] and it was renamed Glass Bros. & Co. Active in the management of the firm were brothers Samuel F. and John H. Glass. The production of a variety of commercial and domestic wares continued into the late 1880s and early 1890s. Examples of the products made under this new name are shown in plates 16.11 through 16.21. Of special interest is the self-sealing

16.12 *Another variation of the Glass Bros. & Co. mark on stoneware pottery produced at their London plant.*

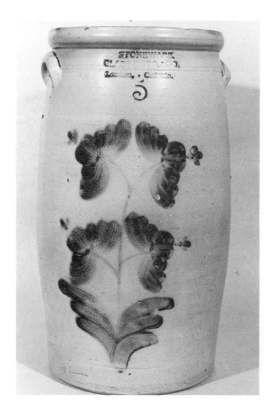

preserve jar in 16.21. This was patented by Glass Bros. & Co., on July 24, 1891, and the jars bear the name and the date, July 1891, on the base.[32] The wire handle fits into a groove on the top of the lid, which creates a tight fit of the lid against the washer and the jar. The self-sealing jar was popular and was produced in at least two sizes and styles, as shown in plates 16.20 and 16.21.

From January 1890 to 1892 the company had a pecuniary worth in credit-rating manuals of $40-$75,000. In the manual of 1893 the business was listed, but without a rating, suggesting either a financial set-back or fire. Beginning in 1894 the business is listed again, but with a reduced pecuniary worth of $10-$20,000. On December 28, 1895, a fire in one of the warehouses destroyed $8,000-$9,000 worth of pottery.[33] Another fire on February 22, 1897, brought the manufacture of pottery to an end. All that remained of the pottery were two big kilns and a brick wall. Losses were estimated at $46,500, but Glass Bros. &

16.13 *Five-gallon stoneware butter churn with elaborate cobalt-blue decoration. Stoneware pottery from the Glass Bros. & Co. firm is not known for elaborate decorations.*

16.14 *A third variation of the Glass Bros. & Co. mark is this example on a five-gallon jug.*

16.15 *A Bristol-ware screw-top canning jar. The top of the lid has the stencilled name of Glass Bros. & Co., London.*

16.16 (left) and 16.17 (above) *Stoneware storage jars with cobalt-blue decoration and the impressed mark of Glass Bros. & Co., London, Ontario.*

16.18 *Plain stoneware teapot made by Glass Bros. & Co., and marked with their firm name on the bottom.*

Co. had only $8,000 worth of insurance.[34] The company continued as a manufacturers' agent in London until 1903.[35]

The site of the plant is between Dundas Street on the north, Hale Street on the east, and Highbury Avenue on the west. Today it is the location of the London Steel Company.

Hyde Park Corner
Joseph Elson began a pottery on the southern half of lot 24, concession 2, London Township, as early as 1842.[36] The site is now located on the northeast corner of Oxford Street and Hutton Road, London. In 1854, Elson was awarded a prize for the best specimen of drainage tile at the Provincial Exhibition.[37] By 1861 his son Peter had taken over the business, although he did not obtain ownership of the workshop until 1878.[38] The census of 1870-71 reports that the pottery worked by the younger Elson employed two men. It produced $1,600 worth of pottery.[39] The pottery was discontinued before Peter Elson's death in 1913.

City of London
For more than half a century pottery was produced in London on lot 29 at the southwest

16.19 *Soda water bottle with porcelain stopper. The name of Glass Bros. & Co., is stamped on the lower part of the bottle.*

16.20 and 16.21   *Two types of self-sealing canning jars made by Glass Bros. & Co. The design of the sealer for these jars was patented in 1891 by the firm.*

corner of Gray & Adelaide Streets. The first potter on the site was Moses Whitehead (Whitehouse), who is listed in an 1857 directory as operating a "drain tile and stoneware manufactory."[40] The next potter reported owning the business was Charles Sibley, who is listed in assessment rolls from 1862 to 1871. The shop was known in 1871 as the London Pottery, a name that it continued to use under successive owners into the first decade of this century.

In 1871 the business was taken over by John Marx (Marks) and William J. Campbell, both former workers at the pottery of Jacob Henry Ahrens, of Paris, Ontario. In 1870-71

the pottery employed four men to produce 10,000 pieces of earthenware valued at $4,800.[41] The workshop used one-and-one-half tons of red lead to make the glaze for the wares.[42] The business does not seem to have been successful, and by 1874 it had been taken over by Charles Pratt, who had settled in the area in 1846 and who had joined the firm in 1871.[43]

Pratt operated the workshop until 1878, when he moved from the city.[44] Pratt exhibited at the International Exhibition at Philadelphia in 1876.[45] The business was operated by Stephen Pearce in 1879, but he did not continue beyond that year. The next year John Fitzmaurice took over the enterprise, but by 1882, it had again changed hands, this time to Peter McGlade and Bernard Fitzmaurice. Both of these men were former workers at a pottery in Paris, Ontario. An 1882 directory names the business as London City Pottery.[46] McGlade left the pottery business in 1883 and opened a furniture business in London, although he continued to own the property for many years.

Bernard Fitzmaurice took another partner, this time John Unger, and formed the firm of Fitzmaurice & Unger, which continued until 1893. The break-up of this partnership may have been related to the sale of the property, but whatever the cause, Bernard Fitzmaurice himself operated the business until 1905.[47] Although it is possible to document the changes in ownership of the business, very little is known about the wares produced. Pieces marked with the impressed name LONDON POTTERY are known, but their direct association with this business, as distinct from other potteries in the city, cannot be confirmed.

A small pottery was established in London in 1897 by Samuel N. Spence and Ernest J. Cook, operating under the name of Spence & Cook. Both of these men were former employees of John Pegler's Star Pottery.[48] The Spence & Cook workshop was located at the rear of 336 Egerton Avenue, a building also used for a blacksmith shop. The partnership did not last beyond 1898.[49]

Delaware

The earliest pottery in the township was operated by John Harvey, who had moved from Yarmouth Township, Elgin County, to Delaware Township in 1850. In that year he purchased a twelve-acre part of lot 6, concession 2.[50] In the years 1864 and 1865 John Britton is reported working as a potter in the area, either as an owner or employee of a workshop.[51]

Later, Samuel Eichenberger (or Erchenberger) operated a pottery on the northwest quarter of lot 6, concession 2, land that he purchased in 1868.[52]

A biographical sketch of Eichenberger in a Middlesex County history states that he was born in Switzerland and immigrated to Canada in 1855. He first settled in Hamilton, but by 1861 had moved further west to Delaware Township. His financial interests in-

16.22 *Large shallow bowl made of red earthenware with a clear lead glaze. Piece is marked on base* RICHARDSON'S EGYPTIAN WARE.

16.23 *Earthenware jar with clear lead glaze. Piece is marked* RICHARDSON'S WARE.

cluded farming as well as the pottery.[53] The pottery was started sometime after 1871 as the census of that year has no record of the business. The workshop was operated by Eichenberger & Stainer in 1878 and possibly into the year 1879.[54] Beginning the next year Eichenberger ran the shop under his own name. The pottery was discontinued in 1891.[55] In 1903 the property was sold.[56] No pottery with Eichenberger's name is known to have been produced.

Kerwood

William & Robert Richardson emigrated from Yorkshire, England, to the United States ca. 1852. They had moved to Canada and settled in Kerwood by 1859, the year William Richardson received a Crown grant for the west half of lot 10, concession 4, Metcalfe Township.[57] The next year he sold ten acres of the southwest corner of the lot to his brother John, who by that time had also immigrated to Canada. John Richardson was a potter by trade. He operated a pottery on the land from 1860 until his death in 1886.[58] In 1861 he received a second prize for the best water filter at the Provincial Exhibition, held at London, Ontario.[59] The 1871 census gives a few details of the business and indicates that by this date the manufacture of bricks and tiles had become an important part of it. In 1870-71 John Richardson worked the pottery for five months of the year to produce pottery ware valued at $400.[60]

John Richardson was assisted by his son, James, until 1872, when James moved to the village of Kerwood to start a brick and tile yard. After the death of John Richardson, his son, Robert T., continued to produce tile, brick, and pottery.

John Richardson made common red earthenware with a clear lead glaze, the lead reportedly having been imported from England. Three examples of Richardson's work are the shallow bowl, marked on its base with RICHARDSON'S EGYPTIAN WARE (plate 16.22), the crock marked RICHARDSON'S WARE (plate 16.23) and the jug marked RICHARDSON'S WARE (plate 16.24).

The brickyard and pottery were sold in 1908 at auction, bringing an end to the pottery-making tradition at Kerwood (see plate 16.25).

Newbury

Oliver White was listed in an 1864 directory as a potter in Newbury, Mosa Township.[61] He did not own land in the township until 1877,

16.24 *Earthenware jug made by John Richardson at his pottery in Kerwood.*

when he purchased eight acres in the southeast corner of lot 18, concession 1.[62] White died in 1881.

Strathroy

The pottery in Strathroy was founded by Albert Diem in 1864 on a one-acre part of the western half of lot 21, concession 4, south of Egremont Road, later incorporated into the town of Strathroy.[63] In the 1870-71 census the pottery was reported as operating all year and producing 15,000 pieces of pottery valued at $1,200.[64] By 1881 Donald and Thomas Brown had taken over the business. In the next year Lena Diem, widow of Albert, then living in the state of Michigan, sold the pottery to the Browns.[65] During the decade 1880-1890

MORTGAGE SALE !

Under and by virtue of the Power of Sale contained in a certain Mortgage, which, with the assignment, will be produced at the time of sale, and in pursuance of leave given by an order ot the Judge of the County Court of the County of Middlesex, dated March 3rd, 1908, there will be offered for sale at the

Albion Hotel, Strathroy,

ON

SATURDAY, MARCH 21, '08

At 2.30 o'clock p. m., the following lands, viz:

Part of Lot number Ten, in the Fourth Concession of the Township of Metcalfe, and described as follows : Commencing at the South Easterly angle of the said lots, thence Northerly along the Eastern boundary of the road allowance forty rods, thence Easterly and at right angles to said road allowance forty rods, thence Southerly and parallel to said road allowance forty rods, thence Westerly along the Southern boundary of said lots forty rods, to the place of beginning, containing ten acres, more or less

The Buildings consist of a Brick House, 1½ storeys high, Frame Barn about 30x50, and Frame Tile and Pottery Shed, about 60 feet square.

The property is situate about seven miles from Strathroy, four from Kerwood, and two from Calvert Post Office.

This is the property long known as Richardson's Tile and Pottery Yard, and the manufacture of a quality of Pottery and Drain Tile equal to any in Ontario has been carried on for a number of years.

There is on the land an almost unlimited quantity of clay suitable, and easily available, for the manufacture of Pottery and Tile, and a successful business can be carried on.

TERMS OF SALE

Ten per cent. of the purchase money to be paid to the Vendor's Solicitor at the time of sale, and the balance within two weeks thereafter.

The property will be offered subject to a reserve bid.

In other respects the sale will be in accordance with conditions of sale which will be read at the time of sale.

For further particulars and information apply to

RICHARD BROCK,
Auctioneer.

ELLIOT TRAVER,
Vendor's Solicitor, Strathroy.

Dated March 4th, 1908.

16.25 *Announcement of the sale of the Richardson pottery in 1908.*

ATTENTION!

ASK YOUR GROCER FOR

White Stone Enamelled

—AND—

Black Vitrified Fruit Jars

· — ALSO —

CROCKS

of every description and price, from 2 cents up. Manufactured at the Strathroy Pottery, 4th Line.

THOS. BROWN,

1215   Proprietor.

APPLES !   APPLES !

16.26 *Advertisement of Thomas Brown's Strathroy Pottery from the 1880s.*

16.27 *Tomato or fruit jar made by Thomas Brown at the Strathroy Pottery. Piece has the impressed mark T. BROWN/STRATHROY.*

Thomas Brown was active in the partnership of Pegler, Hulse & Brown, which was listed as operating in London Township and Strathroy, although Thomas Brown was working in Strathroy during some years. An advertisement in a local Strathroy newspaper from the 1880s is shown in plate 16.26. Pottery with the mark T. BROWN/STRATHROY is rare. An example of a fruit jar is shown in plate 16.27. The Strathroy Pottery was in business until 1899.[66]

LAMBTON COUNTY

Elijah Munger (Monger) operated a pottery in Widder Station (later Thedford) from ca. 1870 to 1878.[67] The pottery was of small size and appears to have gone almost unnoticed by government record-keepers. The workshop was located on lot 18, concession 2, Bosanquet Township.[68] Munger was also a tanner, a profession he appears to have continued while he owned the pottery.

Jonas Cornell, a brick- and tile-maker in Widder Station, was reported in a 1907 directory as operating a pottery. This was probably part of his brick business, which was located along the Sauble River on lot 1, concession 1, Bosanquet Township. There is no evidence that Cornell made any large quantity of pottery.

Footnotes

CHAPTER TWO: THE POTTER'S CRAFT

[1] Daniel Rhodes, *Kilns: Design, Construction and Operation* (Philadelphia, Pa.: Chilton Book Co., 1968). pp. 44-45.

[2] *Ibid.*, pp. 50-51.

[3] *Ibid.*, p. 52.

CHAPTER FOUR: POTTERIES OF EASTERN ONTARIO

[1] Instrument 85, dated January 31, 1823, Augusta Twp., Grenville County Registry Office, Prescott.

[2] Instrument 96, dated March 6, 1823, Augusta Twp., Grenville County Registry Office, Prescott.

[3] *Prescott Herald & Grenville General Advertiser*, August 2, 1837.

[4] Instrument 105, dated November 5, 1840, Town of Prescott, Grenville County Registry Office, Prescott.

[5] Quoted in Shackleton, "Potteries of Nineteenth Century Ontario." Unpublished ms. (Ottawa: Historic Sites Branch, Dept. of Northern Affairs, 1964, p. 89.

[6] Land was owned at the time by his father, Patrick Mooney, cf. Instrument H340, dated November 11, 1839, Town of Prescott, Grenville County Registry Office, Prescott.

[7] *Canadian Agriculturalist*, Vol. 8, 1856, p. 306.

[8] *Ontario Gazetteer & Directory* (Toronto: H. McEvoy, 1869), p. 401.

[9] See will of James Mooney, Sr., which outlines land owned by him at the time of his death. Will was registered in Grenville County Registry Office on January 18, 1855, as instrument B40.

[10] Instrument 40, dated November 22, 1854, Town of Johnstown, Grenville County Registry Office, Prescott.

[11] Census of 1870-71, Grenville County S., Edwardsburgh Twp. District 69, sub-district c, division 1, schedule 6, page 5.

[12] Instrument 6720, dated March 5, 1902, Town of Johnstown, Grenville County Registry Office, Prescott.

[13] Instrument 9535, dated August 9, 1853, City of Ottawa, Carleton County Registry Office, Ottawa.

[14] Philip Shackleton, "Potteries of Nineteenth Century Ontario." Unpub. ms. (Ottawa: Department of Northern Affairs, 1964, p. 89.

[15] Instrument 3880, dated March 3, 1869, City of Ottawa, Carleton County Registry Office, Ottawa.

[16] Census of 1880-81, Vol. 3 (Ottawa: MacLean, Roger & Co., 1882), pp. 446-49.

[17] Instrument 694, dated May 12, 1873, Russell County Registry Office, Russell.

[18] Census of 1880-81, Vol. 3 (Ottawa: MacLean, Roger & Co., 1882), pp. 446-49; Census of 1890-91, Vol. 3 (Ottawa: S.E. Dawson, 1893), pp. 261-62.

[19] Instrument 4904, dated October 10, 1890, Russell County Registry Office, Russell.

[20] The last listing for the pottery is in issues of the *Mercantile Agency Reference Book* in 1890.

[21] *Mitchell & Co's Canada . . . Directory for 1865-66* (Toronto: Mitchell & Co., pub., 1864).

[22] Instrument 9015, dated October 14, 1859, E. Hawkesbury Twp., Prescott County Registry Office, L'Orignal.

[23] Census of 1890-91, Vol. 3 (Ottawa: S.E. Dawson, 1893), pp. 261-62.

[24] *Mitchell & Co's Canada . . . Directory for 1865-66* (Toronto: Mitchell & Co., pub., 1864).

[25] *Mercantile Agency Reference Book* for July, 1872 through July, 1876, list the firm of Merkley & Son in Inkerman.

[26] Census of 1870-71, Dundas County, Williamsburgh Twp., District 71, sub-district c, page 25.

[27] Instrument 1689, dated November 9, 1853, Osnabruck Twp., Stormont County Registry Office, Cornwall.

[28] See T. Ritchie, "Early Brick Masonry Along the St. Lawrence in Ontario," Technical Paper No. 93 (Ottawa: Division of Building Research, National Research Council of Canada, 1960). pp. 115-22.

[29] *Canada Directory for 1857-58* (Montreal: John Lovell, 1857), p. 42.

[30] *Canada Directory* (Montreal: Robert W.S. MacKay, 1851), p. 56.

[31] Census of 1870-71, Stormont County, Osnabruck Twp., District 72, sub-district a, division 1, schedule 6.

[32] Instrument 9907, dated June 1, 1901, Osnabruck Twp., Stormont County Registry Office, Cornwall.

[33] Instrument 3029, dated October 29, 1870, Osnabruck Twp., Stormont County Registry Office, Cornwall.

[34] Census of 1870-71, Stormont County, Osnabruck Twp., District 72, sub-district a, division 1, schedule 6.

[35] *Mercantile Agency Reference Book* for the years 1871 through 1893.

[36] Census of 1851-52, Stormont County, Osnabruck Twp., District 5, page 3, lines 37-39.

[37] Instrument 2412, dated November 24, 1864, Stormont County Registry Office, Cornwall.

[38] Instrument 1887, dated September 20, 1869, City of Cornwall, Stormont County Registry Office, Cornwall.

[39] William C. Ketchum Jr., *Early Potters and Potteries of New York State* (New York: Funk & Wagnalls, 1970), p. 159.

[40] Census of 1870-71, Stormont County, Cornwall, District 73, sub-district d, division 1, schedule 6.

[41] *Ibid.*

[42] *Mercantile Agency Reference Book*, July 1881, July 1891.

[43] Instrument 8891, dated April 8, 1907, Cornwall, Stormont County Registry Office, Cornwall.

[44] *Ontario Gazetteer and Business Directory 1884-85* (Toronto: R.L. Polk, 1884), p. 130.

[45] *J.F. Kimball's Brockville Directory for 1886 and 1887* (Brockville: J.F. Kimball, pub. & comp., 1886), p. 23.

[46] Census of Canada 1890-91, Vol. 3 (Ottawa: S.E. Dawson, printer, 1893), pp. 261-62.

[47] Instrument 1860, dated October 8, 1881, Frontenac County Registry Office, Kingston.

[48] Instrument 2076, dated November 16, 1882, Frontenac County Registry Office, Kingston.

[49] Census of Canada 1880-81, Vol. 3 (Ottawa: MacLean, Roger & Co., 1882), pp. 446-49.

[50] *Foster's Kingston Directory from July 1899 to July 1900* (Toronto: J.G. Foster & Co., pub., n.d.), p. 227.

[51] Martin is reported in the *Mercantile Agency Reference Book* from January 1884 until July 1900, after which time there is no listing, indicating that the pottery business had been discontinued.

[52] Instrument 5878, dated March 3, 1904, Frontenac County Registry Office, Kingston.

CHAPTER FIVE: KILNS OF PRINCE EDWARD AND HASTINGS COUNTIES

[1] William C. Ketchum, Jr., *Early Potters and Potteries of New York State* (New York: Funk & Wagnalls, 1970), p. 166.

[2] Instrument 124, dated October 12, 1849, Hallowell Twp., Prince Edward County Registry Office, Picton.

[3] Census of Canada 1851-52, Prince Edward County, Hallowell Twp., part 1. p. 21.

[4] Instrument 2516, dated October 17, 1855, Hallowell Twp., Prince Edward County Registry Office, Picton.

[5] William C. Ketchum, Jr., *Early Potters and Potteries of New York State* (New York: Funk & Wagnalls, 1970), pp. 166-67.

[6] Instrument 2253, dated October 9, 1864, Hallowell Twp., Prince Edward County Registry Office, Picton.

[7] Census of Canada 1870-71, Prince Edward County, Hallowell Twp., district 59, sub-district d, division 3, schedule 6.

[8] Instrument 3673, dated October 27, 1874, Hallowell Twp., Prince Edward County Registry Office, Picton.

[9] Partnership declaration No. 129, registered on February 16, 1880, Prince Edward County Registry Office, Picton.

[10] Charles A. Hart is mentioned in the above partnership declaration as residing in Belleville; only he continues living there without interruption.

[11] *Census of Canada 1880-81*. Vol. 3 (Ottawa: MacLean, Roger & Co., 1882), pp. 446-49.

[12] Instrument 8271, dated October 5, 1892, Hallowell Twp., Prince Edward County Registry Office, Picton.

[13] Instrument 5683, dated July 14, 1891, Picton, Price Edward County Registry Office, Picton.

[14] Instrument 8745, dated September 15, 1905, Picton, Prince Edward County Registry Office, Picton.

[15] Tax assessment rolls for Belleville for 1892 and 1893, Bleecker Ward.

[16] Instrument G58, dated July 3, 1868, Belleville, Hastings County Registry Office, Belleville.

[17] *The Province of Ontario...Directory* (Toronto: H. McEvoy, compiler, 1869), p. 51.

[18] Instrument G371, dated January 26, 1870, Belleville, Hastings County Registry Office, Belleville.

[19] Philip Shackleton, "Potteries of Nineteenth Century Ontario." Unpublished ms. (Ottawa: Historic Sites Branch, Dept. of Northern Affairs, 1964), p. 6.

[20] Instrument H902, dated October 5, 1871, Belleville, Hastings County Registry Office, Belleville.

[21] Instrument A63, dated December 28, 1872, Belleville, Hastings County Registry Office, Belleville.

[22] Census of Canada 1870-71, Hastings County West, Belleville, district 60, sub-district c, division 1, schedule 6.

[23] Instrument 1530, dated April 3, 1873, Belleville, Hastings County Registry Office, Belleville.

[24] Tax assessment rolls for 1873-75, City of Belleville, Baldwin and Bleecker Wards.

[25] Tax assessment rolls for 1878 and 1879, City of Belleville, Bleecker Ward.

[26] *Census of Canada 1880-81,* Vol. 3 (Ottawa: MacLean, Roger & Co., 1882), pp. 446-49.

[27] *Census of Canada 1890-91,* Vol. 3 (Ottawa: S. E. Dawson, printer, 1893), pp. 261-62.

[28] Instrument A7601, dated March 12, 1925, Belleville, Hastings County Registry Office, Belleville.

[29] *The Canada Directory for 1857-58* (Montreal:

John Lovell, publisher, n.d.), p. 84.

[30] *Directory of the County of Hastings* (Belleville: Mackenzie Bowell, publisher, 1869), p. 220.

[31] *The Province of Ontario...Directory 1899* (Toronto: Might Directory Co., publisher, 1899), p. 1043.

[32] *Census of Canada 1880-81,* Vol. 3 (Ottawa: MacLean, Roger & Co., 1882), pp. 446-49.

CHAPTER SIX: POTTERIES OF EAST CENTRAL ONTARIO

[1] Census of Canada West 1842, Cramahe Twp. C1344, Ontario Archives, Toronto.

[2] William C. Ketchum, Jr., *Early Potters & Potteries of New York State* (New York: Funk & Wagnalls, 1970), p. 177.

[3] *Canada Directory* (Montreal: John Lovell, 1851), p. 66.

[4] *Mercantile Agency Reference Book* (New York: Dun, Wiman & Co.), various dates up to January 1868.

[5] Instrument 529, dated August 2, 1858, Colborne Village, Durham East Registry Office, Colborne.

[6] Tax assessment rolls, Cramahe Twp., 1858.

[7] The tax assessment roll for the Village of Colborne for 1866, no. 54, lists Harvey Fowler as a tanner.

[8] Tax assessment rolls, Village of Colborne, 1869.

[9] Census of Canada 1870-71, Northumberland County E., Cramahe Twp., Village of Colborne, sub-district b, schedule 6.

[10] *Ibid.*

[11] Instrument 1371, dated May 11, 1880, Colborne Village, Northumberland East Registry Office, Colborne.

[12] Instrument 2026, dated July 4, 1888, Colborne Village, Northumberland East Registry Office, Colborne.

[13] Union Publishing Co., *Farmers' & Businessmen's Directory for the Counties of Durham, Hastings, Lennox & Addington, Northumberland, Prince Edward* (Ingersoll: Union Publishing Co., 1893), p. 219.

[14] *Lovell's Business & Professional Directory... for 1896-97* (Montreal: John Lovell & Son, 1896), p. 319.

[15] William H. Smith, *Smith's Canadian Gazetteer* (Toronto: H. & W. Rowsell, 1846), p. 18.

[16] Census of 1845, 1848, 1849, Darlington Twp., Newcastle District, Upper Canada, MS 10, Archives of Ontario, Toronto.

[17] Instrument 309, dated September 25, 1848, Cartwright Twp., Newcastle Registry Office, Bowmanville.

[18] *A Supplement to the Canadian Directory* (Montreal: Robert W. S. MacKay, compiler, 1853), p. 32.

[19] Lease between Charles Bowman and Bailey & Williams, dated June 8, 1846 in collection of Bowmanville Museum, Bowmanville, Ontario.

[20] *Simcoe Standard,* October 3, 1849.

[21] Instrument 1468, dated September 27, 1853, Darlington Township, Newcastle Registry Office, Bowmanville.

[22] Price list of John Brown in the collection of the Bowmanville Museum, Bowmanville.

[23] *Canadian Agriculturalist* 7 (1855), p. 340.

[24] David L. Newlands, "Scragg's Tile Machine," *York Pioneer* 72 (Fall 1977), pp. 31-34.

[25] Instrument 621, dated February 17, 1855, Cartwright Twp., Newcastle Registry Office, Bowmanville.

[26] Census of Canada 1860-61, Durham County, Cartwright Twp., district 4, page 47, lines 25 & 26.

[27] *Ibid.*

[28] Instruments 2106 and 2110, dated May 12, 1862 and May 14, 1862, respectively, Newcastle Registry Office, Bowmanville.

[29] Instrument 447, dated June 22, 1850, Hope Twp., Port Hope Registry Office, Port Hope.

[30] Instrument 3925, dated February 11, 1871, Hope Twp., Port Hope Registry Office, Port Hope.

[31] Instrument 5043, dated March 21, 1876, Hope Twp., Port Hope Registry Office, Port Hope.

[32] Kathleen M. G. Stearns, "Port Hope Pottery." *Canadian Collector* 2 (June 1967), pp. 13-15.

[33] Instrument 45, dated October 9, 1869, Ops Twp., Victoria County Registry Office, Lindsay.

[34] Census of Canada 1870-71, Victoria County, Ops. Twp., district 52, sub-district 6, division 1, schedule 6, page 1.

[35] Ross N. Carr (Mrs.), ed. *Ops — Land of Plenty* (Lindsay: Ops Township Council, 1968), pp. 176-77.

[36] Instrument 4466, dated January 1, 1852, Town of Peterborough, Peterborough County Registry Office, Peterborough.

[37] Instrument 10098, dated March 10, 1856, Town of Peterborough, Peterborough County Registry Office, Peterborough.

[38] *Directory of the United Counties of Peterborough & Victoria, 1858* (Peterborough: T. & R. White, 1858), p. 80.

[39] Census of Canada 1860-61, Peterborough County, North Monaghan Twp., Town of Peterborough, district 1, page 16, lines 18-20.

[40] *Ibid.*

[41] Kingdon, Goodenough, Bacon & Oakley are listed as apprentices in the census referred to in footnote 39; Pethick is listed as a "teamster at Mr. Brownscombe's" in the 1860 tax assessment rolls for Peterborough, no. 151.

[42] *Peterborough Review,* March 22, 1867.

[43] Census of Canada, 1870-71, Peterborough County W., Peterborough Town, district 56, sub-district c, schedule 6.

[44] Tax assessment rolls, Town of Peterborough, 1876, no. 260.

[45] *Peterborough Examiner,* May 11, 1877.

[46] Partnership declaration 187, dated November 22, 1878, Peterborough County Registry Office, Peterborough.

[47] Instrument 163, dated May 1, 1871, North Monaghan Twp., Peterborough County Registry Office, Peterborough.

[48] *Peterborough Examiner,* March 22, 1877.

[49] Instrument 4816, lease, dated March 4, 1880, Peterborough County Registry Office, Peterborough.

[50] Instrument 4967½, assignment of lease, dated October 27, 1881, Peterborough County Registry Office, Peterborough.

[51] Instrument 17565, dated October 25, 1904, N. Monaghan Twp., Peterborough County Registry Office, Peterborough.

[52] Instrument 8296, dated December 5, 1912, N. Monaghan Twp., Peterborough County Registry Office, Peterborough.

[53] Instrument 471, dated January 18, 1871, Mara Twp., Simcoe County Registry Office, Barrie.

[54] Instrument 1253, dated March 13, 1875, Mara Twp., Simcoe County Registry Office, Barrie.

[55] Instrument 470, dated September 9, 1871, Thorah Twp., Durham Registry Office, Whitby; Instrument 425, dated October 28, 1871, Thorah Twp., Durham Registry Office, Whitby.

[56] Tax assessment rolls for 1873, Thorah Twp., no. 291.

[57] Instrument 6026, dated June 24, 1856, Thorah Twp., Durham Registry Office, Whitby.

[58] Instrument 95, dated March 2, 1869, Thorah Twp., Durham Registry Office, Whitby.

[59] Instrument 2749, dated December 18, 1885, Thorah Twp., Durham Registry Office, Whitby.

[60] Instrument 3876, dated May 3, 1898, Thorah Twp., Durham Registry Office, Whitby.

[61] Instrument 4193, dated May 1, 1902, Thorah Twp., Durham Registry Office, Whitby.

[62] Instrument 5256, dated April 18, 1913, Thorah Twp., Durham Registry Office, Whitby.

[63] *Ontario Gazetteer & Directory 1903-04* (Ingersoll: Ontario Publishing & Advertising Co., 1903), p. 60.

[64] Instrument 5659, dated April 18, 1918, Thorah Twp., Durham Registry Office, Whitby.

[65] *Mercantile Agency Reference Book* for July 1876 lists Bemister as a potter. In the tax assessment rolls for Thorah Twp. for 1877 he is listed as a tenant at the pottery on lot 16.

[66] Instrument 1683, dated November 13, 1878, Thorah Twp., Durham Registry Office, Whitby.

[67] In the tax assessment roll for 1905, the pottery site is listed as rented to Chan Sing, who was operating a hand laundry.

CHAPTER SEVEN: THE WORKSHOPS OF YORK COUNTY

[1] *History of Toronto and County of York, Ontario.* Vol. II (Toronto: C. B. Robinson, publisher, 1885), pp. 191-93.

[2] Census of Canada 1870-71, York County W., York Twp., District 44, sub-district c, schedule 6, page 3.

[3] As quoted in Jean Bacso, "Nineteenth Century Potteries in Toronto." Unpublished ms. (Toronto: University of Toronto, 1971), pp. 2-3.

[4] Henry Scadding, *Toronto of Old* (Toronto: Adam, Stevenson & Co., 1873), pp. 431-32.

[5] *Commemorative Biographical Record of the County of York, Ontario* (Toronto: J. H. Beers & Co., 1907), p. 52.

[6] Instrument 9242, Toronto Boroughs & York South Registry Office, Toronto.

[7] Instrument 17136, Toronto Boroughs & York South Registry Office, Toronto.

[8] J. Armstrong, ed., *Rowsell's City of Toronto and County of York Directory for 1850-51* (Toronto: Henry Rowsell, 1850), p. 146.

[9] Jean Bacso, "Nineteenth Century Potteries In Toronto." Unpublished ms. (Toronto: University of Toronto, 1971), pp. 6-7.

[10] Instrument 54872, dated August 23, 1854, Toronto Boroughs & York South Registry Office, Toronto.

[11] Census of Canada 1860-61, York County, York Twp., district 2, ward 2, page 56, lines 23, 24.

[12] *Canadian Agriculturalist* (1858), pp. 207-208.

[13] Census of Canada 1860-61, York County, York Twp., district 3, page 106, lines 30-33.

[14] *Nason's East and West Ridings. . .* (Toronto: James R. Nason, comp. & pub., 1871), p. 70.

[15] Census of Canada 1870-71, York County W., York Twp., District 44, sub-district c, division 2, page 18, entry 67.

[16] Census of Canada 1870-71, York County W., York Twp., district 44, sub-district c, division 2, schedule 6, page 1.

[17] Bacso, "Nineteenth Century Potteries In Toronto." Unpublished ms. (Toronto: University of Toronto, 1971), p. 52*ff.*

[18] Tax assessment rolls for 1870, Albion Twp., Peel County, Ward 2, no. 14.

[19] Census of Canada 1860-61, York County, York Twp., district 4, page 133, nos. 2-5.

[20] *Ibid.*

[21] J. Armstrong, ed., *Rowsell's City of Toronto*

and *County of York Directory* (Toronto: Henry Rowsell, 1850), p. 140.

[22] Bacso, "Nineteenth Century Potteries In Toronto." Unpublished ms. (Toronto: University of Toronto, 1971), p. 9.

[23] *Commemorative Biographical Record of the County of York, Ontario* (Toronto: J. H. Beers & Co., 1907), p. 432.

[24] *Ibid.*

[25] *Ibid.*, p. 442-43.

[26] *Canadian Agriculturalist* (1858), pp. 207-208.

[27] Census of Canada 1860-61, York County, York Twp., district 3, pp. 119, lines 7 & 8.

[28] *Ibid.*

[29] Census of Canada 1870-71, York County W., York Twp., district 44, sub-district c, division 4 lists Joseph Brown as the proprietor of the business.

[30] *History of Toronto and County of York, Ontario* Vol. II (Toronto: C. B. Robinson, publisher, 1885), pp. 213-14.

[31] Co-partnership declaration 708, dissolution of partnership dated March 25, 1907, Toronto Boroughs and York South Registry Office, Toronto.

[32] *History of Toronto and County of York, Ontario* Vol. II (C. B. Robinson, publisher, 1885), pp. 195-96.

[33] Census of Canada 1860-61, York County, York Twp., district 6, page 195, lines 1-9.

[34] *Transactions of the Board of Agriculture of Upper Canada* (Toronto: Board of Agriculture of Upper Canada, 1858), p. 341-42.

[35] *Transactions of the Board of Agriculture and Agricultural Association of Upper Canada 1864-1868* (Toronto: Board of Agriculture & Agricultural Association of Upper Canada, 1866), p. 320.

[36] Instrument 69331, dated September 26, 1857, Toronto Boroughs and York South Registry Office, Toronto.

[37] Census of Canada 1870-71, York County E., York Twp., district 45, sub-district a, division 1, schedule 6, page 1.

[38] *Union Publishing Company's Farmers and Businessmen's Directory for the Counties of Ontario, Peel and York for 1884-85* (Ingersoll: Union Publishing Co., 1884), pp. 318, 560.

[39] Tax assessment roll for 1883, York Twp., no. 258.

[40] Tax assessment roll for 1882, Beverley Twp., Wentworth County, no. 110.

[41] Tax assessment roll for 1885, York Twp., no. 98.

[42] Tax assessment roll for 1905, York Twp., no. 1937.

[43] Toronto Public Library Board, *North Toronto In Pictures 1889-1912*. Local History Handbook Series (Toronto: Toronto Public Library Board, 1974), n.p.

[44] *Commemorative Biographical Record of the County of York, Ontario* (Toronto: H. H. Beers & Co., 1907), pp. 635-36.

[45] *Ibid.*, p. 635.

[46] *Ibid.*, p. 636.

[47] Letters Patent dated February 4, 1928. Company Branch. Ontario Ministry of Consumer & Commercial Relations, Toronto.

[48] Partnership declaration 39849, registered July 4, 1938, Toronto Registry Office, Toronto.

[49] Declaration 42936, dissolution of partnership, dated December 30, 1939, Toronto Registry Office, Toronto.

[50] William C. Ketchum Jr., *The Potters & Potteries of New York State* (New York: Funk & Wagnalls, 1970), pp. 103-4.

[51] Tax assessment rolls for 1857 and 1858, City of Toronto, St. Lawrence Ward, district 4, no. 149.

[52] Census of Canada 1860-61, City of Toronto, St. Lawrence Ward, district 4, no. 149.

[53] Census of Canada 1860-61, Brant County, South Dumfries Twp., Town of Paris, p. 15.

[54] Tax assessment rolls for 1864, City of Toronto, St. Lawrence Ward, no. 1917.

[55] Jean Bacso, "Nineteenth Century Potteries In Toronto." Unpublished ms. (Toronto: University of Toronto, n.d.), p. 32.

[56] *City of Toronto Directory for 1867-8* (Toronto: W. C. Chewett & Co., publishers, 1867), p. 340.

[57] Census of Canada 1870-71, York County, Toronto E., St. Lawrence Ward, district 47, sub-district 6, division a, schedule 6, page 1.

[58] File 2226, Toronto Pottery Co. Ltd., Company Branch, Ontario Ministry of Consumer & Commercial Relations, Toronto.

[59] C. Dean Blair, *The Potters & Potteries of Summit County 1828-1915* (Akron: The Summit County Historical Society, 1965), p. 10.

[60] David L. Newlands, "A Toronto Pottery Co., Ltd. Catalogue," *Material History Bulletin* 5 (Spring, 1978).

[61] Instrument 58181, dated January 31, 1855, Toronto Boroughs and York South Registry Office, Toronto.

[62] Plan 631, Markham Twp., registered July 17, 1885, Toronto Boroughs and York South Registry Office, Toronto.

[63] Instrument 67574, dated May 5, 1857, Toronto Boroughs & York South Registry Office, Toronto.

[64] Census of Canada 1860-61, York County, Markham Twp., district 13, p. 131, lines 41 to 49.

[65] *Ibid.*

[66] Tax assessment rolls for 1868, Waterloo County, Woolwich Twp., no. 30.

[67] Census of Canada 1870-71, York County E., Markham Twp., Markham Village, district 45, sub-district d, schedule 6.

[68] Helen Sutermeister, "Three Early Pottery Sites In Southern Ontario." Unpublished paper (Toronto: Royal Ontario Museum, 1968), p. 3.

[69] *Ibid.*, p. 8.

[70] *Ibid.*, p. 14.

[71] Tax assessment rolls for 1863, York County, Markham Twp., no. 111.

[72] Tax assessment roll for 1876, York County, Markham Twp., no. 641.

[73] *Mercantile Agency Reference Book* for July 1881 through January 1898. (New York: Dun, Wiman & Co.)

[74] Instrument 6928, dated January 13, 1891, Markham Twp., Toronto Boroughs & York South Registry Office, Toronto.

[75] Instrument 12894, dated April 1, 1912, Markham Twp., Toronto Boroughs and York South Registry Office, Toronto.

CHAPTER EIGHT: POTTERS OF WEST CENTRAL ONTARIO

[1] Census of Canada 1851-52, Nelson Twp., Halton County, part 1, page 11, lines 14-19.

[2] *Hamilton, Canada, A Carnival Souvenir* (Hamilton: Hamilton Spectator, August 1903) p. 81.

[3] Instrument 302B, dated May 1, 1854, Nelson Twp., Halton County Registry Office, Milton.

[4] Census of Canada 1851-52, Peel County, Toronto Twp., ward 4, page 65.

[5] Instrument 332E, dated January 1, 1864, Trafalgar Twp., Halton County Registry Office, Milton.

[6] Instrument 1724, dated July 5, 1871, Esquesing Twp., Halton County Registry Office, Milton.

[7] Instrument T5521, dated January 22, 1889, Esquesing Twp., Halton County Registry Office, Milton.

[8] Census of Canada 1860-61, Halton County, Esquesing Twp., district 2, page 29, lines 1-8.

[9] Census of Canada 1870-71, Halton County, Esquesing Twp., district 38, sub-district f, division 4, page 72, no. 275.

[10] *Ibid.*, schedule 6.

[11] Instrument 1802, dated December 1, 1849, Toronto Twp., Peel County Registry Office, Brampton.

[12] Census of Canada 1851-52, Peel County, London Twp., ward 4, page 65, lines 11-18.

[13] Tax assessment rolls for 1863, Hamilton City, St. George's Ward.

[14] Tax assessment rolls for 1865, Hamilton City, St. George's Ward.

[15] Census of Canada 1851-52, Peel County, Toronto Twp., ward 4, page 65.

[16] Instrument 1053, dated November, 1854, Toronto Twp., Peel County Registry Office, Brampton.

[17] Census of Canada 1870-71, Peel County, Streetsville, district 39, sub-district b, schedule 6.

[18] Tax assessment rolls for 1881 to 1885 list Irwin as a "bailiff."

[19] Tax assessment rolls for 1886, Streetsville, no. 109.

[20] Reported in J. Kadoke, "A History of the Pottery Industry in Streetsville." Unpublished ms. (Waterloo: Wilfrid Laurier University, 1977), p. 9.

[21] Tax assessment rolls for 1892, Streetsville, no. 96.

[22] Instrument 111, dated December 16, 1876, Bolton, Peel County Registry Office, Brampton.

[23] Tax assessment rolls for 1904, Bolton, no. 177.

[24] Census of Canada 1870-71, Wellington County, Orangeville, district 34, sub-district i, schedule 6.

[25] Instrument 1661, dated March 26, 1874, Orangeville, Dufferin County Registry Office, Orangeville.

[26] Instrument 3663, dated January 29, 1883, Orangeville, Dufferin County Registry Office, Orangeville.

[27] Tax assessment rolls for Orangeville for years 1888 to 1890.

[28] *County of Wellington Gazetteer & Directory 1879-80* (Elmira: Armstrong & Delion, 1879), p. 135.

[29] *Mercantile Agency Reference Book* for July, 1883 (New York: Dun, Wiman & Co., 1883).

[30] Instrument 976, dated January 16, 1880, Harriston, Wellington N. Registry Office, Arthur.

[31] *Province of Ontario . . . Directory 1892-93* (Toronto: Might Directory Co., 1892), p. 710.

[32] *Mitchell's Canada . . . Directory for 1864-5* (Toronto: J. L. Mitchell, pub. 1864), p. 653.

[33] *Mitchell & Co's Canada . . . Directory for 1865-66* (Toronto: Mitchell & Co., pub. 1865).

CHAPTER NINE: KILNS OF THE GEORGIAN BAY – LAKE SIMCOE REGION

[1] Crown land patent dated August 22, 1866, Simcoe County Registry Office, Barrie.

[2] Census of Canada 1870-71, Simcoe County, Tay Township, district 42, sub-district h, division 1, schedule 6.

[3] Tax assessment rolls for Innisfil Twp. for 1860, no. 264. Simcoe County Archives, Minesing, Ontario.

[4] Instrument 36014, dated July 2, 1863, Innisfil Twp., Simcoe County Registry Office, Barrie.

[5] Instrument 5649, dated September 6, 1860, Derby Twp., Grey North Registry Office, Owen Sound.

[6] *Gazetteer and Directory of the County of Grey* for 1865-66 (Toronto: W. W. Smith, 1865), p. 143.

[7] Instrument 379, dated November 28, 1871, Derby Twp., Grey North Registry Office, Owen Sound.

[8] Census of Canada 1870-71, Grey North, Derby Twp., District 37, sub-district e, schedule 6.

[9] Census of Canada 1860-61, Derby Twp., District 2, p. 13.

[10] Instrument 156, dated March 24, 1870, Sullivan Twp., Grey North Registry Office, Owen Sound.

[11] Instrument 2081, dated December 27, 1872, Town of Hanover, Grey South Registry Office, Durham, Ontario.

[12] Census of Canada 1870-71, Grey South, Bentinck Township, District 36, division a, schedule 6, p. 3.

[13] Instrument 3485, dated April 17, 1882, Normanby Twp., Grey South Registry Office, Durham, Ontario.

[14] Land Patent, dated February 14, 1867, Sydenham Twp., Grey North Registry Office, Owen Sound.

[15] T. Arthur Davidson, *A History of the County of Grey* (Owen Sound: Grey County Historical Society, 1972), p. 305.

[16] Instrument 2751, dated August 1, 1879, Sydenham Twp., Grey North Registry Office, Owen Sound.

[17] Instrument 4591, dated January 31, 1884, Town of Owen Sound, Grey North Registry Office, Owen Sound.

[18] *Gazetteer & Directory of the County of Grey for 1865-6* (Toronto: W. W. Smith, 1865), p. 261.

[19] Census of Canada 1870-71, Owen Sound, Grey North, District 37, sub-district g, Division 3, Schedule 6.

[20] Partnership declaration dated September 19, 1895, filed in Grey North Registry Office, Owen Sound.

[21] *Mercantile Agency Reference Book*, January, 1908, gives the last listing for Horning & Brownscombe. The information for this issue of the book would have been collected in the fall of 1907.

[22] *Directory of the County of Bruce, Canada West* (Montreal: J. W. Rooklidge, 1867), p. 167.

[23] Instrument 3862, dated April 1, 1884, Arran Twp., Bruce County Registry Office, Walkerton, Ontario.

[24] Norman McLeod, *The History of the County of Bruce 1907-1968* (Owen Sound: Bruce County Historical Society, 1969), p. 424.

[25] Grant to Cyrus Eby, Township of Amabel, County of Bruce, Liber 43, folio 199.

[26] Tax assessment rolls for Elderslie Twp. in 1880, no. 63.

[27] Census of Canada 1870-71, Bruce County, Arran Township, District 28, sub-district e, division 3, schedule 6.

[28] Instrument 103, dated September 3, 1867, Arran Twp., Bruce County Registry Office, Walkerton, Ontario.

[29] Census of Canada 1870-71, Bruce North, Arran Twp., District 28, sub-district e, division 3, schedule 6.

[30] Census of Canada 1870-71, Bruce South, Carrick Twp., District 27, sub-district d, division 2, schedule 6.

[31] Instrument 863, dated September 30, 1870, Kinloss Twp., Bruce County Registry Office, Walkerton.

[32] Elsie Woolley, "A Tragedy of the Early Days," in *The Bruce County Historical Society Yearbook for 1972*, p. 29.

[33] *Ibid.*

CHAPTER TEN: POTTERY SHOPS OF WATERLOO COUNTY

[1] Donald B. Webster, *The William Eby Pottery, Conestogo, Ontario, 1855-1907* (Toronto: Royal Ontario Museum, 1971).

[2] David L. Newlands, *The New Hamburg Pottery, New Hamburg, Ontario, 1854-1916* (Waterloo: Wilfred Laurier University Press, 1978).

[3] Instrument 628, Volume G1, dated November 17, 1852. Waterloo Region Registry Office, Kitchener, Ontario.

[4] Census of Canada 1860-61, Village of Waterloo, District 3, page 22, lines 39-44.

[5] Census of Canada 1870-71, District 32, sub-district 15, division e, Waterloo Village, schedule 6, p. 5.

[6] Instrument 1153, Volume G2, dated April 15, 1874, Waterloo Region Registry Office, Kitchener, Ontario.

[7] Tax assessment rolls, Village of Waterloo for 1886.

[8] *Ibid.*, 1890-1907.

[9] Census of Canada 1860-61, Village of Berlin, District 1, lines 22-32.

[10] *Ibid.*

[11] *Ibid.*

[12] *Ibid.*

[13] Census of Canada 1870-71, District 32, sub-district 13, division d, Town of Berlin, schedule 6, p. 3.

[14] *Mercantile Agency Reference Book* (New York: Dun, Wiman & Co., various dates).

[15] Census of 1851-52, District 1, page 45, Waterloo Twp., Waterloo County.

[16] Tax assessment roll for 1853, Ward 1, Waterloo Twp., Waterloo Co.

[17] Instrument 1325, dated December 10, 1856, Waterloo Region Registry Office, Kitchener.

[18] Tax assessment roll for 1863, Ward 1, Waterloo Twp., Waterloo Co.

[19] Tax assessment rolls for 1872 and 1873, Ward 1, Waterloo Twp., Waterloo Co.

[20] Tax assessment roll for 1874, Ward 1, Waterloo Twp., Waterloo Co.

[21] "Deserted Villages in Waterloo County," in *Eighteenth Annual Report of the Waterloo Historical Society* for 1930, p. 168.

[22] Instrument 191, dated November 22, 1853, book B2, folio 713, Waterloo Region Registry Office, Kitchener.

[23] Census of 1851-52, District 2, page 97, Waterloo Twp., Waterloo County.

[24] Census of 1860-61, District 6, page 38, Waterloo Twp., Waterloo County.

[25] Instrument 4029, dated April 9, 1867, book B9, Waterloo Region Registration Office, Kitchener.

[26] Tax assessment rolls for 1866, Ward 2, Waterloo Twp., Waterloo Co.

[27] Census of Canada 1870-71, District 32, subdistrict c, division 2, Waterloo Township.

[28] Instrument 6377, dated December 11, 1875, book B15, Waterloo Region Registry Office, Kitchener.

[29] Instrument 6960, dated November 2, 1877, book B18, Waterloo Region Registry Office, Kitchener.

[30] Instrument 7070, dated February 5, 1878, Waterloo Region Registry Office, Kitchener.

[31] Tax assessment rolls for 1901, Ward 3, Waterloo Twp., Waterloo County.

[32] Instrument 105, dated January 15, 1833, book H, Waterloo Region Registry Office, Kitchener.

[33] By the time of the census of 1851-52, William Schwab is in Clinton Twp., Lincoln County (see census rolls for district 6, Clinton Twp., page 77). Schwab continued to pot, later with the assistance of his son. The family business was discontinued sometime in the 1870s.

[34] Harold Jarvis, "Potters of Lincoln County," *Canadian Antiquities Collector*, 2 (September, 1967), p. 9.

[35] Instument 698, dated March 5, 1834, Liber H, Waterloo Region Registry Office, Kitchener.

[36] Instrument 65, dated June 27, 1834, Liber I, Waterloo Region Registry Office, Kitchener.

[37] Census of Canada 1870-71, District 31, subdistrict F, division a, Waterloo Twp. Waterloo Co., schedule 6.

[38] The last directory listing for Henry Steumpfle as a potter is the *Dominion of Canada...Directory 1899* (Toronto: Might Directory Co., n.d.), p. 1044.

[39] Instrument 1209, dated April 7, 1865, Book AE 2, folio 147, Wellesley Twp., Waterloo Region Registry Office, Kitchener.

[40] Instrument 1718, dated March 7, 1866, book AE 3, folio 128, Wellesley Twp., Waterloo Region Registry Office, Kitchener.

[41] Instrument 6248, dated May 31, 1884, Wellesley Twp., Waterloo Region Registry Office, Kitchener.

[42] Instrument 7009, dated January 7, 1887, book AE 16, folio 331, Wellesley Twp., Waterloo Region Registry Office, Kitchener.

[43] Instrument 7458, dated February 15, 1888, book AE 17, Wellesley Twp., Waterloo Region Registry Office, Kitchener.

[44] *Ontario . . . Directory for 1888-89* (Toronto: R. L. Polk & Co., n.d.), p. 471.

[45] *Huron Expositor,* published in Seaforth, Ontario, in the September 7, 1888 issue, page 1, column 6, reports the operation of Pegler & Winn's pottery.

[46] *Mitchell's Canada . . . Directory for 1864-65* (Toronto: J. L. Mitchell, publisher, n.d.), p. 250.

[47] Webster, *The Eby Pottery*, p. 3.

[48] *Ibid.*

[49] Instrument 370, dated May 2, 1843, Book B, folio 306, Woolwich Twp., Waterloo Region Registry Office, Kitchener.

[50] Abraham E. Weaver, *A Standard History of Elkhart County Indiana*, Vol. II (New York: American Historical Society, 1916), p. 902-3.

[51] Instrument 848, dated July 2, 1857, Book F2, Woolwich Twp., Waterloo Region Registry Office, Kitchener.

[52] Instrument 11170, dated April 10, 1906, Woolwich Twp., Waterloo Region Registry Office, Kitchener.

[53] *Counties of Perth & Waterloo Gazetteer and Directory for 1870-71* (Toronto: James Sutherland, compiler, 1869), p. 210.

[54] Instrument 22, dated March 15, 1853, Wilmot Twp., Waterloo Region Registry Office, Kitchener.

[55] Instrument 789, dated August 11, 1856, Wilmot Twp., Waterloo Region Registry Office, Kitchener.

[56] *The Canada Directory for 1857-58* (Montreal: John Lovell, publisher, n.d.), p. 466.

[57] Instrument 211, dated August 6, 1858, Wilmot Twp., Waterloo Region Registry Office, Kitchener.

[58] Instrument 60, dated September 6, 1856, book H, folio 69, Wilmot Twp., Waterloo Region Registry Office.

[59] David L. Newlands, "The New Hamburg Pottery, "*Canadian Collector* (vol. 12, No. 4, July-August 1977); *The New Hamburg Pottery, New Hamburg, Ontario 1854-1916* (Waterloo: Wilfred Laurier University Press, 1978), pp. 1-53.

[60] *The Canada Directory for 1857-58* (Montreal: Robert McKay, compiler, 1851), p. 204.

[61] W. H. Smith, "Business Directory for Canada West" in *Canada: Past, Present and Future,* vol. 1 (Toronto: Thomas Maclear, 1851), p. 84.

[62] Instrument 1630, dated September 15, 1856, Waterloo Region Registry Office, Kitchener.

[63] Instrument 443, dated August 3, 1854, Wellesley Twp., book 1, folio 22, Waterloo Region Registry Office, Kitchener, records the purchase of the lot and Instrument 75, dated November 2, 1855, Wellesley Twp., Waterloo Region Registry Office, Kitchener, records the sale of the lot.

CHAPTER ELEVEN: POTTERY SHOPS OF PERTH AND HURON COUNTIES

[1] Instrument 103, dated July 11, 1855, Perth County Registry Office, Stratford.

[2] Census of Canada 1860-61, Perth County, South Easthope Twp., District 2, p. 14.

[3] *Ibid.*

[4] Instrument 4879, dated August 24, 1871, Perth County, Town of Stratford, Perth County Registry Office, Stratford.

[5] Tax assessment rolls for 1883, Town of Stratford, nos. 73, 74.

[6] Tax assessment rolls for 1884, Town of Stratford, nos. 1288, 1289.

[7] Instrument 683, dated March 29, 1859, Fullarton Twp., Perth County, Registry Office, Stratford.

[8] *Lovell's Canadian Dominion Directory for 1871* (Montreal: John Lovell, n.d.), p. 299.

[9] *Ibid.*

[10] Vera E. McNichol, *Reveries of A Pioneer* (Kitchener: Dixon Press Ltd., 1966), p. 56.

[11] Instrument 32, dated October 16, 1884, Milverton, Perth County Registry Office, Stratford.

[12] Instrument 6, dated September 26, 1854, Tuckersmith Twp., Huron County Registry Office, Goderich.

[13] Census of Canada 1870-71, Huron S., Tuckersmith Twp., District 25, sub-district e, division 3, schedule 6, page 3.

[14] Instrument 176, Partnership Declarations, Huron County Registry Office, Goderich.

[15] A notice of dissolution was published in the *Huron Expositor* on September 1, 1876.

[16] Issues of the *Mercantile Agency Reference Book* for the years 1873-1876 report this rating.

[17] Instrument 6164, dated November 13, 1900, Tuckersmith Twp., Huron County Registry Office, Goderich.

[18] Instrument 1517, Partnership Declarations, Huron County Registry Office, Goderich.

[19] Instrument 9014, dated October 7, 1919, Tuckersmith Twp., Huron County Registry Office, Goderich.

[20] David L. Newlands, "The Egmondville Pottery 1852-1910," *Canadian Collector,* 10 (Jan.-Feb. 1975) pp. 22-25; "The Huron Pottery Egmondville, Ontario," *Archaeological Newsletter* 128 (January 1976), pp. 1-4; "The Huron Pottery Revisited," *Canadian Collector,* 11 (March-April 1976), pp. 19-22; "A Catalogue of Sprig Moulds From Two Huron County, Ontario, Earthenware Potteries," *Material History Bulletin,* 3 (Spring 1977), pp. 15-30.

[21] Census of Canada 1860-61, Huron County, Hay Twp., district 3, page 31.

[22] Instrument 531, dated January 14, 1871, Hay Twp., Huron County Registry Office, Goderich.

[23] Census of Canada 1870-71, Huron S., Hay Twp., Zurich Village, District 25, sub-district 2, schedule 6.

[24] Instrument 399, dated March 15, 1869, Grey Twp., Ethel Village, Huron County Registry Office, Goderich.

[25] Issues of the *Mercantile Agency Reference Book* up to July 1881 list Spence as operating a pottery in Ethel.

[26] *Union Publishing Company's Farmers' & Businessmen's Directory of Bruce, Grey, Huron and Simcoe Counties . . .* (Ingersoll: Union Publishing Co., 1890), p. 528.

[27] Instrument 2041, dated March 17, 1881, Wingham, Huron County Registry Office, Goderich.

[28] Instrument 2540, dated November 3, 1888, Wingham, Huron County Registry Office, Goderich.

[29] *Mercantile Agency Reference Book,* July 1890.

[30] David L. Newlands, "The David Burns Pottery Site, Huron County, Ontario," *Archaeological Newsletter* 113 (October, 1974), pp. 1-4.

CHAPTER TWELVE: POTTERIES AND POTTERS OF BRANT COUNTY

[1] Instrument 16, dated June 11, 1803, Brant County Registry Office, Brantford.

[2] R. Cuthbertson Muir, *The Early Political and Military History of Burford* (Quebec: La Cie. d'Impr. Commerciale, 1913), pp. 88-89.

[3] Instrument 140, dated March 18, 1857, Brant County Registry Office, Brantford.

[4] The assessment roll for 1857 for Oakland Twp. Village of Scotland, lists Daniel Haines as a potter, presumably in the same household as Marlatt. The 1861 census lists Jacob Mariedetz *(sic)*, sixty years old, and John Garland, thirty years old, also in Scotland. Garland later appears as owner of a pottery in the village of Colborne, Norfolk County, which was later operated by Marlatt's son Abraham.

[5] Census of 1851-52, Brant County, South Dumfries Twp., Village of Paris, pp. 57-58, lines 33-37.

[6] *Ibid.*

[7] *Canada Directory for 1857-58* (Montreal, 1857), p. 503.

[8] General Will No. 56, Brant County Registry Office, probated August 31, 1868.

[9] *County of Brant . . . General Business Directory for 1865-6* (Ingersoll, 1864).

[10] Census of 1860-61, Brant County, South Dumfries Twp., Town of Paris, p. 15, lines 1-4.

[11] *Canadian Agriculturalist,* Vol. 12, 1860, p. 604.

[12] *County of Brant Gazetteer and Directory for 1869-70* (Toronto: 1869), p. 114.

[13] *History of the County of Brant* (Toronto, 1883), p. 678.

[14] *Ibid.*

[15] Assessment rolls for New Hamburg, Wilmot Twp., Waterloo County, list Herman Schmidt in the 1862-64 period as living on Peel Street. The 1864 listing describes his occupation as potter. At this time Henry Schuler would be twenty-two years old, old enough to be an apprentice or junior worker at the pottery. Schmidt is also listed as a potter in *Mitchell's Canada Gazetteer & Business Directory for 1864-65* (Toronto, 1864), p. 493.

[16] Marlatt is listed as a potter in Paris in the *Gazetteer and Directory of the Counties of Haldimand & Brant* (Toronto, 1867), p. 174.

[17] F. P. Goold owned the pottery at this time. For reference to Peter McGlade, see the City of Brantford assessment roll for 1867, Brant Ward, entry 116. Peter McGlade also resided in Brantford in 1868.

[18] *Paris Universal Exhibition . . . Official Catalogue of the Canadian Section* (London, 1878), pp. 274ff.

[19] *County of Brant Gazetteer and Directory for 1869-70* (Toronto, 1869), p. 114.

[20] Instrument 1121, dated March 20, 1865, Town of Paris, Vol. B, Brant County Registry Office, Brantford.

[21] Instrument 1144, dated August 16, 1865, Town of Paris, Vol. B, Brant County Registry Office, Brantford.

[22] *History of the County of Brant* (Toronto, 1883), p. 648.

[23] *Paris Star,* article on Ahrens Pottery, dated April 27, 1972.

[24] Minutes of the Paris, Ontario, Town Council, volume dated 1880-87, p. 223.

[25] *Ibid.,* p. 224.

[26] An almost complete set of the *Mercantile Agency Reference Book,* from 1864 on, can be found in the library of Dun & Bradstreet, Toronto.

[27] *The Gazetteer and Directory of the Southern Division of the Grand Truck Railway for 1889* (Ingersoll, 1889), p. 54, also indicates that J. H. Ahrens & Co., pottery, was in operation at this time, but the location is given as Paris Station.

[28] *History of the County of Brant* (Toronto, 1883), p. 296.

[29] Brantford tax assessment rolls for 1851, Brant Ward.

[30] Instrument 170, dated July 23, 1853, Brant County Registry Office, Brantford.

[31] Brantford assessment rolls for 1853, Brant Ward.

[32] *Canadian Agriculturalist,* Vol. 4, 1852, p. 311.

[33] See article on potteries of Paris, Ontario, in *Canadian Collector* (Nov.-Dec. 1976) for quote on cost of shipping stoneware clay from New Jersey.

[34] *History of the County of Brant* (Toronto, 1883), p. 549-50.

[35] *Brantford Expositor,* May 15, 1857, p. 1.

[36] *Ibid.*

[37] Instrument 2299, dated August 20, 1859, Brant County Registry Office, Brantford.

[38] D. B. Webster, *The Brantford Pottery* (Toronto: Royal Ontario Museum, 1968), fig. 7, p. 20.

[39] *Canadian Agriculturalist,* Vol. 12, 1860, pps. 566, 604.

[40] *Ibid.,* vol. 14, 1862, p. 754.

[41] Webster, *The Brantford Pottery,* p. 8.

[42] Instrument 4321, dated October 29, 1867, Brant County Registry Office, Brantford.

[43] Instrument 4321, dated October 29, 1867, Brant County Registry Office, Brantford.

[44] Instrument 6623, dated December 18, 1872, Brant County Registry Office, Brantford.

[45] Instrument 6716, dated March 8, 1873, Brant County Registry Office, Brantford.

[46] Brantford assessment rolls for year 1873 through 1894.

[47] *Brantford Expositor,* July 27, 1883.

[48] O'Brien no longer appears on the assessment rolls after the year 1905.

[49] Letter from Henry Schuler, former secretary of Brantford Stoneware Manufacturing Co. to Thomas Mulvey, Esq., Asst. Provincial Secretary, Toronto, dated November 8, 1907. Provincial Archives RG 81-1-D General Correspondence.

[50] Instrument 33410, dated January 26, 1907, Brant County Registry Office, Brantford.

[51] *Lovell's Canadian Dominion Directory for 1871* (Montreal, 1871?), p. 227.

[52] *Gazetteer and Directory of the Southern Division of the Grand Trunk Railway for 1889* (Ingersoll, 1889), p. A262.

[53] *Brantford City Directory for 1895-6* (Ingersoll, n.d.

[54] *Lovell's Business & Professional Directory for 1896-97* (Montreal, n.d.), p. 247.

[55] The *Mercantile Agency Reference Book* lists Wendlin B. Schuler as operating a pottery from late

1896 through late 1897, with a worth of not more than $500. No actual credit rating is given during this time.

[56] *Brantford City Directory for 1903-04* (Ingersoll, n.d.), p. 256.

CHAPTER THIRTEEN: FACTORIES OF THE CITY OF HAMILTON– WENTWORTH COUNTY REGION

[1] G. L. Buttrum, "The Ashbaugh Farm" in T. Roy Woodhouse, *Ancaster Heritage* (Ancaster: Ancaster Twp. Historical Society, 1973), p. 112.

[2] Tax assessment rolls for 1856, City of Hamilton, St. Lawrence Ward, No. 48.

[3] *Transactions of the Board of Agriculture and the Agricultural Association of Upper Canada*, Vol. VI, 1864-68 (Toronto: Agricultural & Arts Assn. of Ontario, 1872), p. 62.

[4] *Ibid.*, p. 80.

[5] Tax assessment rolls for 1866, City of Hamilton, St. George's Ward, No. 12.

[6] Partnership declaration No. 249, dated May 28, 1872, Wentworth County Registry Office, Hamilton.

[7] Census of Canada 1870-71, Hamilton City, St. George's Ward, District 24, sub-district A, division 2, schedule 6.

[8] Partnership declaration No. 550, dated March 24, 1876, Wentworth County Registry Office, Hamilton.

[9] File C 23069, Company Division, Ontario Ministry of Consumer & Commercial Relations, Toronto.

[10] Letters Patent, dated April 24, 1902, Foster Pottery Co., Ltd., Company Division, Ontario Ministry of Consumer & Commercial Relations, Toronto.

[11] The corporation was dissolved on March 15, 1912, by order of the Provincial Secretary. See Foster Pottery Co. file, Ministry of Consumer & Commercial Relations, Toronto.

[12] Robert J. Montgomery, *The Ceramic Industry of Ontario*, Vol. XXXIX, part IV. Thirty-Ninth Annual Report of the Ontario Department of Mines. (Toronto: Ontario Department of Mines, 1930), pp. 172-3.

[13] *Ibid.*

[14] Will 4511, probated January 21, 1898, Wentworth County Surrogate Court, Hamilton.

[15] Declaration 2306, dated January 1, 1898, Co-partnership Register, Wentworth County Registry Office, Hamilton.

[16] Will 4511, probated January 21, 1898, Wentworth County Surrogate Court, Hamilton.

[17] M. B. Baker, *Clay and the Clay Industry of Ontario*. Report of the Bureau of Mines (Ontario) (Vol. XV, Part II, 1906), p. 120.

[18] *Ibid.*

[19] Montgomery, *The Ceramic Industry of Ontario*, p. 173.

[20] *Vernon's City of Hamilton . . . Directory for 1903* (Hamilton: Henry Vernon, 1903), p. 199.

[21] *Vernon's City of Hamilton . . . Directory for 1912* (Hamilton: Henry Vernon, 1912), p. 70.

[22] Partnership declaration No. 3885, dated November 10, 1916, Wentworth County Registry Office, Hamilton.

[23] Canadian Potteries Ltd., was incorporated by letters patent on January 9, 1919, and on January 27 they purchased the Canadian Trenton Potteries Ltd., which had been in business in Canada under the latter name for many years. Since business in Canada under the name Canada Potteries Ltd. would have been confusing, the name was changed by order of the Provincial Secretary to Hamilton Potteries Ltd.

[24] *Hamilton Spectator*, September 22, 1947, p. 7, cols. 1, 2.

[25] File 0029410, Company Division, Ontario Ministry of Consumer & Commercial Relations, Toronto.

[26] Partnership declaration 2161, Wentworth County Registry Office, Hamilton.

[27] Instrument 378, dated October 1, 1867, Beverley Twp., Wentworth County Registry Office, Hamilton.

[28] Instrument 643, dated August 24, 1868, Wentworth County Registry Office, Hamilton.

[29] Census of Canada 1870-71, Wentworth N, Beverley Twp., Village of Lynden, district 23, subdistrict A, division 2, schedule 6.

[30] Instrument 3129, dated June 30, 1877, Beverley Twp., Wentworth County Registry Office, Hamilton.

[31] Partnership declaration 1292, dated April 22, 1884, Wentworth County Registry Office, Hamilton.

[32] Instrument 5189, dated March 1, 1884, Beverley Twp., Wentworth County Registry Office, Hamilton.

[33] Instrument 5817, dated October 30, 1886, Beverley Twp., Wentworth County Registry Office, Hamilton.

[34] Instrument 6748, dated May 20, 1890, Beverley Twp., Wentworth County Registry Office, Hamilton.

[35] *Brantford Expositor*, November 16, 1894, p. 1.

[36] Instrument 8830, dated March 14, 1899, Beverley Twp., Wentworth County Registry Office, Hamilton.

[37] Tax assessment rolls 1854-58, Town of Dundas, Wentworth County, Mountain Ward.

[38] Census of Canada 1860-61, Wentworth County, W. Flamborough Twp., Town of Dundas, p. 20.

[39] In the assessment rolls of 1854, Swindle is reported as owning property. The only land he owned in 1847 was lots 11 and 12 in G. Rolph's Survey. See Instrument 64, Liber A, dated July 24, 1847, W. Flamborough Twp., Wentworth County Registry Office, Hamilton.

CHAPTER FOURTEEN: WORKSHOPS OF THE NIAGARA PENINSULA

[1] Instrument A90, dated November 21, 1848, Bertie Twp., Niagara South Registry Office, Welland.

[2] Census of 1851-52, Welland County, Bertie Twp., district 2, page 75, lines 14-17.

[3] Instrument B163, dated May 16, 1856, Bertie Twp., Niagara South Registry Office, Welland.

[4] Instrument 1918, dated May 23, 1854, Town of Thorold, Niagara South Registry Office, Welland.

[5] Census of 1851-52, Welland County, Town of Thorold, page 35, lines 27 and 28.

[6] Instrument 3524, dated October 16, 1855, Town of Thorold, Niagara South Registry Office, Welland.

[7] Instrument 7676, dated June 11, 1859, Town of Thorold, Niagara South Registry Office, Welland.

[8] *The Canada Directory* (Montreal: Robert W. S. MacKay, comp., 1851), p. 408.

[9] Instrument 123, dated April 8, 1869, Town of Thorold, Niagara South Registry Office, Welland.

[10] Tax assessment roll for 1869, Town of Thorold, no. 38.

[11] Census of 1870-71, Welland County, Town of Thorold, District 19, sub-district f, schedule 6.

[12] Census of 1870-71, Peterborough County, Peterborough town, district 56, sub-district c, division 1, page 86.

[13] Instrument 477, dated May 10, 1873, Town of Thorold, Niagara South Registry Office, Welland.

[14] Instrument 294, dated August 30, 1876, Town of Thorold, Niagara South Registry Office, Welland.

[15] W. W. Evans, comp. and pub., *Gazetteer & Business Directory of Lincoln & Welland Counties for 1879* (Brantford: William W. Evans, 1878).

[16] Land Patent, dated June 10, 1842, to John Martindale, lot 131, Niagara, Niagara District.

[17] Instrument 1570, dated July 2, 1849, Niagara, Niagara South Registry Office, Welland.

[18] Instrument 6735, dated October 21, 1823, Niagara North Registry Office, St. Catharines.

[19] Robert J. Sim & Arthur W. Clement, "The Cheesequake Potteries," *Antiques* XLVI (1944), p. 125.

[20] David Rupp, "The Kiln and Red Earthenware Pottery of the Jordan Pottery Site: A Preliminary Overview," *Northeast Historical Archaeology* 7. To be published in Fall, 1979.

[21] Instrument 5171, dated November 5, 1853, Clinton Twp., Niagara North Registry Office, St. Catharines.

[22] Census of 1860-61, Lincoln County, Clinton Twp., District 2, page 27, lines 14-17.

[23] Tax assessment rolls for 1863, Clinton Twp., Lincoln County, nos. 206, 207.

[24] Census of 1870-71, Lincoln County, Clinton Twp., District 21, sub-district e, division 2, schedule 6, page 3.

[25] Census of Upper Canada for 1842, Niagara District, Village of Beamsville.

[26] Instrument 11808, dated October 12, 1857, Niagara North Registry Office, St. Catharines.

[27] Census of 1860-61, Lincoln County, Clinton Twp., District 2, page 2, lines 34-39.

[28] Census of 1870-71, Lincoln County, Clinton Twp., District 21, sub-district e, division 2, schedule 6, page 9.

[29] *Ibid.*

[30] The *Mercantile Agency Reference Book* for January, 1872 was the last reference to the business, which means that it had been discontinued sometime early in 1872.

[31] Instrument 742, dated April 26, 1872, Village of Beamsville, Niagara North Registry Office, St. Catharines.

[32] Census of 1851-52, Lincoln County, Clinton Twp., District 6, page 63.

[33] Instrument 894, dated April 30, 1866, Village of Beamsville, Niagara North Registry Office, St. Catharines.

[34] Census of 1851-52, Lincoln County, Clinton Twp., District 6, page 17, line 47.

[35] Instrument 5505, dated January 31, 1854, Clinton Twp., Niagara North Registry Office, St. Catharines.

[36] Census of 1870-71, Lincoln County, Clinton Twp., District 21, sub-district e, division 1, schedule 6, page 3.

[37] Census of 1890-91, vol. 3 (Ottawa: S. E. Dawson, 1893), pp. 261-62.

[38] Instrument 2163, dated May 12, 1829; Instrument 2164, dated May 13, 1829, Grimsby Twp., Niagara North Registry Office, St. Catharines.

[39] Ruth Tracey, "Report on Culp Pottery Works Site." Unpublished ms. (Toronto: Archaeological & Historic Sites Board of Ontario, 1966), unpaged.

[40] Margaret Home, "John Kulp — Pioneer Potter," *Canadian Collector* 2 (September 1967), p. 11.

[41] Instrument 2582, dated September 14, 1877; Instrument 2583, dated July 6, 1877, Grimsby Twp., Niagara North Registry Office, St. Catharines.

CHAPTER FIFTEEN: POT SHOPS OF THE NORTH SHORE OF LAKE ERIE

[1] Census of 1851-52, Haldimand County, South Cayuga Twp., district 1, page 5, lines 44-46.

[2] *Mitchell & Co's Canada . . . Directory for 1865-66* (Toronto: Mitchell & Col, n.d.).

[3] *Mitchell's Canada . . . Directory for 1864-65* (Toronto: J. L. Mitchell, n.d.), p. 89.

[4] J. A. Bannister, "The Famous Normandale Furnace," in *Historical Highlights of Norfolk County*, new expanded ed. (Hamilton: compiled and published by Bruce M. Pearce, 1973), p. 55.

[5] *Union Publishing Co.'s Farmers' and Businessmen's Directory for the Counties of Brant, Halton, Norfolk, Waterloo, and Wellington* (Ingersoll: Union Publishing Co., 1885), p. 461; *Ontario Gazetteer & Directory, 1903-04* (Ingersoll: Ontario Publishing & Advertising Co., 1903), p. 785.

[6] *Ontario Directory, 1888-89* (Toronto: R. L. Polk & Co., n.d.), p. 834.

[7] *Mitchell's Canada Directory for 1864-65* (Toronto: J. L. Mitchell, n.d.), p. 578.

[8] Census of 1870-71, Norfolk County S, Woodhouse Twp., District 11, sub-district d, schedule 6.

[9] Issues of the *Mercantile Agency Reference Book* for 1895 to 1899 list both Abraham and Clayton Marlatt with pecuniary worth of less than $500 and a credit rating of "limited."

[10] The last credit-rating report listing the pottery was in the *Mercantile Agency Reference Book* of January, 1899, which would include information on businesses operating in the fall of 1898.

[11] Instrument 36304, dated June 1, 1874, Woodhouse Twp., Norfolk County Registry Office, Simcoe.

[12] Instrument 66475, dated October 13, 1886, Woodhouse Twp., Norfolk County Registry Office, Simcoe.

[13] Instrument 95377, dated December 1, 1900, Woodhouse Twp., Norfolk County Registry Office, Simcoe.

[14] Helen Sutermeister, "Three Early Pottery Sites In Southern Ontario." Unpublished ms. (Toronto: Royal Ontario Museum, 1969), pp. 22-34, figs. 16-22, plates 19-34.

[15] Instrument 27994, dated October 18, 1851, Townsend Twp., Norfolk County Registry Office, Simcoe.

[16] Instrument 36712, dated August 24, 1874, Townsend Twp., Norfolk County Registry Office, Simcoe.

[17] Instrument 22091, dated August 29, 1866, Townsend Twp., Norfolk County Registry Office, Simcoe.

[18] Instrument 115294, dated June 12, 1899, Townsend Twp., Norfolk County Registry Office, Simcoe.

[19] *Mitchell's Canada . . . Directory for 1864-65* (Toronto: J. L. Mitchell, n.d.) p. 680.

[20] *Ibid.*

[21] Census of Upper Canada, 1842, London District, Yarmouth Twp.

[22] Instrument 7033, dated January 16, 1832, Yarmouth Twp., Elgin County Registry Office, St. Thomas.

[23] Instrument 512, dated May 17, 1850, Yarmouth Twp., Elgin County Registry Office, St. Thomas.

[24] Instrument 4456, dated September 22, 1868, Bayham Twp., Elgin County Registry Office, St. Thomas.

[25] Instrument 6442, dated March 14, 1876, Bayham Twp., Elgin County Registry Office, St. Thomas.

[26] Instrument 3530, dated September 28, 1898, Bayham Twp., Elgin County Registry Office, St. Thomas.

[27] Census of 1870-71, Elgin County E., Bayham Twp., District 6, sub-district e, division 3, schedule 6.

[28] *Census of 1880-81, Elgin County E.,* Vol. 3 (Ottawa: MacLean, Roger & Co., 1882), pp. 446-49; *Census of 1890-91*, Vol. 3 (Ottawa: S. E. Dawson, 1893), pp. 261-62.

[29] Tax assessment roll, Howard Twp., 1852, no. 429.

[30] Instrument 289, dated November 19, 1864, Morpeth, Kent County Registry Office, Chatham.

[31] Instrument 271, dated November 23, 1868, Howard Twp., Kent County Registry Office, Chatham.

[32] Census of 1870-71, Kent County, Howard Twp., District 3, sub-district a, division 2, schedule 6.

[33] *Canada Directory, 1896-97* (Montreal: John Lovell, 1896), p. 1894.

[34] M. B. Baker, *Clay and the Clay Industry of Ontario*. Report of the Bureau of Mines, Ontario (Vol. XV, Part II, 1906), p. 72.

[35] *Census of 1890-91*, Vol. 3 (Ottawa: S. E. Dawson, 1893), pp. 261-62.

CHAPTER SIXTEEN: POTTERIES OF SOUTHWESTERN ONTARIO

[1] *Census of 1880-81*. Vol. 3 (Ottawa: MacLean, Roger & Co., 1882), pp. 446-49.

[2] *Huron Expositor,* March 16, 1883.

[3] Partnership declaration No. 780, filed November 9, 1883, Oxford County Registry Office, Woodstock.

[4] *Antwerp Universal Exhibition 1885,* Official

Catalogue of the Canadian Section (London, 1885), p. 20.

[5] Partnership declaration No. 850, filed March 19, 1886, Oxford County Registry Office, Woodstock.

[6] London Advertiser, August 7, 1886.

[7] Letter from S. F. Glass to Hon. John Carling. Public Archives of Canada. Department of Finance Records, RG 19.

[8] London Advertiser, August 7, 1886.

[9] Census of 1870-71, Middlesex County E, London Twp., district 9, sub-district c, division 6, schedule 6, page 7.

[10] Ibid.

[11] Co-partnership declaration No. 401, dated February 28, 1880, Middlesex County E. Registry Office, London.

[12] Tax assessment rolls, City of London, 1890.

[13] Partnership declaration No. 1751, dated June 9, 1904, Middlesex County E. Registry Office, London.

[14] Foster's London City and Middlesex County Directory, 1906, (Toronto: J. G. Foster & Co., 1906), p. 347.

[15] Vernon's City of London Directory 1907-08 (Hamilton: Henry Vernon, 1907), p. 548.

[16] Mercantile Agency Reference Book, January 1908.

[17] Issues of the Mercantile Agency Reference Book from January 1908 to July 1933 list the pottery. From July, 1911, onward no credit rating is listed.

[18] City of London and County of Middlesex Directory for 1881-82 (London: J. H. White, 1881), p. 501, 527.

[19] Census of 1870-71, Middlesex County E., London Twp., District 9, division 6, sub-district c, page 22.

[20] The Mercantile Agency Reference Book of January, 1884, is the last issue with any reference to the pottery, suggesting dissolution in 1883, the year the information would have been verified.

[21] The London City and Middlesex County Directory 1886 (London: R. Hills & Co., 1886), p. 231.

[22] Census of 1870-71, Middlesex County E., London Twp., District 9, sub-district c, division 6, page 22.

[23] Ontario Directory, 1884-85 (Toronto: R. L. Polk & Co., n.d.), p. 510.

[24] Census of 1870-71, Middlesex County E., London Twp., District 9, sub-district c, division 6, schedule 6, page 9.

[25] Shackleton, Philip. "Potteries of Nineteenth Century Ontario." Unpublished ms. (Ottawa: Historic Sites Branch, 1964), p. 73.

[26] London Crockery Manufacturing Company,

Letters Patent issued November 10, 1886, Charter Book 18, RG8, Company's Branch, Provincial Secretary Office, Archives of Ontario, Toronto.

[27] Ibid.

[28] London Advertiser, Sept. 7, 1886.

[29] Letter from William Glass to John Carling, dated April 15, 1887. Public Archives of Canada, Ottawa.

[30] Letter of S. F. Glass to John Carling, dated April 13, 1887. Public Archives of Canada, Ottawa.

[31] Liquidator's Report, May 20, 1890. Ontario Archives; London Advertiser, March 15, 1888.

[32] Patent 5645, dated March 26, 1891, Ministry of Consumer and Commercial Affairs, Ottawa.

[33] Daily Free Press, December 18, 1895.

[34] Ibid.

[35] Ontario Gazetteer and Directory 1903-04 (Ingersoll: Ontario Publishing and Advertising, 1903), p. 509.

[36] Census of 1842, London District.

[37] Canadian Agriculturalist, Vol. 6, 1854, p. 342.

[38] Instrument 7083, filed February 5, 1878, London Twp., District 9, sub-district c, division 1, schedule 6, page 4.

[39] Census of 1870-71, Middlesex County E., London Twp., District 9, sub-district c, division 1, schedule 6, page 4.

[40] Canada Directory for 1857-58 (Montreal: John Lovell, 1857), p. 283.

[41] Census of 1870-71, Middlesex County, London City, District 10, sub-district e, ward 5, schedule 6.

[42] Ibid.

[43] Tax assessment rolls, City of London, 1874.

[44] City of London and County of Middlesex Directory for 1881-82. (London: J. Harrison White, comp., 1881), p. 490.

[45] Report of the Canadian Commission at the International Exhibition of Philadelphia, 1876 (Ottawa: The Canadian Commission, 1877), p. 10.

[46] Ontario Directory, 1882-83 (Toronto: R. L. Polk & Co., 1882), p. 1332.

[47] The Mercantile Agency Reference Book January, 1906 gives the last listing for the firm. Information for this issue would have been collected late in 1905.

[48] Foster's London City and Middlesex County Directory, 1897-98 (Toronto: J. G. Foster & Co.,) p. 357, 427.

[49] Western Ontario Gazetteer and Directory 1898-99 (Ingersoll: Ontario Publishing and Advertising, 1898), p. 442.

[50] Instrument 134, dated August 7, 1850, Delaware Twp., Middlesex County W. Registry Office, Glencoe.

[51] Mitchell's . . . Canada Directory for 1864-65 (Toronto: J. L. Mitchell), 1864, p. 146.

[52] Instrument 1943, dated October 13, 1868,

Delaware Township, Middlesex County W. Registry Office, Glencoe.

[53] *History of the County of Middlesex, Canada* (Toronto: W. A. & C. L. Goodspeed, 1889).

[54] Issues of the *Mercantile Agency Reference Book* from July, 1878 through July, 1879 list the firm.

[55] The last rating for the firm is in the *Mercantile Agency Reference Book* of July 1891.

[56] Instrument 6229, dated March 11, 1903, Delaware Twp., Middlesex County W. Registry Office, Glencoe.

[57] Crown Patent, dated September 28, 1859, lot 10, concession 4, Metcalfe Twp., Middlesex County W. Registry Office, Glencoe.

[58] Instrument 4535, filed March 5, 1887, Metcalfe Twp., Middlesex County W. Registry Office, Glencoe.

[59] *Transactions of the Board of Agriculture of Upper Canada 1860-63*, p. 259.

[60] Census of 1870-71, Middlesex County W., Metcalfe Twp., district 7, sub-district d, division 1, schedule 6, page 1.

[61] *Mitchell's . . . Canada Directory for 1864-65* (J. L. Mitchell, 1864), p. 490.

[62] Instrument 4581, dated March 5, 1877, Mosa Twp., Middlesex County W. Registry Office, Glencoe.

[63] Instrument 373, dated February 8, 1864, Town of Strathroy, Middlesex County W. Registry Office, Office, Glencoe.

[64] Census of 1870-71, Middlesex County W., Strathroy Village, district 7, sub-district f, schedule 6.

[65] Instrument 6307, dated October 13, 1882, Town of Strathroy, Middlesex County W. Registry Office, Glencoe.

[66] The last credit rating is in the *Mercantile Agency Reference Book* of January, 1900.

[67] Listed in issues of the *Mercantile Agency Reference Book* from January 1871 to July 1878.

[68] Instrument 1618, dated April 6, 1866, Bosanquet Twp., Lambton County Registry Office, Sarnia.

Appendix One
The Care and Handling of Pottery Collections

Widespread interest in collecting Ontario pottery has developed within the past decade. Crocks which were either discarded or sold at auction for a few dollars are now bringing high prices among a growing number of enthusiastic collectors, whether at an auction or an antique shop. This phenomenon may make it difficult for some individuals or institutions to acquire large numbers of pieces, but it has resulted in the improved care and maintenance of pottery collections.

It is important that the collector and museum curator realize that the quality of care for a collection is not related to the monetary value of the pottery. Important pieces may have a very small value, but are nonetheless

A1.1 *A conservator at work mending an earthenware bowl.*

well worth the special care described in this chapter.

ASSESSING THE CONDITION OF POTTERY

When a piece of pottery is acquired it should be examined carefully and a plan developed for its conservation and regular maintenance. You may want to consult a professional conservator during the assessment process, to alert you to special problems possibly undetected, and to recommend the appropriate treatment for each piece of pottery.

Most large museums have a conservation department where a staff person will be able to advise you on the conservation of earthenware and stoneware pottery (see plate A1.1). The treatments suggested in this chapter have been found to be effective, but the reader should remember that each piece of pottery has its own history and problems. Most pottery will require only a careful initial cleaning and the removal of unsightly incrustations, treatment of flaking or crazing glaze, and the repair of cracks and breaks. After this the collection can be maintained with a regular programme of cleaning and inspection.

CLEANING POTTERY

Dirt and debris can be removed from pottery by washing it in water or wiping the piece with a damp cloth. Avoid the use of strong detergents in the regular maintenance of pottery. Low-fired pottery should not be washed as it will dissolve in water. This type of pottery has to be strengthened by treatment with a consolidant such as soluble nylon (described below) before it can be placed in water.

Glazed ware that is in good condition and well-fired can withstand regular cleaning with water. Pieces which have flaking glaze or heavy crazing should be treated with a consolidant before being washed (plate A1.2). Apply two coats of a 5% solution of soluble nylon dissolved in ethanol. Soluble nylon can be purchased from Crown Bindery Service, Frankford, Ontario, K0K 2C0. (A useful guide to museum and archival supplies has been published by the Ontario Museum Association, 33 Charles St. E., Toronto M4Y 1T1.)

Unglazed pottery, such as flowerpots and lawn vases, should be coated with soluble nylon as described above. Unglazed pieces with a painted surface should be cleaned with the assistance of a trained conservator.

REMOVING INCRUSTATIONS

Incrustations on the exterior of a pot may be caused by the seepage of the former contents of the pot through the clay body or by deposits of calcium sulphate, developed when the pot came in contact with the earth. A 5% solution of HCl (hydrochloric acid) brushed on the pottery will remove the calcium sulphate incrustations. Before beginning the treatment it is essential to determine if the clay body has lime in it, for if so, the pot cannot be treated with acid. If it is safe to use the acid treatment, begin by thoroughly soaking the pot in clean water. Select a small part of the pot as a test area (in as unnoticeable a place as possible) and with a cotton swab or small paint brush apply the acid solution. Work on an enamelled tray and do not let the acid come in contact with your skin. The acid will react with the calcium sulphate and cause an effervescence. When this ceases, wash the pot in running water. Watch out for any evidence of the whiting of lead glaze surfaces. If this happens, discontinue the acid treatment and consult a trained conservator. If the treatment on the test area has not indicated any problems, you can gradually extend the area of treatment until the entire pot has been cleaned. It is best to work on a small area, thoroughly washing the surface in clear water, before going on to a new part of the pot.

MENDING POTTERY

Small hairline cracks in a pot can be strengthened by consolidating the vessel with soluble nylon (described above). If a pot is chipped, the broken piece can be joined by an adhesive such as Ambroid or UHU (see plate A1.3). *Never* use a permanent adhesive such as epoxy resins, for if you make a mistake during repair, it may not be possible to remove the glue without further damage to the vessel.

Pottery which has been broken into several pieces may require special techniques for re-

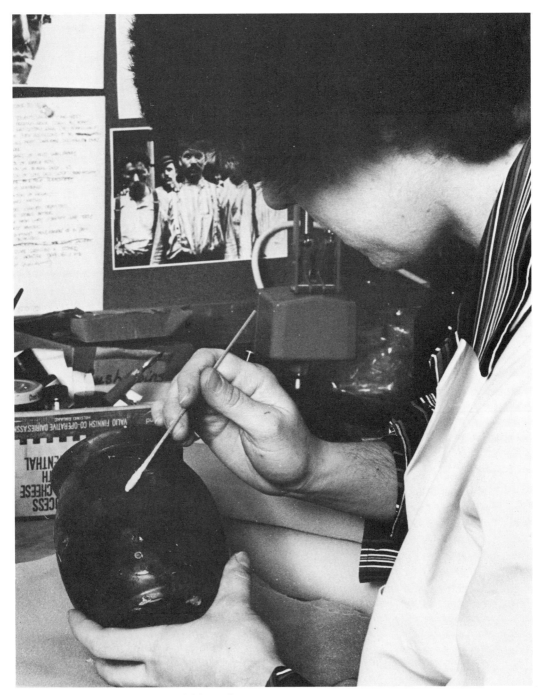

A1.2 *Coating a pot with soluble nylon to strengthen its fabric.*

A1.3 *Broken pottery can be mended with an adhesive such as Ambroid or UHU. Here the broken piece is positioned until the adhesive has "set."*

pair. Major repairs should be done only with the advice and assistance of a trained conservator.

The purpose of repairing pottery is to restore it as closely as possible to its original condition. All repairs should be described in your pottery records and made known when the piece is sold, exchanged or loaned.

REDUCING DAMAGE TO POTTERY
I have met people who not only collect stoneware and earthenware but also use it daily in their home or restored historic house. Although old clay objects have the reputation for being more durable than old metal, bone or organic substances, a piece of pottery may in fact have developed weaknesses because of its composition or past history. There may be hairline cracks or weaknesses along points of attachment of handles, spouts or knobs. Any of the extremities of a pot are subject to greater damage than the main body of the vessel. Other dangers incurred by the use of old pot-

tery include the effects of rapid changes in temperature when used as a baking dish or teapot, the effects of freezing, and damage done to the glaze by strong detergents. Modern ceramics have been developed to withstand the effects of ovens and detergents, but most pieces of nineteenth century pottery were not made for the rigours of the modern home.

It should also be borne in mind that there is a danger of lead poisoning when acid foods or liquids come into contact with lead-glazed pottery. Pottery can also be damaged by uses such as an umbrella holder or flowerpot holder (especially when the flowerpot is too large for the holder in which it has been placed). It is therefore not advisable to use pottery that is of historic importance in the daily routines of the home or restored house.

Some pottery, while not actually being used, is placed in a house or museum where it may be damaged. I have seen many instances where stoneware crocks have been placed in front of a fireplace (see plate A1.4) or in front of a museum exhibit case, where an unintentional kick can permanently damage the piece.

Other dangerous locations are the edge of a table, the foot of stairs, near an opening door, or at the level of coat buttons. An axiom of the museum curator applies in all matters concerning the safety of pottery: "The best way to eliminate or reduce damage to an object is to protect it from any situation that would be a risk."

PHYSICAL HANDLING OF POTTERY
Most pottery damage is caused by improper handling. To reduce damage a collector or museum curator should *never* allow others to pick up their pottery. Pottery should be grasped securely with both hands under the mass of the piece (see plate A1.5). Pottery that is very fragile or difficult to handle because of size or shape should be placed in a padded protective case or on a padded cart before attempting to move it.

A practical reason for permitting only the owner or curator of a pottery collection to handle the wares is the liability and bad feelings that may be created when a valuable piece is broken in an accident. Many dealers and auctioneers have a policy that states that pieces broken by handling or bumping must be paid for by the person responsible.

DISPLAYING A POTTERY COLLECTION

One of the joys of collecting pottery is the beauty of pottery displayed in pleasant and safe surroundings. A display can be both attractive and safe if a few basic guidelines are followed.

Valuable pottery should be displayed in cases where there is controlled accessibility; that is, where only authorized persons can have access to the piece. Less valuable or less important pieces can be displayed on open shelves located so as to discourage handling, touching or other types of physical contact.

A1.4 *Stoneware crocks placed at the front of a fireplace are subject to damage either from the feet of passersby or from intense heat.*

Pottery on open shelves should be cleaned regularly and pieces should not be nested one inside the other, placed in direct contact with other pieces, or crowded because of inadequate display space.

Display areas should be well-lighted to reduce the risk of damage from poor visibility. Damage may also be incurred when a heavy pot is placed on a small mount. This may make the pottery more visible to the interested observer, but if improperly used, may cause the pot to fall when bumped or shaken by vibrations of foot traffic, car traffic or airplanes.

STORAGE OF POTTERY

Pottery should be stored in a place that is well-lighted, clean, and away from extremes of heat or moisture. Storage facilities should be carefully chosen and equipped, guided by the same concern that you would show for an

A1.5 *Both hands should be used to carry a piece of pottery. The hands should be under the mass of the vessel.*

exhibit area (see plate A1.6). Pottery should be stored in transparent polyethylene bags (.006 inches in thickness) to protect it from dust, while permitting the viewer to see the contents of each bag. An identifying tape label can be applied to each bag and placed so that a piece on a shelf can be identified without being handled.

INSURANCE
As pottery continues its rapid increase in dollar value, even a small collection may represent a considerable investment. Insurance companies are expressing greater concern about the protection of fine arts collections, because of the highly speculative nature of the collections and the increased number of burglaries and thefts.

Whether or not to insure a pottery collection is a matter of conscience, based on calculated risks. Every individual or institution must decide about the need for fine arts insurance coverage based on the assessment of their own situation. If a collection is easily replace-

able and of relatively low value, it might be covered by insurance on the contents of a house, but a large and irreplaceable collection may require a separate fine arts insurance policy, as an insurance company may be reluctant to include it, together with television sets or stereos, in a general house contents clause. It is always advisable to discuss the value and importance of a large pottery collection with your insurance agent, so that if insurance is recommended, the proper policy can be negotiated. The final decision of whether a museum collection should be insured or not lies, of course, with the governing body of the institution, because the trustees carry the ultimate responsiblity of what is, in fact, public property. However, the museum curator must be aware of the insurance situation and must be knowledgeable enough to make recommendations in this respect if he deems this necessary.

If one decides to obtain insurance, it should also be kept in mind that premiums can rise in

A1.6 *A good storage area for pottery should have wide shelves with plenty of room for the wares. Notice that each pot has been enclosed in a polyethylene bag to protect it from dust and corrosive debris.*

relation to the risks to which a collection is exposed and reference is therefore made to the preceding sections, which deal with damage to pottery as well as with its physical handling, display and storage. Further, market increases in the value should be followed closely so that a new policy can be negotiated if the coverage is no longer adequate.

RECORDKEEPING

A record of all pottery is important for research, shipping and insurance purposes. A convenient and flexible record system for earthenware and stoneware pottery consists of a five-inch by eight-inch master card, and a manila folder (to contain the supporting documentation) for each piece of pottery. The master cards should be filed in numerical order following the order of acquisitions. A straight numbering system will suffice for the individual collector. Museums, however, are advised to follow general museum practice and use a chronological system, because a straight numerical system may become ineffi-

A1.7   A sample master file card for a pottery collection.

cient as collections grow over the years. The recommended system will include the year, as well as the order of acquisition; for example, 79.14 will represent the *fourteenth* acquisition in *1979*. If the acquisition consists of five items, 79.14.1 will refer to the first item and 79.14.5 to the last item in the acquisition. (See also the section under "Physical Marking of Pottery.")

It is recommended that collectors and curators keep a record of numbers in a notebook or loose-leaf folder, with a brief description leading to the manila folder so that a master card that has been misplaced or lost can be reconstructed.

A large collection, and this refers particularly to museums, will also require one or more additional card records under subject entries, such as the name of makers or manufacturers or the type of pottery. If such cards have to be handwritten or typed, a brief reference to the master card will suffice.

The master card should include the following information (as illustrated in plate A1.7):

1. An accession number of each piece of pottery.
2. A black & white photograph of the pot, either thirty-five millimetres or two and

---

```
968.14.1                              CANADIANA
                                      earthenware

Two gallon open earthenware crock of light
buff clay; rim inside measurement 22.5 cm;
height 25.7 cm; base diameter 18.7 cm.

Pronounced crazing of glaze on inside of
crock; hair-line crack across front; two
chips in rim, one about 4 cm long and
second about 5 cm long.

Crock marked with impressed name J.W. TAYLOR
BEAVERTON
--------------------------------------------

Purchased from John Q. Smith,
Smithtown, Ontario, July 10,
1968.  Price $40; valued at
$250 in 1979.

Loaned to Smalltown Museum from
February 10-April 20, 1970.
```

one-quarter by two and one-quarter inches in size. The purpose of the photograph is not to highlight the aesthetic features of the piece but to show characteristics that will help to document the piece's condition and identify the piece, should it be misplaced or stolen.

3. A written description of the pot, including measurements, the physical condition, a record of any repairs or treatments given and any other features important for identifying the piece.
4. The source of the pottery, including the date acquired, from whom, and the price.
5. A list of former owners. This is of special importance if the pottery has come from outside Canada.

It should be noted, as indicated on the sample master card on plate A1.7, that the set-up of all the cards should be consistent so that certain information is always entered in the same area of a given card. The information required can thus be obtained at a quick glance and the uniformity of the entire master card record system is assured.

Supporting documents for each piece of pottery should include a proper receipt of purchase, which should also state the names and addresses of both the buyer and seller. A pedigree is valuable for historical research, securing your claim to legal ownership, and retracing the development of the market value of the piece for insurance purposes. Supporting documents may also include correspondence, notes, loan agreements, condition reports, invoices for repairs, comments by scholars and qualified laymen, and similar material.

In the case of museums, which are likely to receive donations, the gift agreement should also be placed in the folder with the supporting documents. This is an important contract, which should contain the full names and addresses of both parties and be signed and dated by both the donor and the donee to establish proper transfer of ownership. No strings or conditions should be attached to a gift and the agreement should be headed by the simple statement that the donor gives "the object(s) listed herein and this document transfers full title and ownership of such item(s)

without the need for further formality." Additionally, as much information as possible regarding the past history of the gift should be obtained from the donor. Such a document may also have value for the private collector although it is difficult, admittedly, to make such an arrangement with a friend, the person most likely to make a donation.

When dealing with a larger collection of several hundred pieces or more, it is recommended that the folders be filed under the names of the dealers or donors from whom the material has been acquired. Museums should establish this as a standard practice, because such filing is essential to provide information regarding the identity and the number of pieces obtained from a certain source. Such a procedure requires that the acquisition or accession number always be included in the sheet files so that it can be connected with the numerical master card.

It is recommended procedure to keep the original acquisition records, such as purchase receipts and gift agreements, outside the home in a safe place separate from the pottery collection. Copies should be filed in the respective folders so that the information is available at any time.

When a pot is sold the master card and supporting documents should accompany the piece to its new owner. I am convinced that if all private collectors adopted the usage of precise and thorough recordkeeping, as is general museum practice, a properly documented piece (and this fact should be advertised when the pottery is offered for sale) will have a much higher value than a similar piece that is not so documented. From the point of view of the professional collector, the development of careful documentation of pottery improves the general integrity of the dealing profession and increases the possibility of identification and return of stolen pieces.

THE PHYSICAL MARKING OF POTTERY

The acquisition or accession number should be affixed physically to the item as soon as possible after its acquisition, preferably on the base where it is not immediately visible and will not mar the appearance of the piece of pottery. Do not use pressure-sensitive tape to

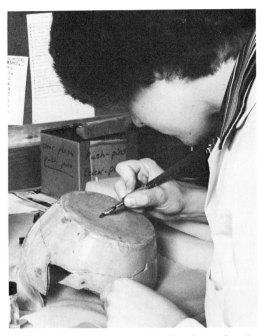

A1.8 *Pottery should be marked with an identifying number to indicate ownership.*

mark pots, as the tape may damage the surface of the piece. Likewise, inscribing your initials on a pot will permanently damage the piece. A simple and effective way to mark pottery is with india ink (see plate A1.8). Never use india ink, or chemical markers that become visible under ultra-violet light, directly on an unglazed or porous fabric, or the ink or chemical will be absorbed into the clay and will be difficult to remove later. A very porous fabric may also cause the ink to blot, destroying the clarity of the mark. India ink applied directly to a glazed surface will rub off. To overcome these problems cover a small part of the base (one centimetre by three centimetres or one-half-inch by one and one-half inches) with a 5% solution of PVA (polyvinyl acetate). When this has dried, the identifying number can be written on the PVA with a stiff nib pen. When the ink has dried a second coat of PVA should be applied to make the number waterproof. PVA is an inexpensive consolidant that can be purchased from BDH Chemicals, 350 Evans Avenue, Toronto, M8Z 1K5.

SECURITY

An increase in the number of burglaries and thefts of fine arts materials (under which Ontario earthenware and stoneware should be classified) has resulted in greater concern for the security of collections.

Whether your collection is in a house or museum the general rule is: security is most easily maintained by limiting accessibility to any area where your pottery is displayed or stored. Where there is a large and valuable private collection, a separate locked room may be required. An alarm system or other surveillance device may be recommended for particularly valuable collections. Local and regional police and your insurance company are the best sources of information on security for your collection.

A private collector should not publicize the extent or importance of a collection in the media. This is not to suggest that pottery should not be loaned to institutions for public display, or be available for serious study. However, the greater the public knowledge of a private collection, the greater the risk may be of burglary or theft. Private collectors who loan material to museums or other cultural institutions should be cautious about having their name appear as the source of the loan.

LOANING POTTERY

It is usually better for a private collector to lend his pottery for a special exhibition at a museum or art gallery rather than to share his collection through publicity in the media. If an individual or institution agrees to lend pottery, it should be emphasized that the owner of the pottery collection has the right to request from a potential borrower fair and reasonable conditions for the protection of the collection. These conditions should govern everything that may affect the pottery, from the time it is packed and shipped until it is returned.

Lending pottery to individuals is not recommended because they will not be able to provide the safety and security available to an institution. Further, they will only in rare instances have a floater insurance policy to protect the material in transit. If an individual is interested in a particular piece or a collection

ROYAL ONTARIO MUSEUM

Loan Conditions

1. *The borrower will exercise the same care in respect to loans as it does for the safekeeping of its own property.*
2. *Objects on loan shall remain in the condition in which they are received. They shall not be unframed, unglazed or removed from mats, mounts or bases, cleaned, repaired or transported in damaged condition except:*
   a. *With the permission of the lender*
   b. *When such is imperative to prevent further damage.*
   The lender will immediately be informed about any loss, breakage or deterioration.
3. *Loans shall remain in the possession of the borrower and/or other organizations participating in the exhibition in question for the time specified on the face of this loan agreement. Loans received for an indefinite period of time for display in permanent exhibits, may not be withdrawn by the owner within six months.*
4. *Unless the lender expressly elects to maintain his own insurance, the borrower will insure the loan wall-to-wall under its fine arts policy, for the amount indicated on the face of this loan agreement, against all risks of physical loss or damage from any external cause while in transit and on location during the period of the loan. The policy referred to contains the usual exclusions of "all-risks" policies.*
5. *The object or objects described on the face of the loan agreement, will not be reproduced in any media without the permission of the lender. However, permission to photograph for publication connected with the exhibition, for publicity, telecasts and slides for educational use is assumed, unless stated otherwise by the lender.*

A1.9 *The standard loan conditions of the Royal Ontario Museum, Toronto.*

of pottery, he can visit a museum, or make arrangements with an individual owner to visit him in his home. It is general museum practice *never* to lend museum material to individual borrowers.

When lending to museums, the collector should first ascertain whether the respective institution can provide the proper protection, whether it carries a fine arts floater insurance policy, and whether it has a staff knowledgeable in packing and shipping practices. The institution should also have developed proce-

dures to govern loans and should be able to provide the lender with a copy of its standard loan condition on request.

The lender would be wise to study the conditions before he commits himself to the loan. The loan conditions of the Royal Ontario Museum (see plate A1.9) may serve as a guideline. Every museum will, of course, phrase its conditions in its own way but those conditions should always include the following points:

1. The borrower guarantees that he will provide the same care that he gives to his own material.

2. The borrower agrees not to clean or repair the pottery without the permission of the owner.
3. The material will not be loaned to another party by the borrower without the permission of the owner.
4. The borrower promises to inform the owner immediately of any loss or damage to the pottery.
5. The borrower promises to insure the material from the time it leaves the home of the owner until it is returned to him (known as "wall-to-wall insurance") for the value stated on the loan agreement.
6. The borrower promises not to reproduce the pottery without the permission of the lender.

Such conditions should be on the reverse of the loan agreement which constitutes the contract between the lender and the borrower. The face of the agreement should carry the following information:

1. Name and address of lender.
2. Date of agreement.
3. Name and address of receiving institution.
4. Itemized list of all pottery being loaned, including the lender's accession number and value for each piece of pottery. Your record system will be useful here.
5. Date for commencement and termination of loan.
6. Signature of lender.
7. The signature of the Director of the borrowing institution, or of his authorized representative.

If the lender wishes to remain anonymous, such information should also appear on the face of the agreement.

With regard to the lender's claim of the value of the pottery, it should be pointed out that no advantage will be gained by over-evaluating a piece of pottery. In case of loss or damage, the borrower's insurance company will only settle for the fair market value of the piece.

The loan contract or agreement should be in the hands of the lender before he releases his property, so that he has an opportunity to study the entire document before he makes a final commitment. If the material is physically picked up at his home he should also request a detailed receipt, to be signed by the representative who has come to collect the pottery. If the material is shipped to the borrower, the lender should immediately be informed in writing about the arrival and the condition of his pottery.

PACKING AND SHIPPING POTTERY

Any piece of pottery that travels is exposed to the risk of damage, no matter how conscientious a borrower may be, because he has no control over situations that could occur in transit. Nevertheless, certain risks can be reduced if proper precautions are observed. It therefore becomes essential to carefully consider in advance the questions of packing and shipping.

As the borrower must carry all expenses in connection with the loan, the owner should insist on the services of professional packers, and it is recommended that such packers be experienced in handling and packing fine art objects (see plate A1.10). Individual collectors

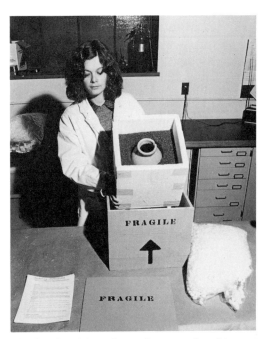

A1.10 *Careful packing of pottery for shipment requires the services of a person experienced in the shipment of fine arts materials.*

should not pack their own pottery, because of the fragility of the material and the particular skills that are required in this respect. In addition, if any damage occurs in transit due to poor packing, they run the risk that the insurance company of the borrower may not honour their claim.

If an owner wishes, however, to familiarize himself with the techniques of packing and shipping pottery for one reason or another, he will find an invaluable reference guide in Per E. Guldbeck's book, *The Care of Historical Collections* (Nashville, Tennessee: American Association for State and Local History, 1972).

The owner should be present when his pottery is being packed. Prior to this, however, he should examine each piece and its condition compared with that described in the records. If there is any noticeable change in the condition of a piece of pottery, then this should be noted in the records and the piece should be rephotographed before it is shipped. The photograph should become part of the record and should be consulted when the pottery is returned.

Shipments of pottery should only travel by public transport and not in private cars because this is one of the conditions of the fine arts floater policies of museums. If an accident occurs in a private vehicle an insurance company may hesitate to honour any claim. Further, such shipments should not be forwarded or returned by parcel post but always shipped with an accompanying waybill to provide proper evidence of the existence of the shipment. The services of a shipping agent should be used in this respect and the borrower provided with his name.

The owner should insist that the packing material be retained by the borrower and the shipment returned in exactly the same manner in which it was received unless, of course, the borrower states valid objections with respect to packing and shipping. On return of the shipment, the owner should, again, carefully examine the condition of each piece of pottery and, in case of damage, present a claim in writing to the borrower.

THE EXPORT AND IMPORT OF POTTERY

The export and import of moveable cultural property is now subject to provisions of the *Cultural Property Export and Import Act* (Bill C-33). The purpose of this legislation is to preserve and maintain in Canada collections of the best objects of national cultural significance. At the same time the law contains provisions prohibiting the import into Canada of cultural property illegally exported from foreign states, where the foreign state has signed a cultural property agreement with Canada.

Information on the act is given in the guide, *An introduction to the Cultural Property Export and Import Act,* available from Canadian Customs or from the Department of the Secretary of State, Ottawa. Anyone who wishes to export Ontario Pottery that is subject to control should obtain an export permit from the two designated regional customs offices in Ontario: Regional Collector, Customs and Excise, 55 Bloor Street West, P.O. Box 10, Station "A", Toronto, Ontario, M5W 1A3; and Regional Collector, Customs & Excise, 1615 Carling Avenue, Ottawa, Ontario, K2A 3Y1.

Appendix Two
Glossary of Ceramic Terms

Bat — A flat slab of clay for pressing onto or into a plaster or clay mould. Made with a knocker, *q.v.*.

Biscuit or bisque — Clay that has been fired once, the piece being unglazed.

Blister — Bubbles or gas produced in the body or glaze of a pot during firing, the bubbles being formed from impurities in the clay body, excessive moisture, or impurities in the glaze.

Blunger — A device similar to a pugmill *q.v.*, but used to make a liquid slip.

Body — The clay or clay mixture of a piece of ceramics, also called the "fabric" or "ware"; the main part of a vessel.

Bristol ware — An opaque glaze with zinc oxide as the main flux. Bristol glazes were developed in England, as an alternative to lead glazes.

Brown ware — A term used to describe redware glazed to a brown colour, or stoneware with a brownish finish.

Cane ware — In Ontario, used to describe a bright-yellow glazed earthenware, especially popular in the late nineteenth and early twentieth century. Its use in Ontario should not be confused with the unglazed stoneware also called cane ware, and first introduced by Josiah Wedgwood in the eighteenth century.

Casting — Making pottery by pouring slip into a plaster mould (cast). When the clay has hardened the mould is taken apart and the pottery removed to continue to dry.

Ceramic — Any object made of clay, including porcelain, stoneware or ironstone.

Charging — The loading (packing) of a kiln with pottery.

Coggle — A small clay or plaster wheel mounted on a handle and used for making an impressed repeating decoration around the outside of a pot.

Combing — Parallel incised lines made by a comb of wood; combing is used to decorate a pot dipped in slip or a plain redware fabric.

Crazing — Unintentional fine cracking of a glaze on a clay body due to the glaze not "fitting" the clay body, i.e., the composition of the glaze is such that in firing, the glaze expands at a different rate from the clay.

Demijohn — In Ontario, used to describe any vessel with a wide body and a narrow neck.

Drawing — Unloading of fired ware from a kiln.

Earthenware — Clay pottery with a porous fabric in the biscuit state; the pottery is opaque and it may be white or coloured. In the nineteenth century in Ontario, the term earthenware was generally used to describe redwares, *q.v.*, yellow wares, *q.v.* and plain white clay fabric or "white wares," *q.v.*, often without distinction.

Engobe — A slip coating on a clay fabric.

Fabric — The clay mixture of a piece of pottery, also called the "body" or "ware."

Fire clay — A coarse clay that can withstand very high temperatures, used for saggars, and linings of chimneys and kilns.

Flaking — The peeling or scaling of slips or glazes, due to unsuitable composition of the slip or glaze for the particular clay used in the fabric.

Flint-enamelled ware — A general term for lead-glazed ware. There is no evidence that any special glazing was used for this ware, but rather that the term became popular among customers of the potteries and so was used in popular literature.

Fluxes — The ingredients of a glaze which promote melting.

Frit — A mixture of silica and fluxes that is melted and then run into cold water to make it hard. The frit is then ground to a powder and added to certain glazes to make them more durable.

Glaze — An impervious glassy substance

used to cover a ceramic body to prevent it from leaking, to make it more durable, to make it more attractive, or to protect it.

Green ware — Unfired clay body.

Grog — Crushed burnt clay or fire clay added to unfired clay to make it less plastic; grog is also added to clay used in making saggars.

Growler — A stoneware drinking mug, usually decorated with raised relief and cobalt-blue colour.

Incising — Scratching an identifying mark or decoration into the surface of a green (air dry) pot.

Jigger — Revolving wheel which holds a clay or plaster mould on which pottery shapes are made. (See also jolley.)

Jolley — An arm that holds a profile tool and is lowered into a mould to shape a piece of pottery. A jolley is used in conjunction with a jigger.

Kiln — A furnace or oven for the heating and hardening of ceramics.

Kiln furniture — Various small pieces of clay used to separate wares in the kiln during firing to prevent them from fusing during the melting of the glaze. (See also *spur* and *cockspur* and *wedge*.)

Knocker — A plaster block about 6 inches in diameter, attached to a clay handle; used to make a bat, (q.v.).

Majolica ware — Originally a tin-glazed earthenware with an overglaze of bright colours. In Ontario the term majolica was used for any earthenware with coloured glazes, especially fancy wares.

Mocha — A form of "dipped" earthenware with bands of coloured slip (brown, black, blue, green or pink) and with distinctive "seaweed" or "fern"-like decoration.

Pancheon — A steep-sided and deep bowl used in the kitchen.

Pugmill — A mill for cleaning and blending clay into a homogeneous mixture.

Redware — Pottery made from red firing clay that is fired in an oxygen-free atmosphere. In Ontario most local clays fire to a redware or yellow ware, *q.v.*.

Rib — A gauge made of wood or pottery used to form the outline of a pot as it is thrown on a wheel.

Rockingham-type wares — Wares covered with a rich purple-brown glaze, but many small potters in Ontario used this term to describe any ware covered with a dark brown ("rock") glaze, and therefore the term is often synonymous with brown ware, *q.v.*.

Saggars — Containers made of fireclay and used to hold pottery during firing in a kiln; saggars prevent the wares from sticking when the glaze melts.

Salt glaze — A "glaze" on stoneware formed by throwing common salt on wares during firing. The salt decomposes and combines with silica and alumina in the clay to form a glassy finish called "salt glaze."

Sgraffito — A decorative technique whereby a coating of slip is scratched through to give a pattern on a different-coloured fabric beneath.

Sherd (Shard) — A fragment of pottery.

Slip — Liquid clay mixed to a consistency of thick cream.

Slipware — Pottery decorated with slip of a contrasting colour.

Sprig (sprig mould) — A raised clay decoration made in a clay or plaster mould. The resulting plaque, called a "sprig," is applied to the unfinished ware.

Spur & Cockspur — Clay supports used to separate wares in a kiln to prevent them from touching during the melting of the glaze. (See also Kiln furniture.)

Stoneware — Clay which when fired is impervious to water and vitrifies at temperatures above 1200°C. Stoneware clay used in Ontario during the nineteenth century was imported from England or the United States.

Terra cotta — Fine-textured reddish-coloured unglazed or glazed pottery, usually used for architectural details and garden ornaments.

Throwing — The forming of a pot by hand on a potter's wheel.

Waster dump — Dumps of broken and misshapen pottery found at the site of a pottery. The waster material was the result of damage during firing.

Weathering — The storage of clay under natural conditions to "age" it and make it easier to work.

Wedges — A wedge-shaped clay support used to separate pottery in a kiln during firing to prevent the pottery from touching. (See also Kiln furniture.)

Wedging — The working of clay by cutting and slamming and kneading on a table. Wedging is done to make the clay homogeneous and to remove air pockets before the clay is formed into a pot.

Yellow ware — Pottery made from clay which fires to a buff colour, appearing a bright yellow colour under a clear lead glaze. Local clays in Ontario fire to a yellow ware or a redware, *q.v.*

Appendix Three
Checklist of Ontario Pottery Marks

The purpose of this list is to provide the collector and historian with a list of maker's marks which appear on pottery produced in Ontario during the nineteenth century.

Most of the earthenware and stoneware produced in the province was never marked, and this list is therefore representative neither of all potters working in the province, nor of the different decades during which pottery was produced in Ontario.

The marks listed were either observed by me, or reported in reliable published sources. In most cases the mark can be related to a section of the book that tells the history of the particular workshop. I have not listed marks of particular stores that often had pottery with their advertisement placed on the ware, but instead have restricted this list to marks of potters.

The list is not exhaustive, and more marks will no doubt come to public attention in future years. What I can claim is that this list is the most complete one yet published on Ontario pottery marks.

I have listed the marks in alphabetical order, and where possible, have included close-up photographs showing the marks and possible variations. In many instances the marks are associated with capacity numbers, the latter indicating the liquid capacity of the particular container. I have disregarded the capacity mark in determining the variations of each maker's mark that has been found.

The use of C.W. for Canada West would normally have stopped after Confederation in 1867, but in some factories was continued as long as twenty years later. The presence of C.W. is therefore not in itself a reliable guide to distinguishing pre-1867 manufactured pottery from that manufactured after that date.

The terms *earthenwares* and *stonewares* are used as defined in the Glossary of Ceramic Terms. The term *earthenware* includes redwares, creamwares and white paste earthenwares.

A discussion of the different types of maker's marks can be found in chapter Two.

The general plan for this checklist is a modification of the style established by Geoffrey Godden in *Encyclopedia of British Pottery & Porcelain Marks* (New York: Bonanza Books, 1964). I am indebted to Geoffrey Godden for permission to continue his very successful format in this checklist of Ontario pottery marks.

The numbering system used here is sequential.

AHRENS

J. H. AHRENS (& CO.), Paris, Brant County. 1860-1883. Earthenwares.

1 *Impressed mark.*

1a *Incised on picture frame made by W. E. Welding of Brantford. (I = "Jacob")*

ALBION POTTERY

See C. Saunders.

B.P. CO.

See Belleville Pottery Co.

B.S. MFG CO. LTD.

See Brantford Stoneware Mfg. Co., Ltd.

BAILEY

F. BAILEY, Cartwright Twp., Durham County. 1855-1862. Earthenwares.

2 *Impressed mark.*

BAILEY

JAMES T. BAILEY, Bowmanville, Durham County. 1851 - ca. 1855. Earthenwares. Formerly Bailey & Brown.

3 *Impressed mark.*

BALLARD

O. L. BALLARD, Cornwall, Stormont County. 1864-1869. Stonewares. Subsequently Flack & Van Arsdale, q.v.

4 *Impressed mark.*

BEECH

G. BEECH, Brantford, Brant County. Ca. 1851-1869. Stonewares.

**Made by G. Beech
April 1862
Brantford
Canada West**

5 *Incised signature on picture frame.*

5a *Incised signature on picture frame.*

BELLEVILLE

BELLEVILLE STONEWARE CO., Belleville, Hastings County. Ca. 1870 -

ca. 1879. Stonewares. Subsequently Hart Bros. & Lazier, q.v.

6 *Impressed mark.*

BELLEVILLE

BELLEVILLE POTTERY CO., Belleville, Hastings County. 1901 - ca. 1914. Stonewares. Formerly Hart Bros. & Lazier.

7 *Stamped mark.*

7a *Stamped mark.*

BEMISTER

WALTER BEMISTER, Beaverton, Ontario County. Ca. 1888-1904. Earthenwares. Formerly James Bemister & Son.

W. BE[ ]

8 *Part of inscribed signature on base of garden stand recovered from Bemister's property. See plate 6.10.*

BIERNSTIHL

ADAM BIERNSTIHL, Bridgeport, Waterloo County. Ca. 1867-1900. Earthenwares.

**Emilie
Biernstihl
Bridgeport**

9 *Painted signature on inside of earthenware bowl. See plate 10.8.*

BOCK

JACOB BOCK, Waterloo, Waterloo County. 1820s. Earthenwares.

**Waterloo
Upper Canada
September 17, 1825
Jacob Bock, potter**

10 *Incised signature on base of tobacco jar.*

10a *A jar identical to No. 10 but with a different inscription.*

BOEHLER

BOEHLER & WEBER, Huron Pottery, Egmondville, Huron County. 1873-1876. Earthenwares. Formerly Valentine Boehler pottery.

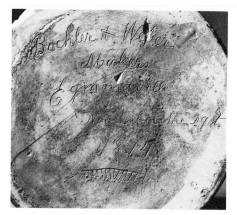

11 *Incised signature on stand of water container. See plate 11.1.*

BOEHLER

JOSEPH BOEHLER, New Hamburg, Waterloo County. 1874-1894. Earthenwares. Formerly Xavier Boehler pottery.

12 *Impressed mark. Joseph Boehler was the nephew of Valentine Boehler, founder of the Huron Pottery. See Boehler & Weber.*

BOWMANVILLE

JAMES BAILEY, Bowmanville Pottery, Bowmanville, Durham County. 1851-57. Earthenwares. Formerly Bailey & Brown.

13 *Impressed mark.*

BRANTFORD

BRANTFORD STONEWARE MFG. CO., LTD., Brantford, Brant County. 1894-1906. Stonewares and white wares. Formerly W. E. Welding, q.v.

14 *Impressed mark.*

14a *Impressed mark.*

14b *Impressed mark. Probably used during Welding period also.*

BROWN

J. & W. O. BROWN & CO., Weston, York County. 1860 - ca. 1881. Earthenwares.

15 *Impressed mark. May also have added line (indistinct in the photograph) of "Patented 1859."*

BROWN

J. & J. BROWN, Weston, York County. 1900-1907. Earthenwares. Formerly Brown Brothers.

J & J BROWN

16 *Impressed mark. For reference to this, see Collard,* Nineteenth Century Pottery & Porcelain in Canada, *p. 336.*

BROWN

T. BROWN, Strathroy Pottery, Strathroy, Middlesex County. 1881-1899. Earthenwares.

17 *Impressed mark.*

BROWNSCOMBE

JOHN (JAMES?) BROWNSCOMBE, Kinloss, Bruce County. 1870 - ca. 1882. Earthenwares.

Mr. J. Hodgin. 1879
Kinloss
J B

18 *Harvest jug with applied decoration on both sides.*

18a *Miniature jug with applied decoration. See plate 9.8.*

BROWNSCOMBE

SAMUEL BROWNSCOMBE, Kinloss, Bruce County, and later Owen Sound, Grey County. 1882-1907. Earthenwares.

19 *Painted mark in cobalt blue.*

BROWNSCOMBE

W. BROWNSCOMBE, Peterborough, Peterborough County. 1852-1868.

Earthenwares. *Subsequently Brownscombe & Goodfellow, q.v.*

20 *Impressed mark.*

BROWNSCOMBE

BROWNSCOMBE & GOODFELLOW, Peterborough, Peterborough County. 1880-1881. Earthenwares and stonewares. *Formerly W. Brownscombe.*

21 *Impressed mark. Frank Goodfellow was the son-in-law of William Brownscombe.*

21a *Impressed mark.*

BURGARD

F. BURGARD & SON, Huron Pottery, Egmondville, Huron County. 1900-1910. Earthenwares.

22 *Painted marks and signatures on jugs, especially miniature jugs. See plate 11.9.*

BURNS

DAVID BURNS, Holmesville, Huron County. Ca. 1860 - ca. 1900. Earthenwares.

23 *Incised signature on base of candle holder reads "D. Burns/Maker."*

BURNS

BURNS & CAMPBELL, Toronto. 1879-1881. Stonewares. *Formerly N. Eberhardt. Subsequently James R. Burns, q.v.*

24 *Impressed mark.*

BURNS

JAMES R. BURNS, Toronto. 1881-1887. Stonewares. *Formerly Burns & Campbell.*

25 *Impressed mark.*

CAMPBELL

R. CAMPBELL'S SONS, Hamilton Pottery, Hamilton. Ca. 1890-1928. Earthenwares & stonewares. Formerly Robert Campbell & Co. Subsequently Canada Potteries Ltd., q.v.

26 *Mould mark.*

CAMPDEN

See Orth.

CANADA

CANADA POTTERIES LTD., Hamilton. 1928-1929. Earthenwares & stonewares. Formerly R. Campbell's Sons. Subsequently Hamilton Potteries, q.v.

27 *Mould mark.*

CORNWALL

CORNWALL POTTERY, Cornwall, Stormont County. Pottery made by either O. L. Ballard, q.v. or Flack & Van Arsdale, q.v.

28 *Impressed mark reported on crock and jug. See Circa 76, Vol. 2, No. 4, p. 24.*

CULP

See Kulp.

DAVIS

JOHN DAVIS & SON, Davisville Pottery, Davisville, York County. Ca. 1890 - ca. 1928. Earthenwares.

29 *Mould mark.*

DAVIS

JOSEPH DAVIS, Davisville. 1845-1890. Earthenwares. Member of firm of John Davis. Subsequently, John Davis & Son.

**Joseph
Davis
Maker
Sept. 1878**

30 *Incised on base of earthenware pot.*

DERBY

DERBY POTTERY, Kilsyth, Grey County.
Ca. 1869-1909. Earthenwares.
Mark attributed to Walmsley & McCluskie
or Alexander Sinclair.

DERBY

31 *Impressed mark on base of individual*
tea service.

EBERHARDT

EBERHARDT & HALM, Toronto.
1863-1865. Stonewares. Formerly Warner
& Co., q.v. Subsequently N. Eberhardt.

32 *Impressed mark.*

EBERHARDT

N. EBERHARDT, Toronto. 1865-1879.
Stonewares. Formerly Eberhardt & Halm.
Subsequently Burns & Campbell, q.v.

33 *Impressed with location "C.W."*

33a *Impressed mark with location*
"ONT."

FLACK

FLACK & VAN ARSDALE, Cornwall
Pottery, Cornwall, Stormont County.
1869-1907. Stonewares. Formerly
O.L. Ballard.

34 *Impressed mark.*

FLACK & VAN ARSDALE
CORNWALL, O

34a *Impressed mark.*

G

See Glass Bros. & Co.

G.B. & Co.

See Glass Bros. & Co.

GILBERT

EBAN T. GILBERT, Port Ryerse, Norfolk
County. Ca. 1886-1900. Earthenwares.

35 *Impressed mark.*

GLASS

GLASS BROS. & CO., London
1888-1897. Stonewares. Formerly London
Crockery Manufacturing Co.

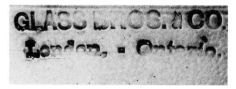

36 *Impressed mark.*

36a *Stamped mark.*

36b *Stamped mark.*

36c *Stencilled mark.*

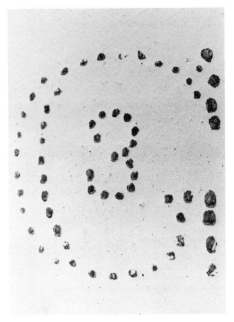

36d *Painted mark.*

**GLASS BROS. & CO.
LONDON ONT.**

36e *Mould mark.*

36f *Mould mark.*

GOOLD

*F. P. GOOLD (& Co.), Brantford, Brant
County. 1859-1867. Stonewares. Formerly
Morton, Goold & Co. Subsequently
Welding & Belding, q.v.*

37 *Impressed mark.*

37a *Impressed mark.*

GRAY

GRAY & BETTS, Tillsonburg, Oxford County. 1883-1886. Stonewares. Formerly F. B. Tillson. Subsequently Gray & Glass, q.v.

38 *Impressed mark.*

GRAY

GRAY & GLASS, Tillsonburg, Oxford County. March to August 1886. Stonewares. Formerly Gray & Betts.

GRAY & GLASS TILSONBURG

39 *Impressed mark.*

GROH

JOHN GROH, Kossuth, Waterloo County. 1863 - ca. 1873. Earthenwares.

40 *Impressed mark. Letters PR presumably refer to "potter."*

H.B. & L.

See Hart Bros. & Lazier.

HAMILTON

HAMILTON POTTERIES, Hamilton. 1930-ca. 1947. Earthenwares & stonewares. Formerly Canada Potteries Ltd.

41 *Impressed mark.*

41a *Mould mark.*

HANDLEY

HANDLEY BROTHERS, Picton, Prince Edward County. 1891-1894. Earthenwares. Subsequently H. Handley, q.v.

HANDLEY BROTHERS PICTON

42 *Impressed mark. See* Ontario Showcase, *August 1, 1966, Vol. 2, No. 5.*

HANDLEY

H. HANDLEY, Picton, Prince Edward County. 1894-1899. Earthenwares. Formerly Handley Brothers.

43 *Impressed mark.*

HANDLEY

See also White & Handley.

HART

W. HART & CO., Picton, Prince Edward County. 1849-1855. Stonewares. Subsequently S. Skinner & Co., q.v.

44 *Impressed mark.*

HART

HART BROS. & LAZIER, Picton, Prince Edward County (1879-1887), and Belleville, Hastings County (1879-1901). Stonewares. Picton factory formerly G.I. Lazier, q.v.; Belleville factory formerly Belleville Stoneware Company, q.v., subsequently Belleville Pottery Co., q.v.

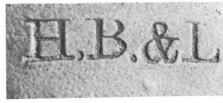

45 *Impressed mark, Picton or Belleville.*

45a *Impressed mark, Picton or Belleville.*

45b *Impressed mark, Picton.*

45c *Impressed mark, Picton.*

45d *Impressed mark, Picton.*

H.B. & L.
BELLEVILLE
ONT.

45e *Impressed mark, Belleville.*

45f *Impressed mark, Belleville.*

HART BROS. & LAZIER
BELLEVILLE
ONT.

45g *Impressed mark, Belleville.*

HUMBERSTONE

S.T. HUMBERSTONE, Newton Brook Pottery, Newton Brook, York County. 1872-1902. Stonewares.

46 *Impressed mark.*

46a *Impressed mark with "NEWTON BROOK."*

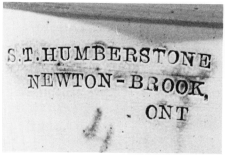

46b *Impressed mark with "ONT".*

I.H.A.

See J. H. Ahrens.

J.B.

See John (James) Brownscombe.

James

See John (James) Brownscombe.

KENNEDY

J. A. KENNEDY, Brantford, Brant County. 1889-1897. Earthenwares.

47 *Impressed mark.*

KULP

JOHN KULP, Grimsby, Lincoln County. 1829-1868. Earthenwares.

48 *Incised signature.*

LAZIER

G. I. LAZIER, Picton, Prince Edward County. 1864-1879. Stonewares. Formerly S. Skinner & Co. Subsequently Hart Bros & Lazier, q.v.

49 *Impressed mark.*

LENT

B. LENT, Jordan Station, Lincoln County. Late 1820s - early 1830s. Earthenwares.

50 *Impressed mark on sherds.*

50a *Impressed mark on sherds.*

B. LENT

50b *Impressed mark on shoulder, milk pitcher.*

LONDON

LONDON CROCKERY MFG. CO. LTD., London. 1886-1888. Stonewares. Subsequently Glass Bros. & Co., q.v.

51 *Impressed mark.*

LONDON

LONDON POTTERY MFG. CO., 95 Rectory St., London. 1905 - ca. 1933. Stonewares. Formerly Hulse & Son.

LONDON POTTERY LONDON, ONT.

52 *Impressed mark.*

MARKHAM

MARKHAM POTTERY, Markham, York County. 1855-1884. Earthenwares.

53 *Slip-applied signature. Piece probably attributable to P. Ensminger or Cyrus Eby. See plate 7.24a, b, and c.*

MARKS

See John Marx.

MARLATT

*J. M. MARLATT (& CO.), Paris Pottery,
Paris, Brant County. 1859-1868.
Earthenwares & stonewares. Subsequently
Schuler & McGlade, q.v.*

54 *Impressed mark.*

54a *Impressed mark, with addition of
"& CO."*

MARX

*JOHN MARX, Paris, Brant County.
Ca. 1887 - ca. 1883. Earthenwares.
Employee of J. H. Ahrens, Paris Pottery.*

55 *Incised signature on earthenware
picture frame.*

McGLADE

*SCHULER & McGLADE, Paris, Brant
County. 1868-1873. Stonewares. Formerly
J. M. Marlatt. Subsequently H. Schuler, q.v.*

56 *Impressed mark. Mark has names of
the partnership reversed.*

MOONEY

*JAMES MOONEY, Prescott, Grenville
County. Ca. 1847 - ca. 1856.
Earthenwares.*

57 *Impressed mark.*

MORTON

*MORTON & CO., Brantford, Brant
County. 1849-1856. Stonewares.
Subsequently Morton & Bennett, q.v.*

58 *Impressed mark.*

58a *Impressed mark.*

MORTON

MORTON & BENNETT, Brantford, Brant County. 1856-1857. Stonewares. Formerly Morton & Co. Subsequently J. Woodyatt & Co., q.v.

**MORTON & BENNETT
BRANTFORD C. W.**

59 *Impressed mark.*

MORTON

MORTON, GOOLD & CO., Brantford, Brant County. 1859. Stonewares. Formerly J. Woodyatt & Co. Subsequently F. P. Goold & Co., q.v.

60 *Impressed mark.*

ORANGEVILLE

O. W. KETCHUM, Orangeville Pottery, Orangeville, Dufferin County. Ca. 1865-1880. Earthenwares & stonewares.

61 *Impressed mark or mould mark.*

ORTH

DANIEL ORTH, Campden, Lincoln County. Ca. 1851-1903. Earthenwares.

**D. Orth
1892**

62 *Incised signature on earthenware dog.*

See Collard, Nineteenth Century Pottery & Porcelain In Canada, p. 345.

**Campden
D. Orth
1878**

62a *Incised signature on base of miniature spittoon in collection of Jordon Museum of the Twenty, Jordan.*

OWEN SOUND

HORNING & BROWNSCOMBE, Owen Sound Pottery Co., Owen Sound, Grey County. 1894-1907. Earthenwares.

**Owen Sound
1904**

63 *Painted mark on miniature jug. See plate 9.5.*

PICTON

See W. Hart, S. Skinner, G. I. Lazier for Picton pottery owners from 1849 to 1887. Stonewares.

64 *Impressed mark.*

RICHARDSON

JOHN RICHARDSON, Kerwood, Middlesex County. 1860-1886. Earthenwares.

65 *Impressed mark.*

65a *Impressed mark.*

SAUNDERS

C. SAUNDERS, Albion Pottery, Bolton, Peel County. 1898-1904. Earthenwares.

66 Impressed mark.

SCHULER

See McGlade & Schuler.

SCHULER

H. SCHULER, Paris, Brant County. 1873-1884. Stonewares. Formerly Schuler & McGlade.

67 Impressed mark.

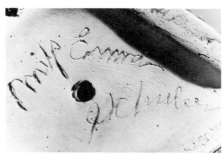

67a Incised signature on base of stoneware dog. Emma Schuler was daughter of H. Schuler.

SCHWAB

W. SCHWAB, Beamsville Pottery, Beamsville, Lincoln County. 1853 - ca. 1875. Earthenwares.

68 Impressed mark.

SIMCOE

SIMCOE STREET POTTERY, Beaverton, Ontario County. 1876-1904. Earthenwares. Made by either James Bemister or Walter Bemister, q.v.

SIMCOE STREET POTTERY BEAVERTON

69 Impressed mark.

SKINNER

S. SKINNER (& CO.), Picton, Prince Edward County. 1855-1864. Stonewares. Formerly W. Hart & Co. Subsequently G. I. Lazier, q.v.

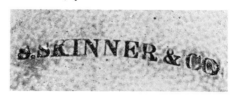

70a Impressed mark. P.O. may refer to "Post Office."

SMITH

ANTHONY SMITH, Paris, Brant County.

1867-1877. Earthenwares. *Employee of J. H. Ahrens, Paris.*

A. SMITH

71 *Impressed and incised marks on picture frame. See Collard,* Nineteenth Century Pottery & Porcelain In Canada, *p. 347.*

SMITH

R. SMITH, Paris, Brant County. 1861-1865. Earthenwares. *Employee of J. H. Ahrens.*

72 *Incised signature on picture frame.*

STAR

STAR POTTERY, John Pegler or Hulse & Son, proprietors, 95 Rectory Street, London. 1892-1905. Stonewares. *Subsequently London Pottery Mfg. Co., q.v.*

73 *Mould mark.*

TARA

JAMES McCLUSKIE, Tara Pottery, Tara, Bruce County. 1867-1884. Earthenwares. *Mark also found on bricks in houses in the Tara area.*

74 *Impressed mark.*

TAYLOR

J. W. TAYLOR, Beaverton, Ontario County. 1873-1875. Earthenwares.

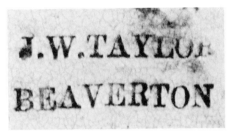

75 *Impressed mark. See* Circa 76, *Vol. 2, No. 4, p. 11.*

TILLSON

F. B. TILLSON, Tillsonburg, Oxford County. Late 1870s - ca. 1883. Stonewares.

76 *Impressed mark.*

TILSONBURG

TILSONBURG POTTERY CO., Tillsonburg, Oxford County. 1880s. Stonewares.

**TILSONBURG
ONT.
POTTERY CO.**

77 *Impressed mark.*

TORONTO

*TORONTO POTTERY CO., Toronto.
1899-1924.* Stonewares.

78 *Stamped mark.*

WAGNER

*JOSEPH WAGNER, Berlin Pottery, Berlin,
Waterloo County. Ca. 1869 - ca. 1880.*
Earthenwares.

79 *Impressed mark (indistinct). Probably
"JOSEPH WAGNER, BERLIN
POTTERY."*

79a *Impressed mark (indistinct). Probably
same as above.*

WARNER

WARNER & CO., Toronto, 1856-1863.
Stonewares. *Subsequently Eberhardt &
Halm, q.v.*

80 *Impressed mark.*

WEBER

*J. B. WEBER, Huron Pottery, Egmondville,
Huron County. 1876-1897.* Earthenwares.
*Formerly Boehler & Weber. Subsequently
F. Burgard & Son, q.v.*

**J.B. WEBER
HURON POTTERY
EGMONDVILLE—ONT.**

81 *Impressed mark.*

WELDING

*WELDING & BELDING, Brantford, Brant
County. 1867-1872.* Stonewares.
*Formerly F. P. Goold & Co. Subsequently
W. E. Welding, q.v.*

82 *Impressed mark.*

WELDING

W. E. WELDING, Brantford, Brant County.

*1873-1894. Stonewares. Formerly Welding
& Belding. Subsequently Brantford
Stoneware Manufacturing Co., Ltd.*

83 *Impressed mark.*

83a *Incised signature on picture
frame with impressed name of
BRANTFORD. A presentation piece
for J. H. Ahrens, Paris, Brant
County, q.v.*

WHITE

*WHITE & HANDLEY, Brockville, Leeds
County. 1884 - ca. 1890. Stonewares.
Also known as White, Handley & Co.*

84 *Impressed mark.*

WOODYATT

*J. WOODYATT & CO., Brantford, Brant
County. 1857-1859. Stonewares. Formerly
Morton & Bennett. Subsequently Morton,
Goold & Co., q.v.*

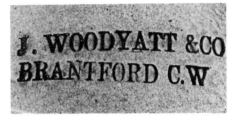

85 *Impressed mark.*

Selected Bibliography

Bacso, Jean. "Nineteenth Century Potteries In Toronto." Unpub. ms. Toronto: University of Toronto (1971).

———. "Toronto Stoneware." *Canadian Collector* 9 (May-June 1973): 28-32.

———. "The Davisville Pottery." *York Pioneer* 1975: 32-38.

———. "Potters of the Don Valley." *York Pioneer* 71 (Spring 1976): 20-28.

Badone, Donalda. "The Humberstone Potteries of North York." *Canadian Collector* 13 (November-December 1978): 44-48.

Baker, M. B. *Clay and the Clay Industry of Ontario.* Toronto: Bureau of Mines, 1906.

Barbeau, Marius. "Canadian Pottery." *Antiques* 39 (June 1941): 296-99.

Brears, Peter C. D. *The English Country Pottery: Its History and Techniques.* Newton Abbot, England: David & Charles, 1971.

———. *The Collector's Book of English Country Pottery.* Newton Abbot, England: David & Charles, 1974.

Brink, Helen. "The Earthy Craft In Early Ontario." *Ontario Potter* 1 (Spring-Summer 1976): 4-7.

Collard, Elizabeth. *Nineteenth Century Pottery and Porcelain In Canada.* Montreal: McGill University Press, 1967.

Crowfoot, H. L. "Daniel Orth." *Canadian Collector* 6 (September-October 1971): 20-21.

Home, M. "John Kulp — Pioneer Potter." *Canadian Collector* 2 (Sept. 1967): 11.

Irvine, Barbara. "Potting In Ontario." *Canadian Collector* 9 (Sept.-October 1974): 27-29.

Jarvis, Harold. "Potters of Lincoln County." *Canadian Collector* 2 (September 1967): 9-10.

Ketchum, William C. Jr. *Early Potters and Potteries of New York State.* New York: Funk & Wagnalls, 1970.

———. *The Pottery and Porcelain Collector's Handbook.* New York: Funk & Wagnalls, 1971.

Montgomery, Robert J. *The Ceramic Industry of Ontario.* Toronto: Ontario Department of Mines, 1930.

Newlands, David L. "The David Burns Pottery Site, Huron County, Ontario." *Archaeological Newsletter* 113 (October 1974): 1-4.

———. "The Egmondville Pottery." *Canadian Collector* 10 (Jan.-Feb. 1975): 22-25.

———. "Potteries of Ontario." *Ontario Potter* 1 (Fall-Winter 1975): 25-28.

———. "The Huron Pottery, Egmondville, Ontario." *Archaeological Newsletter* 128 (January 1976): 1-4.

———. "The Egmondville Pottery Revisited." *Canadian Collector* 11 (March-April 1976): 19-23.

———. "The Ahrens Pottery." *Canadian Collector* 11 (Sept.-Oct. 1976): 33-37.

———. "The Potters of Paris, Ontario." *Canadian Collector* 11 (November-December 1976): 48-51.

———. "The Brantford Pottery: The Early Years." *Canadian Collector* 12 (Jan.-Feb. 1977): 22-27.

———. "Ontario Potteries — The First Decade of Study." *Archaeological Newsletter* 141 (February 1977): 1-4.

———. "A Catalogue of Sprig Moulds From Two Huron County, Ontario Earthenware Potteries." *Material History Bulletin* 3 (Spring 1977): 15-30.

———. "The Brantford Pottery: The Later Years." *Canadian Collector* 12 (Mar.-April 1977): 22-27.

———. "The Potteries of Waterloo County, Ontario: 1." *Ontario Potter* 2 (Spring-Summer 1977): 3-6.

———. "The New Hamburg Pottery." *Canadian Collector* 12 (July-Aug. 1977): 36-39.

———. "The Potteries of Waterloo County, Ontario: 2." *Ontario Potter* 3 (Fall 1977): 2-5.

———. "Rare and Unusual Ontario Pottery." *Canadian Collector* 12 (Nov.-Dec. 1977): 25-29.

———. "The Hamilton Pottery." *Canadian Collector* 13 (March-April 1978): 29-34.

———. "A Toronto Pottery Company Catalogue." *Material History Bulletin* 5 (Spring 1978): 12-35.

———. "The Potteries of Waterloo County, Ontario: 3." *Ontario Potter* 3 (Spring/Summer 1978): 2-5.

———. "A Country Craft: The Potteries of Grey County." *Rotunda* 11 (Summer 1978): 34-39.

———. "Toronto Pottery at Sharon Temple." *York Pioneer* 73 (Fall 1978): 20-22.

———. *The New Hamburg Pottery, New Hamburg, Ontario 1854-1916.* Waterloo: Wilfrid Laurier University Press: 1978.

———. "The Rise and Fall of Ontario's Potteries," in *Everyday Life In 19th Century Ontario* (Toronto: Ontario Museums Assn., 1978), pp. 99-102.

———. "Potter by the Maitland — David W. Burns." *Rotunda* 12:1 (Spring 1979), pp. 32-36.

Newlands, David L., and Breede, Claus. *An*

Introduction to Canadian Archaeology. Toronto: McGraw-Hill Ryerson Ltd., 1976.

Parker, Bruce A. "Potteries of the Brothers Glass." *Canadian Collector* 13 (Sept.-Oct. 1978): 44-48.

Rupp, David. "The Kiln and Red Earthenware Pottery of the Jordan Pottery Site: A Preliminary Overview." *Northeast Historical Archaeology* 7 (Spring 1979).

Shackleton, Philip. "Potteries of Nineteenth Century Ontario." Unpub. ms. Ottawa: Historic Sites Branch, Dept. of Northern Affairs (1964).

Stearns, K. H. G. "Port Hope Pottery." *Canadian Collector* 2 (June 1967): 13-15.

Sutermeister, Helen. "Three Early Pottery Sites In Southern Ontario." Unpub. ms. Toronto: Royal Ontario Museum, (1969).

Taylor, David, and Taylor, Patricia. *The Hart Pottery, Canada West.* Picton: Picton Gazette Pub. Co., 1966.

Taylor, Patricia. "Sam Hart's Canadian Stoneware." *Canadian Collector* 2 (March 1967): 6-8.

Tracy, Ruth. "Report on the Culp Pottery Works Site." Unpub. ms. Toronto: Archaeological and Historic Sites Board of Ontario, 1966.

Turnbull, Margaret. "Late Starters, The Glass Brothers." *Canadian Collector* 5 (November 1970): 26.

Webster, Donald B. *The Brantford Pottery 1849-1907.* Toronto: Royal Ontario Museum, 1968.

_____. "Pennsylvania and Ontario Earthenwares: A Comparative View." *Rotunda* 2 (Winter 1969): 26-33.

_____. *Early Slip Decorated Pottery In Canada.* Toronto: Charles J. Musson Ltd., 1969.

_____. "Beaver Teapots." *Canadian Collector* 4 (June 1969): 14-16.

_____. *The William Eby Pottery, Conestogo, Ontario 1855-1907.* Toronto: Royal Ontario Museum, 1971.

_____. "Earthen Pottery." *Canadian Collector* 6 (May 1971): 56-58.

_____. *Early Canadian Pottery.* Toronto: McClelland & Stewart, Ltd., 1971.

_____. "On the Digging of Potteries." *Antiques* CVI (Sept. 1974): 430-433.

_____. "Pottery — Earthenware and Stoneware." In *The Book of Canadian Antiques.* (Toronto: McGraw-Hill Ryerson Ltd., 1974): 240-253.

INDEX